SUZUKI RG 500
THE RACING MYTH
1974-1980

MASSIMO CUFFIANI

FOREWORD BY PHIL READ

The first RG 500 Suzuki's were factory ones, raced by Sheene, Paul Smart, Pat Hennen (from 1977 - Ed.) and Jack Findlay in 1974/75.

In 1976, to my delight and excitement and that of many other riders, Japan's Suzuki factory produced replica's of their factory RG 500's for the world markets.

For me this was a great relief to obtain two of the new and competitive Suzuki RG 500cc bike as MV Agusta had withdrawn their GP race Team and loaned my MV bikes to Ago (Agostini -Ed-) from the funding of Marlboro for that 1976 GP season. Ago also had a RG 500 which he raced at the Italian GP at Mugello from which he retired when Sheene and I had passed him to drawn away.

By good chance I employed an Australian ace mechanic to work on my RG's. As it happened Geoff Howie was the boyfriend of my nanny, who later she become his wife. Geoff did brilliant work on my RG motors to very nearly make them as fast as the factory Sheene Suzuki's.

Having spent four season racing the factory MV Agusta 500cc four-stroke machines, when in 1975 I just lost my third world title for them due to an electrical retirement when leading the Finnish GP that allowed Ago to win the world title on the factory Yamaha 500.

Although I had more gross points than him, that season the results were calculated by counting half ones results plus one.

The most exciting race in which I was involved was the Italian GP at Mugello (1976 Nations GP - Ed.), one of the most exciting and demanding race circuits. Geoff and I had made much improvement to my No.1 Suzuki bike. We opened and polished the cylinder ports, re-set the ignition timing, lightened the pistons and with the help of my friend, Roberto Marchesini, he produced for me a set of magnesium wheels. These lighter wheels allowed the bike to turn faster. That was a great help to allow me get closer and pass the factory Suzuki's of Sheene.

At this GP I had a slow start to loose many places to the ace Suzuki riders Barry Sheene, Agostini, Virginio Ferrari, Teppe Lansivuori and Pat Hennen and a few other riders, but within a few laps I was able to get behind the leading pair of Ago and Sheene. I passed Ago and then Sheene. After ten laps Sheene and I had pulled clear of the field, when during the remaining 20 laps to the finish we ducked and dived passed each other until the last lap when I had a 2 second lead but nearly lost the bike as its rear tire skidded sideways through a fast corner, allowing Sheene to slip passed me. I closely followed him till the last corner, then out braked him to lead the race on the edge of the track just before the finish line to stop him slip-streaming me. The extra power of his factory bike didn't need this, allowing him to win by 0.10 seconds.

Did I make a mistake by passing Sheene into the last corner or could I have won by drafting him to gain extra speed to pass him before the finish line? I will never know!!!

We shared the fastest lap at 2'07.60 at a speed of 92 mph. Now the 2018 MotoGP fastest lap at Mugello is around 22 seconds less, which is an incredible speed and shows the great advancement of racing motorcycle engineering and the skill of the current riders.

Unfortunately during the next Belgium GP at Francorchamps my main sponsor Life Helmets went bankrupt owing me the half of my contracted amount. Without these funds I had no way of continuing to race with the overheads I would have incurred for team manager, Alberto Pagani and three team members salaries, plus transport costs of my large coach transporter and my Rolls Royce.

So I was very unset to be forced to leave the GP series to its future winner and world champion, Barry Sheene, on his factory RG 500 Suzuki.

We were happy to spend the rest of the racing season at well paid International events in the UK and Continent, where my RG 500 never failed me, including a Senior TT win in 1977 with a Suzuki engine borrowed from Suzuki GP, prepared by the great Bob White.

During the last three years I have been fortunate to have the use of the renowned Steve Wheatman's 1976 RG 500 Suzuki at Classic events throughout the Continent with high speed parades in the World GP Bike Legends events.

© Massimo Cuffiani

FOREWORD BY DARIO BALLARDINI

People who love racing but not the Suzuki RG 500 are probably heartless or – more likely - were born too late to experience its magic. Very few bikes have ever made such a deep impression on the World Championship as that of the square four-cylinder from Hamamatsu. Before its arrival, the ordinary privateer rider had absolutely no chance of competing - with any kind of honour - with official factory riders.

The paddock of the 500 was always a kind of exhibition fair full of weird and wonderful handmade creations including Yamaha 500s made by installing four 250 thermals on the 700 GP four-cylinder engine originally created for the 200 Miles; Yamaha 350 two-stroke engines; a few two-cylinder Suzukis and a pair of Königs driven by the same four-cylinder sidecar boxer made from an engine created for nautical competitions; the two-cylinder Harley-Davidson 500 and the surly three-cylinder Kawasaki 500, protagonists in some timid trip; and the brave four-stroke Paton 500...

The list could go on and on, but obviously there was a huge gap. In the first half of the 1970s, only the two four-stroke MV Agusta 500s and the official factory two-stroke four-cylinder Yamaha 500, which made their debut for the first time in 1973 with Jarno Saarinen, were capable of winning.

But then the square four-cylinder Suzuki arrived on the scene to upset the status quo. In 1974, it aroused quite a lot of curiosity as would be to be expected for a company that committed itself directly. It also raised a lot of puzzlement. In 1975 this bike aroused considerable fear because, despite still fragile, it began to win.

And then in 1976 and 1977 it filled that great void when the great Barry Sheene rode it to win the world title twice in a row. The real revolution, however, was not this but rather the fact that, since 1976, the RG had become available for privateer riders who suddenly found they could buy a winner not too far different from the working teams' bikes: their RG was the same as those used the year before by the riders of the official factory team and was also based on a winning formula, which was used season after season. And since even the official factory teams were actually privateer teams, managed by the Manufacturers only indirectly, a lot of materials from the previous year remained in Europe and ended up to being incorporated into the fairing of some rich privateers – assuming your definition of luxury for a world championship is official factories setting up their workshops in camping tents or the van-workshop launched by Team Gallina in 1978, looked at as a spaceship at the time. How times have changed!

The Suzuki RG, however, was the "harbinger of change" and marked a real turning point. This bike 'wrote' the pages of a history of motorcycling whose authors were not just the champions but also "honest workers of the handlebars". The champions still had to keep alert though, because now major feats were within the reach of privateer riders such as Boet Van Dulmen, winner of the 1979 Finland GP, and the many others who gave the official factory teams a run for their money on more than one occasion.

What's more, since the RG was now ubiquitous, it became an excellent 'test-lab' for the frame manufacturers who attempted repeatedly – though without any significant breakthrough - to get that "extra added value". Several created futuristic methods, for example, the explosive Roberto Gallina with his power steering; many inserted spoilers. And then there were numerous experiments by the motorists - made possible by the simplicity of the two-stroke! Yes, the Suzuki RG certainly has a glorious history – maybe even a soul. And it is fascinating to retrace its footsteps on the pages of this book from its beginnings up until 1980, the final year before the arrival of the Gamma version, which Marco Lucchinelli and Franco Uncini rode to win the world title in 1981 and 1982 respectively.

The history of the RG is really seductive and one which has cast its spell over Massimo Cuffiani. Even though his day job is not to write books but to develop the styling of motorcycles that go into production, as the RG played a big part in his childhood, he has written this book as a declaration of his love for this bike and the entire world it represents. He has gone beyond any craftsman in his commitment, and passion, and in the meticulous attention paid to the technicalities, history, and detail. Cuffiani has truly put his entire soul into - or perhaps had it stolen by - the RG.

© Massimo Cuffiani

WHY I DID THAT! BY MASSIMO CUFFIANI

When I started writing this book, one of my motivations was the beauty of this bike, both aesthetic and technical. But not only this... I slowly realized that beyond the bike, there were men who had driven it and brought it to success. A symbiosis that made it great.

I started thinking about those riders, too, and it was inevitable that unforgettable moments of my childhood would come back to me. For this I will always be grateful to my father, who, despite his fear bikes and all their implications, made sure I never missed a race at the Enzo and Dino Ferrari racetrack in Imola, my hometown. I grew up on Imola 200 Miles and Bike World Championships.

Then, inevitably, I longed to meet these men I saw riding and who made me move and spend so many evenings imitating them, trying to make the little stool in my bedroom bank.

I immediately thought of four Italians ... the "fantastic four" of my memories:

Ferrari, Lucchinelli, Rossi, Uncini (strictly in alphabetical order).

Each of them brings back special particular memories. Rossi for example, the first person I interviewed, will always be Graziano Rossi and not Valentino's father. An uncompromising rider, who could share the desire he had to stay in front of everyone and perhaps did not have the recognition that he deserved. And he will also be remembered as that "crazy guy" that ran around the paddock with the hen! Interviewing him was great fun, with all his forgotten stories and anecdotes of those crazy old times.

The author on the saddle of the Uncini's RG 500 MK IV 1979. Note the front axle with anti-dive fork and Brembo brake unit with front floating disc, used by the Recanati champion in 1981. The fairing is a 1982 RGB

archivio © Massimo Cuffiani

The author on the saddle of the Uncini's RG 500 MK IV 1979 in Adria circuit. The best over the counter bike competing in 1979

archivio © Massimo Cuffiani

Then I interviewed Virginio Ferrari. I remember him as the champion who, for the first time after Agostini, was about to bring the World Championship prize back to Italy and managed to beat champions like Roberts and Sheene.

A person with truly kindly manner which was quite the antithesis of the determination and speed he showed on the track. Rather than an RG rider, I thought he was one of Suzuki's designers after looking at his technical expertise!

It was then the turn of Franco Uncini, a very friendly man, who managed to dedicate some of his time to me, despite his many MotoGP commitments. I have two unforgettable memories of Franco, even though I was very young: great and victorious in the World 500 with the "light blue" Suzuki, and lying lifeless on the ground after the crash with Gardner's bike.

Two opposite feelings that nevertheless created in me the idea of a superhero Uncini, who managed to beat Lucchinelli and the Americans and to survive an accident where anyone else would die.

Finally, there's Marco Lucchinelli. Always impossible to get hold of despite being in Imola so often!

I've always thought of "Lucky" from the outside as Graziano, another "crazy guy" who is all or nothing.

He was uncompromisingly the ultimate showman who reminded me a lot of my other myth, Barry Sheene.

I remember that when on a school trip in 1981, we used to boast that Lucchinelli was from Imola, even if as an "adopted" son. And it was something incredible to win a 500 Motorbike World Championship thanks to him.

I would like to thank these four "heroes" for their availability and above all for letting me delve into something that I only saw from the outside as a child.

SUZUKI RG 500 - THE RACING MYTH | SUM

THE MYTH IN ACTION	10	INTRODUCTION
	18	1974 RG 500 XR14
	24	1975 RG 500 XR14
	36	1976 RG 500 XR14
	50	1977 RG 500 XR14
	64	1978 RGA 500 XR22
	76	1979 RGB 500 XR27B
	94	1980 RGB 500 XR34
BIKES IN HISTORY	112	DRAWINGS
	124	THE COLLECTION IMOLA CLASSIC
THE TECHNIC	172	ENGINE
	184	FRAME
	194	AERODYNAMICS
THE PROTAGONISTS	200	RIDERS
	210	INTERVIEWS
STATISTICS	230	RACES FINAL RESULTS
	240	ANNUAL DATA

INTRODUCTION

The history of **Suzuki RG 500 XR 14 starts in the mid-60s,** when the racing bikes were "exotic".
Four, five, six-cylinder motorcycles, with double-digit gear ratios, filled the grids in each category, such as the **1967 Suzuki RK67 50 cm3** with 14 gears.

And then the International Motorbike Federation changed the rules by introducing several restrictions in 1969, such as the maximum number of cylinders and gears, thereby eliminating real masterpieces of technology from the tracks.
As a result, for several years after that, GP grids were also packed by old single-cylinder or road engines converted and installed on racing frames – something that led to the undisputed domination by teams with large budgets, such as MV Agusta.

RG 500
THE MYTH
IN ACTION

© Massimo Cuffiani

At that time and up until 1973, the Kawasaki H1R and the Suzuki TR 500 dominated the scene, a two-cylinder 2-stroke developed starting from the road T 500 up to the Yamaha TZ 500. The Company, at the beginning of 1973, beat competitors with its four-cylinder 2-stroke driven by the lamented Jarno Saarineen, winning the World 500 first two races. Probably, it was right that the tragedy at Monza, where Saarineen died along with Renzo Pasolini, deprived Yamaha of the world title, which withdrew from competitions as a sign of mourning.

In the middle of that year, Suzuki decided to build a revolutionary racing bike to beat Yamaha and increase sales in Europe, so they began the development of the new GP 500 and hired the young British rider Barry Sheene so as to be ready for **the assault on the 1974 World Championship.**

Makoto "BIG Mac" Suzuki was one of its developers, alongside Makoto Haze, the designer already responsible for the square four cylinders in the 125 and 250 of the 1960s: RS 67 125 cm3 and RS65 250 cm3.

1974 RG 500 XR14

1974 RG 500 XR14

As Makoto Suzuki recently confessed in an interview: "People thought we were crazy, since two-stroke engines were only used with small displacement," he recalls. "The decision was made for us, and we did not have any option, so we looked at our small-displacement bikes. We had already built some square four engines and V4 125 cm3 and 250 cm3 for races, so we made them bigger. We started the project in July 1973 with the goal of being ready for the 1974 season, with only four people working there, two for the engine and two for the chassis". Although racing GPs are back to four-stroke nowadays, **the bike that Suzuki built showed that the two-strokes were perfect for producing high power output.**
While this was good news for the engine development team, the chassis engineers had to face some tough challenges.
"With the bike we aimed to get over 100bhp, but we reached 110bhp at the end," said Makoto Suzuki, "and this would have been a problem for the chassis. In the US we competed with the XR11, a 750 cm3 three-cylinder with lots of power and a whole series of chassis problems. In the US we suffered from ripped tyres, broken transmission chains, and pack suspension; it was terrible, the development of chassis lagged far behind that of the engine."

"For the RG 500 we used the knowledge of the XR11 to build a good chassis, but the engine was very difficult to drive and hard in fueling. Its power was increased from 8,000 to 10,500 rpm, even if the GP mechanics could intervene on these characteristics with mufflers and main jets, directly in the track. At that time there was a lot of experimentation and development, we were looking for inspiration from all over the world, even from household items."

"The original drain pads of the RG 500 were modified green tea cans, then I looked at the correct format and I introduced this technology into the GP bike."

Suzuki took the view that it was not the riders' but the manufacturers' championship which mattered. If the rider wins he can only say that the rider is a world champion, if you win the manufacturers' championship you can say that 'Suzuki is world champion'.

Barry Sheene was very upset because the over the counter motorcycles were identical to the official factory ones! But for Suzuki it was just perfect, as we won seven manufacturers' championships in a row" laughs Makoto Suzuki.

"The only difference was the fact that the official factory bikes had titanium and magnesium screws, while the standard bikes had the steel or aluminium ones. The engine was 100% identical; we just changed the name of the prototype to production.

You could buy a production RG 500 and win a GP, as Jack Middelburg did in 1981.

That was the last time a privateer rider won a 500 GP, however he drove an RG 500 Mk VI based on the XR22. You can imagine Barry Sheene's frustration.

Barry won the title in 1976 with the XR14, but we kept the XR22 in 1977 in the event that other producers came out with something special", explains Makoto Suzuki. "Yamaha in particular was a concern for us, but it had only introduced the exhaust valves so we kept it under wraps until 1978. Moreover, our over the counter RG 500 was proving very popular and we did not want to undermine it, even if we needed to beat the Suzuki privateer riders,

1977 RG 500 MK II

1978 RG 500 MK III

1981 RG 500 MK VI

1982 RGB 500 MK I

who began to compete with the official factory bikes."
"Some had developed their XR14 so well that they were incredibly fast and more than capable of competing with the XR22. The XR22's power was similar to that of the XR14 at around 124bhp, although its engine was lighter and this made the bikes more manoeuvrable.

Weight was an important factor in the GPs in the 1970s and 1980s because, although there was a minimum weight of 100 kg, the bikes never achieved it – our best was 108 kg.

With 124 bhp and 108 kg, the XR22 was just a beast!"

After developing the XR14 and then the XR22, Makoto Suzuki was finally able to experience all this power with his own hands.

"I drove the XR22 for half a lap in Japan, but only once – that once was enough for me.

I went out of the pits and did a 200 degree bend but the tachometer had not even started to measure, as it only started at 5,000 rpm. On the straight I gave it full throttle and suddenly the rpms appeared. The bike did a wheelie and I went back to the pit. It was terrifying. That made me really appreciate the skills of riders like Barry Sheene.

The 'square four' continued to dominate the 500 GP races, winning two other world titles (1981 with Marco Lucchinelli and 1982 with Franco Uncini) and a total of 50 races, plus seven consecutive manufacturers' championships. But all good things must come to an end and **in 1987 the square four-cylinder RG 500 was replaced by the V4 RGV 500**, an inevitability because the competition then used two-stroke V engines."

"The 'square four' had excellent weight distribution and bags of power.

It was a straightforward engine that was reliable and worked very well, but its power was limited, which is why it was replaced by the V4, "Makoto Suzuki explains.

"The supply manifold was limited in size, but on a V4 it is not. The more fuel and more air you can fit into the engine, the more power you get, which is why the introduction of the V4 immediately increased the power from 133 bhp to over 145 bhp".

The RG 500 became such a benchmark for the GP 500 motorcycles in the late '70s that Honda bought a new one when they returned to racing, no doubt through a third party, to be used as a direct comparison in the development of the NR 500 V with oval pistons.

The official factory XRs, along with the over the counter RG versions, were being developed for about nine years after their GP debut and in over the counter for many seasons later.

Suzuki officially retired in 1984, starting the development of the V4, Gamma series, with the success of Kevin Schwantz in 1994 and Kenny Roberts Jr. in 2000.

1980 RG 500 MK V

1983 RGB 500 MK II

1978 RG 500 MK III. This was the version for privateer riders.

1974 - RG 500 XR14

While other projects fell by the wayside, the two-cylinder Suzuki XR05 continued to run in the '73 and '74 seasons, allowing XR14 designers to take stock of the competition. It is hardly surprising that Hase was also the designer of the Suzuki 125 and 250 square four-cylinder engines in the 1960s. The great success of the Suzuki 125 RS67 four-cylinder then led to the not so victorious version, RZ65 250. Known as "whispering death", because of its characteristic to seize up without any of the usual warning signs, the 250 never finished a race better than the third place throughout his short career and the project was shelved after just one season. The square engine layout also made it possible to use rotary disk carburettors. Actually, **the engine consisted of four cylinders of 125 cm^3** and since each cylinder had its own crankshaft and crankcase, engine tuning was facilitated, in fact, it was enough to take a single cylinder and measure the results to test the engine bench.

Each of the four crankshafts controlled the primary gear, but this led to some initial difficulties. To solve the initial problems of the crankshaft unreliability, a forced lubrication system was created by means of an oil pump. It was mounted under the front carburettors, with its own tank made in the tail. The XR14 had a six-speed gearbox and five-pass cylinders. **In 1974 the engine reached 95 hp at 11.200 rpm, 137 kg empty weight.**

The RG 500 was a motorcycle that broke all the patterns in the premier class and decreed the end of the dominant four-stroke along with Yamaha.

MV Agusta, however, did not give up and because of their perseverance and technical knowledge, they kept the four-stroke four-cylinder 100 hp competitive for two more years, winning the title with Phil Read in 1974 and finishing in second place behind the Yamaha of Giacomo Agostini in 1975 (actually, Read obtained more points during the year, but the final score was based on the best six out of ten races and Agostini won thanks to the scraps).

It is fair to say that initially the XR14 was not without its faults with its vertical shock absorbers and the abundant fairing needed to wrap the protruding carburettors. In 1975, the XR became a little more pleasant (to look at), with inclined shock absorbers and better balanced fairing appearance. In an attempt to reduce the frontal area of the fairing, the original frame did not include the lower tubes, this meant that the exhaust and lower fairing were higher off the ground. This chassis had made a good impression on the Suzuki test track, but when the bike was tested on fast and sometimes rough tracks during competitions, it became obvious that the handling was not up to scratch and so two tubes were added at the bottom. Finally, a closed cradle frame, the third version in less than a year and designed by Ron Williams of Maxton Engineering, would be used for the remainder of 1974.

The engine vibrated badly and many of the external pieces broke off or got dislodged throughout the first year, thus causing premature withdrawals.

RG 500
THE MYTH
IN ACTION

© Massimo Cuffiani

1974 Sheene with Read

The bike debuted in **1974** at the Clermont Ferrand, **French GP,** driven by **Barry Sheene and Paul Smart**, with the **official factory SUZUKI MOTOR CO Team** and by the Australian **Jack Findlay,** with the **Italian Suzuki SAIAD Team**.

Sheene qualified 4th and finished the race with an excellent 2nd place, five seconds behind Read the winner, while Findlay finished 12th and Smart retired after only one lap.
In Austria, in the third race, at Salzburgring, another podium: 3rd Sheene and 4th Findlay, with Smart not even classified after a bad start. Sheene was unlucky in the Italian race as his gearbox seized up while in third place and he was catapulted onto the asphalt.
For the Dutch TT, in the Netherlands, SAIAD gave an XR14 to its rider, Guido Mandracci. The Italian, who usually rode the two-cylinder Suzuki TR 500, classified in 18th place. Sheene, however, was already well up on the leaderboard, when a vibration warned him of an impending gearbox failure and decided to retire after some careful deliberation. As Sheene had guessed, it was discovered during the check afterwards that a shaft had sheared its mounting bolts making it like an unexploded bomb inside the engine.
Suzuki then made some quick changes before for the next GP only a couple of weeks later. An engineer returned to the parent company and built four new shafts in a new type of steel. They were mounted in time for the race and there were no further problems.

Then there was a bitter pill for Sheene and Suzuki team in Belgium. Sheene had lowered his best time in the Spa Francorchamps track by twelve seconds and was comfortably following the race leader Phil Read on MV Agusta at half race when the Suzuki gearbox lever broke, forcing Sheene to retire again. Mandracci also had an official factory XR14, but he failed to qualify.

In Sweden, Sheene was leading the race quietly but on the second lap the bike broke due to a gearbox failure and put him on the ground. Phil Read, who was just behind Sheene, was able to avoid his compatriot, while Agostini hit the bike, came off and fractured his collarbone, losing the chance to fight for the World Title.

1974 was a competitive season of varying fortunes and an unreliable engine, but the biggest problem was bike driveability.

In the middle of the season, Suzuki welded an extra tube to increase stiffness. The XR14-Sheene combination was without doubt very competitive, but it just did not last long enough to win the races.

1974 Nations GP – Paul Smart with his official factory Suzuki before Agostini at the Rivazza bend

The final classification of the **1974** World Championship was as follows:
Read 82 p., **Bonera 69 p., Länsivuori 67 p., Agostini 47 p., Findlay 34 p., Sheene 30 p.**

In the manufacturers' championship **Suzuki finished third with 52 p., with Yamaha first at 87 p. and MV Agusta second at 87 p. also.**

1975 - RG 500 XR14

In 1975 Suzuki had a very strong team with its two riders of the calibre of Sheene and Teuvo Länsivuori. Rumour was that the leading champion of the 500 Phil Read had left the MV to join the Suzuki Team, but he finally remained with the Italian four-stroke for another year. Sheene was confident for the 1975 World Championship, he had spent a lot of time trying the XR14 during the whole previous winter, solving those annoying little problems that had caused him to have to retire so often during the previous season. The new frame was easy to drive and its many engine tests had provided even more power. Other more obvious changes had been made in the inclination of the rear shock absorbers, so as to obtain more stroke together with finer adjustments; and in the replacement of the round section swingarm, including a rectangular section box unit and right resistance.

The engine remained virtually the same as in 1974: 5-port cylinder, bore and stroke 56 x 50.5 mm, with a peak of 100 hp at 11,200 rpm, 135 kg empty weight.

The frame was new, instead of a bent top tube, a straight pipe had been used (which was basically what Suzuki had done with the welded pipe added in 1974).
The 1975 GP season began at the end of March at Paul Ricard racetrack for the French GP, with Länsivuori only. The beginning of the year was actually quite disastrous for Barry Sheene, as he was seriously injured in Daytona during the 200 Miles tests where he fell at 280 km/h. Länsivuori led the first race ahead of Agostini until a gearbox problem forced him to retire.
Sheene's recovery was only just in early stages and, in spite of this, he took part in the second GP, the Grand Prix of Austria at Salzburgring and qualified sixth just a month after the accident. The race officials, however, stopped him from competing, as he was not able to push start his Suzuki.
In that race, Länsivuori got an excellent second place with a superb race. Sheene showed up again at the German Grand Prix, but had to retire due to problems with the ignition, while Länsivuori ascended the podium again, this time finishing third, and the new Suzuki rider, Stan Woods, was 5th.

1975 NATIONS GP (Imola) - Barry Sheene

archivio © Claudio Ghini

For the following des Nations GP in Imola, Suzuki fielded Sheene, Länsivuori, Toracca, Woods and Gallina (later to become Team Nava Olio Fiat team manager). Länsivuori could not compete because of a collarbone he had broken during tests. In Italy the bikes were not very reliable, but Toracca finished fourth in his debut, after being the best Suzuki on the grid with the third time placement. Woods instead finished the race 5th. Sheene, however, before retiring on the second lap due to a gearbox failure, had given the winner Agostini a hard time.

Halfway through the season in the Netherlands, Suzuki attended with three official factory riders: Sheene, Länsivuori and John Newbold. Newbold had only competed with the old XR05 so far, but it was decided by Suzuki's management that he could race with the reserve bike in Assen. After the Italian GP in Imola on May 18, there was a bit of pause, with the Isle of Man TT race in the middle of it, now defected to by great champions. This interval allowed Barry to recover and get in shape at Assen for the Dutch TT on June 28th.

Sheene got Pole Position and remained close to the Agostini's Yamaha, overtaking it on the exit of the last corner, on the last lap, beating it at the photo finish, despite the same time of 48'01"00 for both.

1975 NATIONS GP (Imola) - Roberto Gallina

archivio © Claudio Ghini

Sheene won his first GP500 - for himself and for Suzuki.
Moreover, Suzuki had Newbold and Länsivuori in 4th and 5th place, respectively.

1975 The Finnish Teuvo Länsivuori

1975 GP SWEDEN (Anderstorp)
Sheene romping home to his second win

archivio © Claudio Ghini

1975 DUTCH TT (Assen) - Barry Sheene on Agostini's tail. He finally went on to beat him in a photo finish

1975 John Newbold in the paddock of Spa, Belgium

1975 Barry Sheene doing one of his incredible wheelies

1975 GP SWEDEN (Anderstorp) - Barry Sheene first before Read and Williams

archivio © Claudio Ghini

1975 Barry Sheene with his XR14

In the Belgium GP on SPA's very fast track with an average of 200 km/h, Sheene still showed that he could win, but two laps from the end the engine broke down again. However, it set his personal new track record at an average of over 218 km/h. Despite the victory at the Dutch TT, the bike was still not reliable enough, but even so, it did not stop

Sheene from getting his second win of the season at the Swedish GP

and two second places for Newbold in Belgium and Länsivuori in his native Finland respectively.

The final classification of the **1975** World Championship was as follows: **Agostini 84 p.**, Read 76 p., Kanaya 45 p., **Länsivuori 40 p.**, Williams 32 p., **Sheene 30 p.** In the standings of the manufacturers' championship, **Suzuki was third with 76 p.** behind Yamaha 87 p. and MV Agusta 78 p.

The season ended with some entries for the 1976 season: an improved version of the XR14, a 750 cm3 version for the F750 races and an over the counter version RG 500.
The over the counter RG 500 was confirmed, but Suzuki came out with shocking news for 1976...

archivio © Claudio Ghini

1976 - RG 500 XR14

Things seemed to be going perfectly for Sheene just before the 1976 World Championship, but then, at the start of the season, **Suzuki completely withdrew their support from him.** This was because they had to develop the new GS road bike range but did not have enough money to run a racing team at the same time and so had to officially announce that they were withdrawing from competitive racing.
Peter Agg, President and Administration Manager of Heron Team, came up with a plan involving financial support from Texaco to keep Suzuki racing. He managed to persuade them to supply him with official factory machines and parts, while he took over responsibility for the World Championship.
He chose Merv Wright as Team Manager, who had been working at Suzuki the previous year. **The riders were Barry Sheene**, with his father, Franko, and Don Mackay as his mechanics; **John Newbold**, with Martyn Ogborne as his mechanic; and **John Williams** supported by Bob White.
Such was the progress made in performance that the Sheene 1975 XR14, like its 1974 predecessor, was almost obsolete within a season.

The characteristic feature of the 1974-75 XR14s was its peaky, short-stroke engine but from 1976 onwards they became the 54x54 mm. Only Sheene rode this bike however, while John Newbold and John Williams were happy to carry on with the XR14 of previous years with a higher rpm engine configuration.

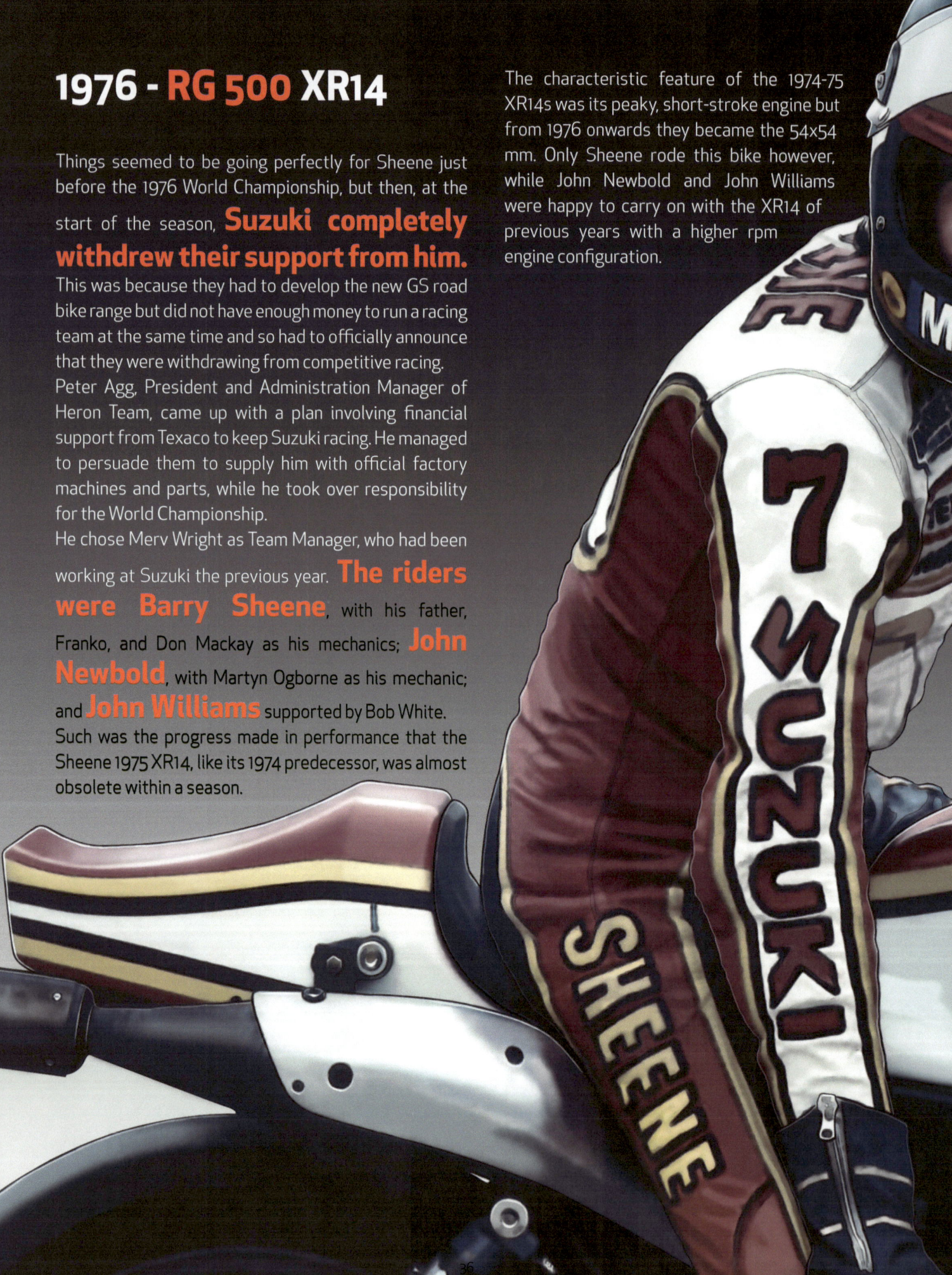

1976 - Sheene's bike in the paddock.
Note the 7 Spoke Morris wheels used instead of the traditional 5 Spoke Campagnolo ones, and the tyre pairing with a slick on the back and treaded on the front.

archivio © Claudio Ghini

The 54 x 54 engine produced very little extra horse power but did deliver a much wider spread of power thus making it easier to ride throughout the long distances encountered in a GP race.
The smaller bore reduced the likelihood of seizure, while the increased stroke made bigger port barrels possible. The oil pump was removed following extensive modification to the crank material and the subsequent improvement in reliability.
The cylinders now had seven port barrels.
The oil pump was removed following extensive changes to the crank material and subsequent improvement in reliability.

The engine now delivered **114 hp at 11,000 rpm with a curb weight of 132 kg.**
Even the chassis was modified and lost 8 kg.
The rear shock absorbers were moved forward and now the pivot of the swing arm was in front of the rear wheel axle.
Kayaba also supplied a new 35mm nitrogen-loaded pneumatic fork, which, along with all the other modifications, contributed to making the XR14 more driveable and prepared to compete for final victory.
The front brake discs were increased from 270 mm in diameter to 290 mm, while the rear ones were decreased from 250 mm to 240 mm.

In 1976, the customer version was also available, a very popular and successful bike that helped Suzuki to gain the first twelve positions in the final ranking (although it should be remembered that Agostini, 7th at the end, also rode with an MV Agusta).

Pat Hennen and Marco Lucchinelli finished 3rd and 4th, with even Hennen, who obtained the first victory for an American in the 500 World Championship in Finland, with the over the counter RG 500. Sheene took part in 6 races and won 5 of them. In the end, if it had not been for Agostini's victory at the Nürburgring with MV Agusta, Suzuki would have won all the races.

Sheene made sure that no other member of the Suzuki team got their hands on the latest changes and this was to be the cause of huge tensions within Heron Suzuki Team.

To make matters worse, there was an incident involving Sheene and French privateer talent Michel Rougerie. Rougerie was struggling to qualify for the Belgian GP at SPA due to technical difficulties, so Sheene lent him one of his bikes enabling the Frenchman to reach 5th position in front of other members of the Heron Team.

1976 Lucchinelli testing the RG 500 MK I on a public road

1976 NATIONS GP (Mugello) - Giacomo Agostini made his debut with Suzuki RG 500 MK I

archivio © Claudio Ghini

Since the beginning of the 1976 GP season, **the majority of the 500 grid consisted of Suzuki factory mounted XR14s or over the counter RG 500s.**

This production machine was available to all those who could pay the price of £5,000, then about 8 million Italian Lire - not bad for such a racing GP bike.
Suzuki was unique in this, as Yamaha did not produce a customer version of the OW 500 series for privateers until 1980, and even then it was in no way a competitive racing bike.

archivio © Claudio Ghini

1976 NATIONS GP (Mugello) - Giacomo Agostini during the practice. Note the tank with the original Suzuki colours. During races he would use the one with his personal colours

archivio © Claudio Ghini

Although the consumer version RG 500 MK I was built to the 1975 specifications, several riders and trainers made good use of their "square four", often carrying on competitive races and even beating the official factory riders.

In the first 1976 race, the French GP, the privateer and future 500 GP champion Marco Lucchinelli, won a superb third place on a customer version RG 500, beaten only by the victorious Sheene on the official factory Suzuki and by Cecotto with the Yamaha, which had previously belonged to Agostini. Lucchinelli, by the way, also achieved the fastest lap.

In Austria, during the second GP, Sheene dropped back by several seconds, but Lucchinelli, once again, put on a show with an incredible comeback on his over the counter Suzuki RG 500, which enabled him to get the second position ahead of Read.

At the GP des Nations also Agostini moved to riding a customer version Suzuki, as he had been disappointed by the performance of his MV Agusta.

His RG 500 allowed him to get the pole position and lead the race with 2 seconds before Sheene until he retired from the race.

Finally, Sheene beat Read.

1976 Barry Sheene in action

Another victory in the Netherlands for Sheene, with Agostini still starring with his Suzuki until the second to last lap, when he was forced to pull in due to a mechanical failure. Sheen's only setback occurred in the Belgian GP, when a problem with his Suzuki slowed him down after dominating the race and relegated him to second position behind his teammate John Williams.

That first championship-winning year, however, was not entirely a bed of roses for Sheene.

During a test at his local Snetterton track, the front brake pads jumped out of their seating at the end of the straight and Barry had no choice but to run into the grass bank at full speed. A mechanic had "merely" forgotten to put in the retaining pins thus allowing the pads to simply fall out. Fortunately, Sheene suffered no injuries from this accident and only had to finish in the top five at the Swedish GP the following weekend to win the championship title.

Just imagine Sheene's state of mind. He was just about to go out to start practice when he noticed that a pad had been mounted incorrectly. After the Snetterton accident, there was no doubt that whole team was under tremendous pressure. Sheene's bike had been rebuilt with the wrong steering plates. In addition, the back-up bike had been fitted with the wrong gearbox. However, these problems were solved, **Sheene won the Swedish GP and thus his first GP 500 title.**

archivio © Claudio Ghini

1976 Three pictures of Länsivuori. Note the Campagnolo hydroconic front brake assembly

1976 GP AUSTRIA (Salzburgring) - Barry Sheene in pole position close to Cecotto with Yamaha. In the background Stu Avant with the RG 500 MK I, Agostini with the MV Agusta and with the #5 John Williams

1976 GP SWEDEN (Anderstorp) - Lucchinelli (32) followed by Coulon (51), Sheene, Ankonè and Gustavson

Sheene, now a world champion, was not satisfied with the prizes offered by the last three races and so he did not take part in them. Even Read quit the season early due to the bankrupt of his sponsor Life Helmets, and gave his customer version Suzuki to Länsivuori. **The year 1976 saw also the very last win for a four-stroke bike, with Agostini** winning his final race at the West German GP on the Italian four-cylinder **MV AGUSTA**.

The final classification of the **1976** World championship was as follows: **Sheene 72 p., Länsivuori 48 p., Hennen 46 p., Lucchinelli 40 p., Newbold 31 p., Coulon 28 p.**, Agostini 26 p.(only with MV Agusta).

In the manufacturers' championship **Suzuki was first with 90 points**, ahead of Yamaha with 48 points, and MV Agusta with 26 points.

1976 Phil Read in action

RG 500
THE MYTH
IN ACTION

1977 - RG 500 XR14

The 1977 500 World Championship opened with several major pieces of news: for the first time, the final classification would be drawn up by taking into account all the results; four-stroke bikes would no longer race; and, most importantly, there would be no Isle of Man TT Races, which would be replaced by the British GP at Silverstone.

Moreover, because of the two deaths in 1976, the Italian track at Mugello was again replaced by Imola. Le Mans was replaced by Paul Ricard (French GP), the Nurburgring by the Hockenheim track (West German GP) and Montjuic by Jarama (Spanish GP). Yamaha again officially signed up Baker and Cecotto and a third unofficial bike entrusted to Agostini, with the support of the parent company.

The **Heron Suzuki team** replaced Newbold and Williams with the American **Pat Hennen** and the 1976 British Champion **Steve Parrish**. Roberto Gallina's Suzuki team, the **Gallina-Nava-Olio Fiat Team**, signed up two RG500 privateers **Virginio Ferrari** and **Gianfranco Bonera**.

There were no major technical changes for 1977. The diameter of the Kayaba front fork was increased to 36 mm, while the front discs were increased to 295 mm in diameter with the rear one to 240 mm. The fairing was the biggest change on the bike, which now delivered **119 hp at 10,800 rpm for 135 kg.** The first version, nicknamed "Donald Duck", had had a more inclined front fairing and a light deflector in the lower part of its sides. The tail was similar to that of the XR23 RG 700, with exhausts still visible.

Various versions of the fairing came out that year and one of them was criticised by Hennen at Imola in the des Nations GP when he crashed into the Tamburello bend after losing control of the front wheel. He reported that the bike became unrideable as if the wheel had risen.

Several other tests were subsequently carried out, including by Sheene, involving the insertion of a range of different new parts. A new tail was brought in to protect riders more from the exhausts along with a new fairing without the deflector and with a less inclined and more rounded front fairing.

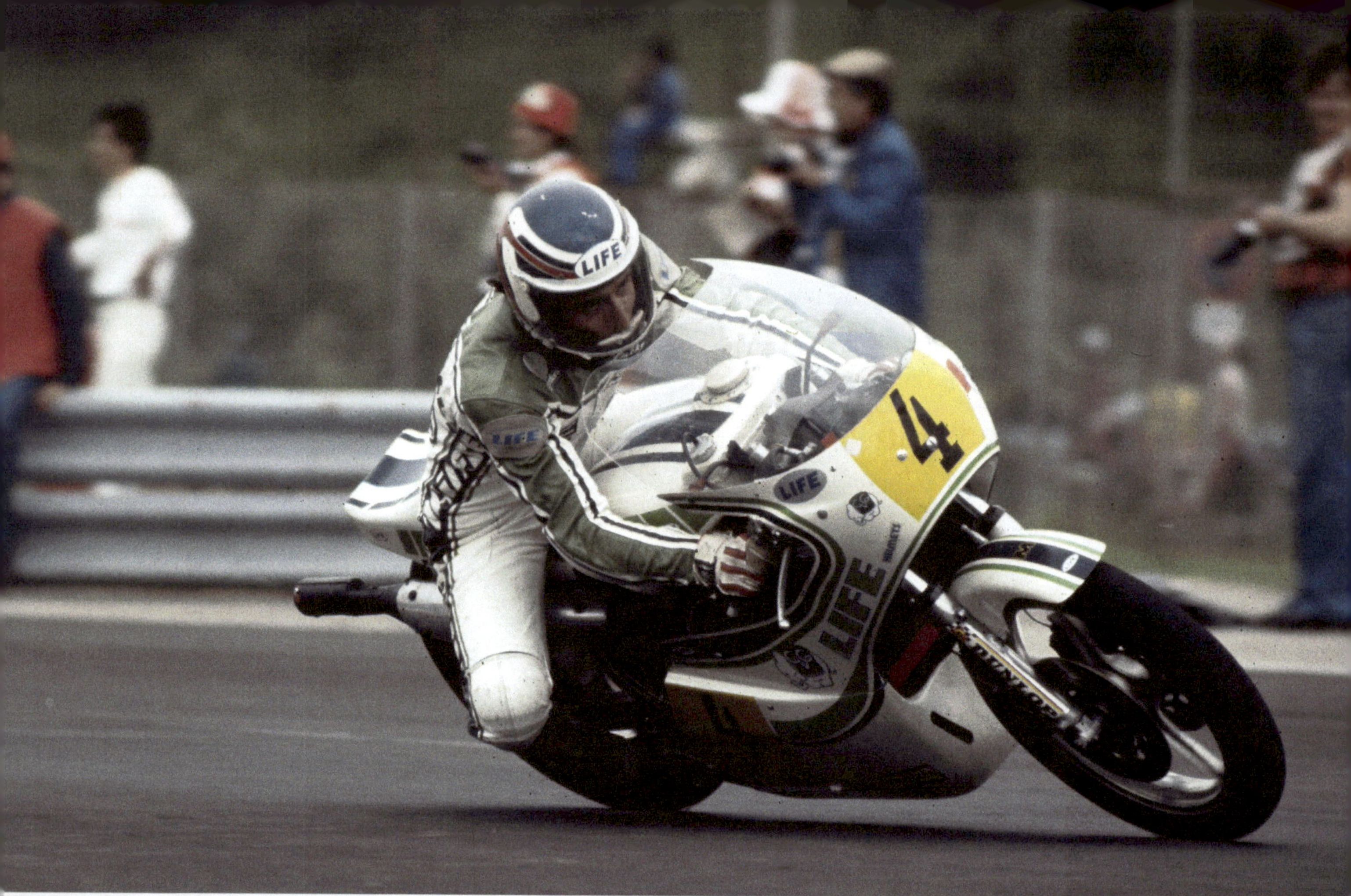
LIFE
4

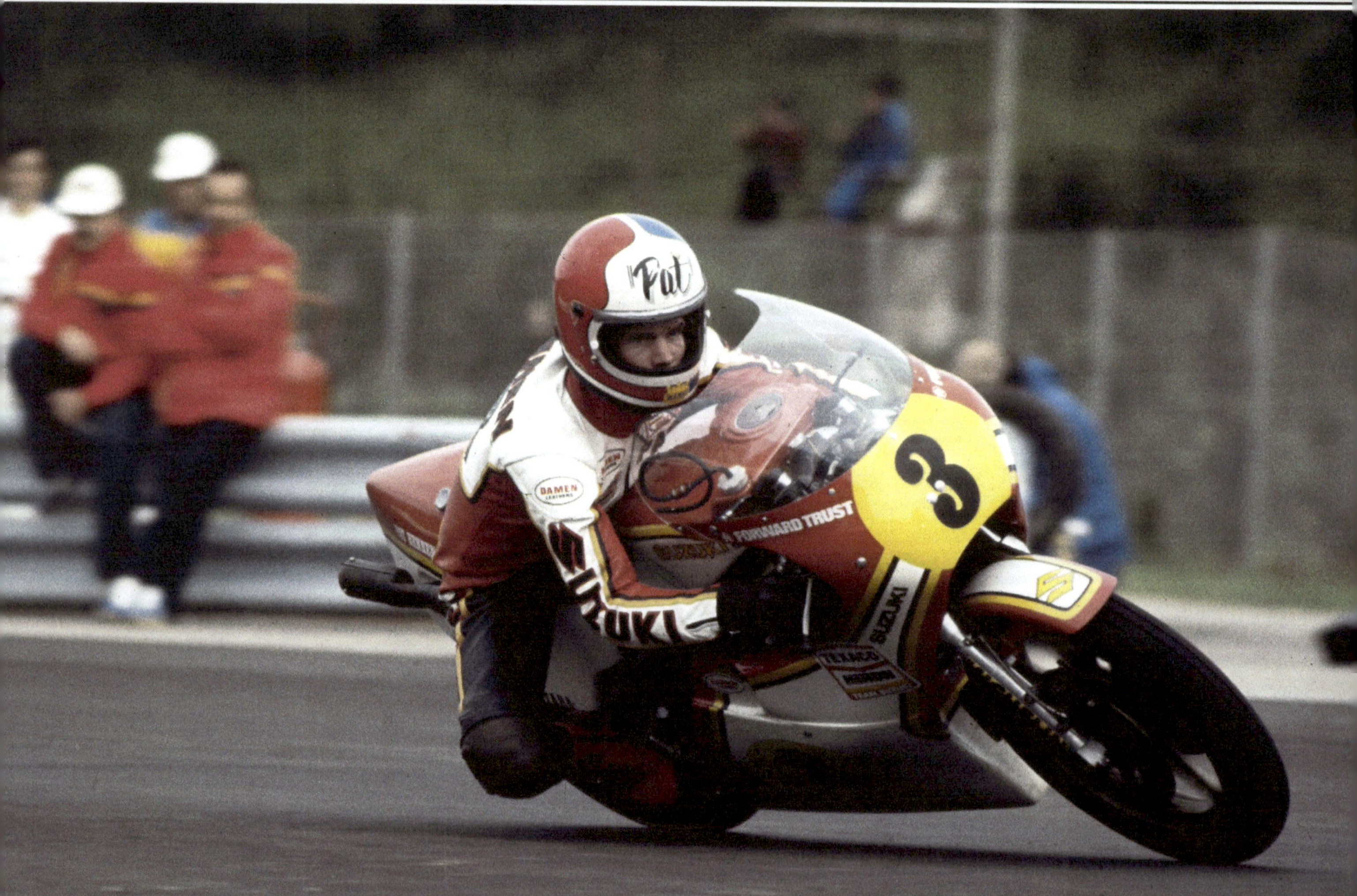
Pat
3
FORWARD TRUST
SUZUKI

1977 Nations GP (Imola) – Different styles at the Variante Bassa, Lucchinelli (4), Länsivuori (2), Hennen (3), Coulon (6)

1977 An intense Roberto Gallina helping his rider Virginio Ferrari to mount his RG 500

1977 Nations GP (Imola) – Ferrari before Barry Sheene in the Variante Bassa and while lining up on the starting grid

archivio © Claudio Ghini

1977 Finland GP (Imatra)- The English Steve Parrish with his official factory Suzuki – Heron Team

In 1977 Suzuki came out with a new motorcycle, the **RG 700 XR23, a 652 cm3 version of the RG 500**.
Basically, it was an RG 500 with increased bore. Suzuki used this bike only in the British "open events" and it was nothing more than a kind of 'lab' to test frames with a more powerful engine. During racing and testing, the Suzuki XR23 was a major advance in research which led to important developments for the frames of the future RG 500. In the 1977 Championship, Suzuki's only rivals were the new official factory Yamahas, led by Steve Baker and Johnny Cecotto.

Cecotto won two races and he was the only non-Suzuki winner in 1977.
Will Hartog was the only non-official factory rider to win a "normal" GP in 1977, obtaining the first place in his home GP, the Dutch TT, and showing the potential of the over the counter RG 500 with Sheene and Hennen in second and third place.
Jack Findlay won the Austrian GP, although it should be remembered that this race was boycotted by all top riders because of the fatal accident involving Hans Stadelmann in the 350cm3 category. In fact, none of the riders who finished the season in the top 14 took part in that race. Pat Hennen won the last race of the season.
Sheene won 6 out of the 11 races and became world champion for the second time in a row.

1977 GP Finland (Imatra) - Gianfranco Bonera with his Gallina Nava Olio Fiat Team Suzuki

archivio © Claudio Ghini

1977 Tepi Länsivuori at the starting grid

1977 The SAIAD racing dept. in Turin, Italian Suzuki importer

1977 Ferrari before Sheene

1977 GP Finland (Imatra) - Sheene's bike. Wil Hartog is in the background.

archivio © Claudio Ghini

Final ranking of the **1977** Riders' World Championship was: **Barry Sheene 107 p.**, Steve Baker 80 p., **Pat Hennen 67 p.**, Johnny Cecotto 50 p., **Steve Parrish 39 p.**, Giacomo Agostini 37 p., **Gianfranco Bonera 37 p., Philippe Coulon 36 p., Teuvo Länsivuori 35 p., Wil Hartog 30 p.**

1977 Barry Sheene is the World Champion for the second year running

In the manufacturers' championship **Suzuki was first with 157 p.** ahead of Yamaha with 114 p.

RG 500
THE MYTH
IN ACTION

1978 - RGA 500 XR22

For the 1978 season Suzuki had a severe problem; the official factory Yamaha driven by Kenny Roberts.
Yamaha was determined to win the 500 cm3 World Championship and Roberts had already proven his skills in the United States and was ready to win in Europe.
Suzuki could only fight the US "Martian" by carefully selecting his riders and making their best with **the new XR22 bike.**

© Massimo Cuffiani

In the **winter of 1977** in Hamamatsu, Barry Sheene tried **the first version of the XR22** that would debut in the 1978 World Championship.
As you can see in the picture below, several comparisons were made between different versions available.
In the picture on the left you can clearly see how the "Golden Shock" rear shock absorbers already show the auxiliary tank mounted on top of the main body, that is inverted if compared with the 1977 XR14.

1978 Team Gallina NAVA OLIO FIAT

The Texaco Heron Suzuki team dropped Steve Parrish and kept **Barry Sheene and Pat Hennen.** The Nava Oil Fiat Suzuki team, managed by Roberto Gallina, used two official factory XR14s assigned to the former Yamaha rider **Steve Baker** and to **Virginio Ferrari.** After the victory in the 1977 Dutch TT, Suzuki Netherlands decided to compete with an official factory bike and their rider was, of course, the Dutchman **Wil Hartog.**
The team was managed by Ton Riemersma, Hartog' manager, along with the Dutch distributor Nimag. The new Suzuki motorcycle was named the XR22, better known as the RGA 500. The bike was a decisive step forward compared to the glorious XR14.
Suzuki made major changes to the engine remaining faithful to the "square four" scheme, with bore and stroke 54 x 54 mm, but the analogies ended there. In order to make the engine more compact and give it a lower centre of gravity, **the front cylinders were moved downwards**.
This change in the cylinders' layout also made the engine shorter and improved cooling.
It also allowed Suzuki to redesign the gearbox: **XR22 included a removable gearbox**, which meant that it was possible to remove the gear assembly by removing only six screws. This made it possible to change the ratio in about 20 minutes and, by laying the bike on its left side, you could do it in 15 minutes. The lower centre of gravity reduced the tendency to wheelie and improved the cornering distance.

The maximum power went up to **122 hp at 11,000 rpm, with an empty weight of 136 kg.**

Even the frame underwent some changes: the **Kayaba front forks** became **37 mm in diameter** with stroke reduced to 130 mm, the **front brakes were increased** by 5 mm in diameter going **from 295 mm to 300 mm** while the rear disc was decreased by 10 mm in diameter, going from 240 mm to 230 mm. These changes were possible because the tyres were improved and became more able to cope with high braking forces.

The **fairing** was redesigned and **equipped with a pair of side deflectors** and a lower front part to ease the air flow around the fairing. These improvements gave the bike more aerodynamic load and more stability on the straight.

> **1978 Barry Sheene with his RGA 500 XR22**

archivio © Claudio Ghini

1978 Nations GP (Mugello) - Sheene with his legendary 7 before Cecotto (4) with Yamaha; below, Pat Hennen (3) precedes Kenny Roberts (2) again with Yamaha.

The 1978 season started with the Venezuelan GP on the San Carlos track. After qualifying, the two Heron Suzukis were caught in the grip of Yamaha (Cecotto, Roberts, Sheene, Hennen, Baker and Katayama).
The premonition of a difficult race overcame Suzuki. Cecotto, the Venezuelan, initially brought satisfaction to his fans by leading the first part of the race.
Sheene, on the other hand, was 6th after the first lap, deliberately letting the others pass him on the first hairpin bend:

> "I knew it was better not to commit too much at the beginning in order to save energy for the end of the race".

Roberts retired on the second lap with engine seizure, and then later Cecotto retired because his front tyres were too soft. Katayama led the race for eight laps, then retired after coming off his bike.

The race ended with the victory of Sheene and four Suzuki in the first four positions: Sheene, Hennen, Baker and Parrish. No official factory Yamaha finished the race.

1978 Graziano Rossi with Suzuki RG 500 MK III - OECE Team.

Hennen won the following race, the Spanish GP in Jarama, with Roberts second and Sheene fifth.

Sheene missed the top of the standings, overtaken by his teammate Hennen. This was now the start of a new rivalry between Sheene and Hennen; having Hennen as teammate has never been exciting for Sheene even before the start of the season and now that Hennen was leading the championship the situation got worse.

After the French GP, with Hennen second and Sheene third, the relationship between the two teammates broke down, with Sheene accusing Hennen of having copied his tyre choice. Although the Suzuki parent company had asked everyone to work as a team, the reality was rather different.

For the Mugello Nations GP, Sheene arranged to give Team Gallina an XR22 for Steve Baker, but this also did not help Sheene. Roberts won the race, with Hennen second, and Luchinelli third with a customer version RG 500 MK III, Baker fourth and Sheene only fifth.

Later, Sheene went to the Chimay track in Belgium to compete in an international competition which did not count towards the World Championship, while Hennen went to the Isle of Man to compete in the TT.

The US rider's decision looked quite irresponsible and it seemed risky to race on such a dangerous track while competing for the World Championship.

But Hennen was running after the big money prizes of the TT to cover his expensive extras and mechanics. After a few laps in the Senior TT, Hennen was leading ahead of Tom Herron, with the new lap record, when his bike unseated him at the Bishop's Court.

Hennen fell over at top speed in 6th gear, suffering serious injuries that forced him to withdraw permanently from competitions.

1978 Barry Sheene

1978 AGV Nations Cup Imola - Will Hartog with the official factory Suzuki, Heron Team

archivio © Claudio Ghini

With Hennen out of the game, Suzuki immediately looked for someone to replace him and to help Sheene in his fight to conquer the third World Championship title.
The right man was the Dutch ace **Will Hartog**. Hartog won the Dutch TT in 1977 with his over the counter RG 500 and his first race on the official factory XR22 would have been the Dutch TT. Hartog had some problems with brakes, as the Heron mechanics advised him to insert the brake pads they used. During the first lap Hartog made a mistake, as his bike did not brake as well as his old RG 500, but he still managed to finish the race in fifth position. The Dutch GP was won by Cecotto, before Roberts and Sheene.

In the following GP, that of Belgium in Spa, the Heron Team gave an official factory XR22 to the Frenchman Rougerie.
At the same time, for this race, Hartog's mechanics used the RG 500 pads improving the performance.
Hartog had one of his famous lightning starts that brought him to the top of the group.
Hartog and Sheene got ahead of the pack immediately when the rain began to fall, but Roberts recovered on Sheene and this gave Hartog a chance to take a bigger advantage.
In the final laps Hartog slowed down trying to help Sheene – he had been hired by Suzuki for this - but the stable orders were clear and told him to go and win.

1978 Pat Hennen at the starting grid

archivio © Claudio Ghini

On the last lap Roberts passed Sheene and Hartog increased the gap between himself and his competitors. Hartog was very happy after his second win in a Grand Prix, but Sheene attacked him after the race: he was furious with Hartog because he had not helped him, but Hartog only did what the Suzuki team manager ordered him.

After Belgium, the teams went to Karlskoga for the Swedish GP and this track suited the characteristics of the two Suzukis, an extremely difficult track where skilful handling was more important than top speed.

Cecotto reached Pole Position with Yamaha, but he and Roberts were never a threat to the Suzuki in this race. Hartog again got off to a good start and halfway through the race, as per his team's orders, he slowed down and signalled to Sheene with his leg where he should overtake him. Sheene took over control of the race faithfully followed by Hartog.

The end of the race was quite awkward: Sheene was so happy about his second win after the Grand Prix of Venezuela that he raised his hands 50 meters before the finish line, throttling back and losing speed. Hartog was so close that he had to brake so as not to overtake Sheene.

For the Swedish public Hartog was the real winner but, with his help, Sheene reduced the gap between himself and Roberts to just three points in the general ranking. At the next Finnish GP in Imatra, the race started again with a great start by Hartog who took the lead at the first corner from the 5th place on the grid.

Roberts managed to overtake Hartog once, but Hartog crossed the finishing line in triumph. Sheene retired on the fourth lap, however, limiting the damage as Roberts also retired at the eighth lap due to ignition problems.

The Silverstone British GP was in the hands of the weather. The air was heavy with rain although the race started on a dry track. Hartog rocketed forward as usual but on the second lap Roberts took the lead with Hartog second, Rougerie third and Sheene sixth. After a couple of laps the first drops of rain began to fall and Roberts almost lost control of his bike at the Woodcote corner. At the end of the 12th lap, conditions became difficult for the rider.

Katayama was agitated communicating to the commissioners to stop the race but at the same time Cecotto, Sheene and Hartog entered the pits to change tyres. Roberts and Katayama had to do the same thing as on the following lap.

With the change of tyres Roberts had a great advantage over the Suzuki, because the Yamaha had a "quick release" system of the front wheel. It took Roberts only 2.5 minutes to change tyres, while Team Suzuki took 7.5 minutes. Because of the various entrances in the pits no one understood anymore who the leader was, but Roberts was the first to get the checkered flag.

When Roberts, Manship and Sheene got on the podium they clashed with Marco Lucchinelli, who was regarded by many as the race's winner.

The West German GP was the last race of the season and would be the decisive one for establishing the World Champion. Roberts was the championship leader and Sheene was second; for the Briton to become world champion meant winning with Roberts in no better than fourth place.

To increase Sheene's chances of success, Suzuki also gave Virginio Ferrari an official factory XR22, so they were four at the Nurburgring: Sheene, Hartog, Rougerie and Ferrari. The tactic provided was very simple: insert the other three XR22s between Sheene and Roberts.

Ferrari immediately took the lead in the race followed by Cecotto, Roberts, Sheene, Lucchinelli and Katayama. Hartog strangely had a bad start and was seventh, but he was already in fourth place by the middle of the first lap. Unfortunately, Hartog's recovery made him overconfident, which lead to his overdoing it and falling off, thereby losing his third place in the World Championship to Cecotto.

The rest of the race saw Ferrari in the lead, then Cecotto and Roberts who controlled the race by keeping the position that would guarantee him the victory in the Championship. Sheene ultimately ranked fourth and after the race he was the first to congratulate Roberts on his first world title.

1978 Barry Sheen before Hennen

The final classification of the **1978** World championship was as follows:
Roberts 110 p., **Sheene 100 p.**, Cecotto 66 p., **Hartog 65 p.**, Katayama 53 p., **Hennen 51 p.**, **Baker 42 p.**, **Länsivuori 39 p.**, **Lucchinelli 30 p.**, **Rougerie 23 p.**

In the manufacturers' championship **Suzuki was the first with 149 p.** ahead of Yamaha with 136p.

1979 - RGB 500 XR27B

Motorcycle fans waited for the 1979 World Championship with apprehension, imagining a spectacular season: Suzuki and Yamaha, in fact, would make maximum effort to become world champions. Just as in 1978, Yamaha deployed three official factory bikes: **Kenny Roberts**, **Johnny Cecotto** and young French **Christian Sarron** supported by the French importer Sonauto, while **Katayama** switched to **Honda**, which had just returned to racing for the first time since 1968, with a **500 bike cm3, 4-stroke V4**.
Graziano Rossi moved from Suzuki to the newly launched Morbidelli 500.
Suzuki would field five RGB 500 official factory bikes for three teams: Team Texaco Heron Suzuki with **Barry Sheene**, **Steve Parrish** and Irishman **Tom Herron**; Team Gallina Nava Olio Fiat with **Virginio Ferrari** and Team Nimag Suzuki with **Wil Hartog**. In 1978 Hartog raced the second half of the season for Team Heron Suzuki and was offered a place in the team for 1979.
For Hartog, however, the races were still a hobby (even though he was one of the top riders) and he wanted to remain faithful to Ton Riemersma, his manager and sponsor for a few years and to the Dutch importer Nimag.
In 1979, Suzuki wanted to regain the World Championship Title, and to do this they brought out a **new 500, the RGB 500 XR27B.**

© Massimo Cuffiani

RG 500
THE MYTH
IN ACTION

1979 Barry Sheene with his XR27BFR

So as to leave nothing to chance, Suzuki invited Sheene, Hartog and Ferrari to try out their new bike in Japan in winter testing. The bike itself remained essentially the same, although the engine now had melted cylinders with steel bushings treated with Nikasil pressed inside. Inside the engine the cylinders had no longer mounting bolts in common with the heads, but they were screwed independently into the crankcase, while the heads were fixed by six screws on the cylinders. The power had been increased to **124 hp at 11,000 rpm** for an empty weight of **136 kg**.
The front discs had also been increased and reached 310 mm in diameter, while the rear had been decreased to 220 mm.
The bike's most important modifications were in the frame. The upper main tube was now straight towards the swing arm, without bends. To reduce the bike's tendency to do wheelies, Suzuki produced a version, **the XR27BFR, with the radiator in the front part of the fairing.**

This made it possible to put more weight on the front wheel, but also raised the centre of gravity. During the test in Japan, Sheene was very happy with the XR27BFR, while Ferrari and Hartog did not like its driveability because its higher centre of gravity made it very difficult on corners. The new stiffer frame, however, caused problems of diving while braking, which Suzuki tried to solve with **a hydraulic anti-dive system in the front fork.**

1979 VENEZUELA GP (San Carlos) - Parrish's motorcycle with new engine

1979 Barry Sheene with his RGB 500 XR27B

Team Gallina was the first to use a 16" front rim to improve handling, while other teams thought this would not work. It was not used regularly during the season due to inadequate development on tyres.
Another important fact for Suzuki was the confirmation that **the RG 500 MK IV over the counter bike was a great one** and this was demonstrated by the victory of Boet van Dulmen in Finland and his podium alongside his compatriot Jack Middelburg in the GP of Sweden.
The first race of the year was the Venezuela GP, not attended by Roberts due to an accident during the tests in Japan.
For most of the race it seemed that no one could beat Hartog, until the twelfth lap, when his front wheel froze and he came off.
Sheene won the race, Ferrari was second after a gripping duel with Herron, using tyres with 1978 compound and 18" rim at the front.

Suzuki started the championship with great results, placing its bikes in the first six positions.
The second race, the Austrian GP, took place at the Salzburgring. During the qualifying, Roberts, on his return, immediately showed that he was in good shape.
The race was full of twists and turns: Ferrari had to replace the defective front tyre with the only spare, a slick carved for the wet conditions. Despite this, he immediately led the race, followed by Roberts and Hartog.
Ferrari battled for a long time until the tyre collapsed, delivering the victory to Roberts, but he managed to defend the second position from Hartog.
Sheene finished twelfth due to problems with the anti-dive system, Cecotto fell and broke the kneecap saying goodbye to the championship.
Hartog won the next race, the West German GP at Hockenheim and led the race from start to finish using his Suzuki's speed in long straights.
Behind him the fight was between Roberts, Van Dulmen (with the over the counter RG 500 MK IV), Sheene and Ferrari.
Van Dulmen and Sheene retired due to engine failure, so Roberts won the second place ahead of Ferrari.

1979 NATIONS GP - (Imola) - Sheene precedes Heron at the Tosa bend

1979 Summer tests on the Imola racetrack:
Above - Franco Uncini shows his RG 500 MK IV to an F1 delegation present at Imola, including Bernie Ecclestone;
Left - Ferrari tries some modifications on Team Gallina's XR27B. Note on the right the XR23B (RGB 700), the Suzuki for the 750 class

1979 NATIONS GP (Imola) - Yet another flying start by Hartog (3), followed by Ferrari (11), Lucchinelli (9), Parrish (12), Herron (20), Van Dulmen (16), Sheene (7), Roberts (1), Baldwin (27), Middelburg (62), Rolando (33), Uncini (8).

archivio © Claudio Ghini

archivio © Claudio Ghini

1979 NATIONS GP (Imola) - Tosa bend. Ferrari precedes Sheene and Baldwin

The fourth round of the World championship, the des Nations GP, took place at Imola.
Roberts won again, with Ferrari second, despite a very bad crash at the Tamburello bend, during practice.
Due to chassis problems, during the four rounds of tests, he tried various types of chassis, including the XR22 version of 1978 and that of the 1979 customer version, which however did not fit well with the new engine. Ferrari managed to keep the championship lead in this place. Herron was ranked in third position ahead of Sheene with Hartog retiring after a fall.
The race at the Jarama track, the Spanish GP, was a battle between Roberts and Hartog for most of the race, in front of the American "rookie" Mike Baldwin who was

third (RG 500 MK IV), with Ferrari fourth, Uncini fifth (RG 500 MK IV), Van Dulmen sixth (RG 500 MK IV) and Middelburg seventh (RG 500 MK IV).
The Suzuki customer version demonstrated its value and proved that an official factory bike was not necessary to finish high up on the classification. Tom Herron did not take part in the race due to a fall during qualifying.

Despite this injury, he decided to take part the following weekend in the "North West 200" in his native Ireland.
It was the last race for Herron, who fell off on the last lap of the 1000 cm3 class on his RGB 500.
For Team Herron Suzuki it was the first time that one of his official factory riders died during race.

1979 Barry Sheene

archivio © Claudio Ghini

Franco Uncini proved his worth, in the year of his debut in the 500cc World Championship, bringing his **over the counter RG 500 MK IV** to victory in the international race at Salzburgring in Austria.

In Yugoslavia Suzuki had problems with the bikes' handling. Ferrari actually declared, **"We should try the 16" tyres again, they would make the bike more agile"**.
Roberts won the race ahead of Ferrari, Uncini, Hartog and Van Dulmen. Ferrari was still confirmed as he was the only one able of holding their own with Roberts, while Uncini won his first prize, proving himself to be the fastest privateer.
The next race, the **'Dutch TT'** which is the Dutch GP, was a Suzuki show once again.
Ferrari won a duel at the last bend with Sheene, ahead of Hartog, Van Dulmen, Uncini, Coulon, Middelburg and Roberts.

1979 GP YUGOSLAVIA - (Rjieka) – Race prize giving: 2nd Ferrari, 1st Roberts, 3rd Uncini

In Sweden Roberts resumed the lead in the world rankings, finishing fourth behind Sheene, Middelburg, Van Dulmen, with Ferrari retiring due to a broken bearing. In Finland Ferrari lost further points when, due to imperfect engine tuning, he decided to retire.
The "extreme privateer" Van Dulmen won with the RG 500 MK IV, ahead of the young American Mamola, who had been entrusted with a Suzuki, and Sheene, with Roberts sixth due to an error on the bend.
The following **British GP in Silverstone saw the epic duel between Roberts and Sheene** with the former winning by just a few centimetres, and Hartog third after his initial battle for the win. Ferrari was fourth.
There was only the French GP at Le Mans to go.
To win the title, Ferrari had to win the race and Roberts had to score no points.
He started immediately as leader but fell on the thirteenth lap giving Roberts, who ended the race in third position, his second title. Sheene won the race before an increasingly effective Mamola.

The final classification of the **1979** World Championship was as follows:
Roberts 113 p., **Ferrari 89 p., Sheene 87 p., Hartog 66 p., Uncini 51 p.**

In the ranking of the brands **Suzuki was first with 165 p.** ahead of Yamaha 138 p. and Morbidelli 2 p.

1980 - RGB 500 XR34

The 1979 World Cup had just ended and two sensational divorces marked the pre-championship 1980. After years of successful collaboration and, above all, two World championship titles, **Barry Sheene fell out with Suzuki and walked out.** The divorce was quite painless for both: the Hamamatsu House still had excellent riders and Sheene, flanked by the Japanese colossus of Hi-Fi AKAI joined Yamaha as non-official factory driver with special assistance. The second divorce involved the vice-champion 1979 Virginio Ferrari, who left the Suzuki of Team Gallina for the Belgian team of Serge Zago with their 500 "special" Yamahas. Even this deal didn't last, however.

As from 1980, Yamaha began to imitate Suzuki by supplying motorcycles to private customers such as the YZR 500, at a price of about 20% higher than the Suzuki RG 500.

The new model that Suzuki used in 1980 was the RGB 500 XR34, in two versions: XR34H with traditional rear suspension and XR34M with the new "Full Float" rear suspension with single shock absorber.

RG 500
THE MYTH
IN ACTION

© Massimo Cuffiani

1980 Randy Mamola - Heron Suzuki Team

The fork was increased to 40 mm in diameter, with only 120 mm of travel and kept the "anti-dive" system. Suzuki calculated that the torsion resistance under fork load increased by 50%, reducing its stroke by only 20%. The power increased by another hp reaching 125 hp at 10,800 rpm, with a curb weight of 144 kg.
There were five official factory Suzukis.

Two for the **Texaco Heron Team** with **Randy Mamola** and the New Zealander **Graeme Crosby** as riders, Rex White as team manager, Geremy Burgess and George Vulkanovich as Mamola's mechanics, Mick Smith and Dave Cullen as Crosby's mechanics, chief engineer Martyn Ogborne. The two other official factory bikes were for **Team Gallina Nava-Olio Fiat** with **Marco Lucchinelli** and **Graziano Rossi** and one for the Dutch team **Riemersma-Nimag** with **Wil Hartog**.

1980 Graeme Crosby - Heron Suzuki Team

1980 Marco Lucchinelli - Gallina Team

archivio © Claudio Ghini

The choice between the two rear suspension versions divided the riders during the championship. **The Full Float system** was used for the first time at the Spanish GP with the **XR34M1**, used by Mamola, Rossi and Hartog, but it was then replaced by the revised version **XR34M2.**

1980 Graziano Rossi - Gallina Team

After 1979, the **Gallina Team** still used the **16" front rim**, while the British preferred the 18" one because it gave more tyre options.

archivio © Claudio Ghini

1980 Franco Uncini with his RG 500 MK V

With this bike, Mamola won the Belgian and British GP, while Crosby raced again with the XR34H.
Hartog, instead, returned to the XR34H version at the French GP, and then used the XR34M2 again from the Finnish GP by winning it.
In the Nava Team, Rossi used the XR34M1 version from the Spanish GP, while **Lucchinelli** initially raced with the H versions, passing from the Finnish GP to the **XR34M2 and winning the last GP of the season in West Germany at the Nurburgring.** Also, the H version underwent development during the season, Suzuki actually made three versions: **XR3400H, XR3402H, XR3403H**, with the latter that differed for the steering head set back by 20 mm and the 20 mm lengthened swing arm.

The 1980 season began with the cancellation of the first two GPs: Venezuela for economic reasons and Austria because of snow.

The first GP therefore was the des Nations in Misano, which was won by Roberts with the Suzuki official factory bikes withdrawn with the exception of Rossi's, and Uncini achieving a great second position with a customer version Suzuki.

1980 NATIONS GP (Misano) - Uncini with his brother and team manager Henry and mechanic Ciamberlini.
In the background the "Mr. Fixit" Carlo Biffani

archivio © F.Uncini

1980 Italian Championship - Misano
5 Suzukis in the front row (from left): Rolando, Perugini, Uncini, Lucchinelli, Rossi.

1980 Marco Lucchinelli in action with his XR34H

1980 GP FINLAND (Imatra) - Mamola

The next Spanish GP in Jarama saw Lucchinelli again in pole position. At Misano he had to retire when he was in second position, but here he ended up behind Roberts and ahead of Mamola.
In the French GP, Roberts won again, and the rest of the podium was reversed with Mamola second to Lucchinelli at the photo finish. At Assen victory still eluded Suzuki, with Rossi and Uncini taking second and third positions in a race that was decided by choice of tyre and won by the privateer Middelburg on a Yamaha.

1980 GP GERMANY WEST (Nürburgring) - Lucchinelli out ahead on his own and on his way to victory

1980 Lucchinelli third in the World Championship

Finally, in Zolder at the Belgium GP Mamola won ahead of Lucchinelli, also because of stability problems with Roberts' bike.
The Finnish GP, on the dangerous Imatra track, saw Hartog win with the official factory Suzuki, ahead of Roberts and Uncini. This allowed Uncini to move up the standings ahead of Lucchinelli who had retired because of a burning gasket head while he was in the lead with a wide gap. The British GP following this was no more fortunate for Roberts, beaten by Mamola with Lucchinelli third and Rossi fourth. At this point, only the Nürburgring West German GP remained, where Roberts and Mamola tried their best to win the title

separated by 13 points. Lucchinelli won authoritatively after initially duelling with Mamola who was then forced to slow down due to engine failure. Crosby came second, followed by Hartog, Roberts and Mamola.

Final riders' classification 1980: **Roberts 87 p., Mamola 72 p., Lucchinelli 59 p., Uncini 50 p., Rossi 38 p.**

In the ranking of the brands, **Suzuki was first with 108 p.** ahead of Yamaha 102 p. and Kawasaki 13 p.

DRAWINGS
of motorcycles of greatest significance

© Massimo Cuffiani

Year - 1975
Model - RG 500 XR14
Rider - Barry Sheene
Power - 100 HP
Max speed - 284 km/h

RG 500 BIKES IN HISTORY

Year - 1974
Model - RG 500 XR14
Rider - Jack Findlay - GP Sweden
Power - 95 HP
Max speed - 275 km/h

© Massimo Cuffiani

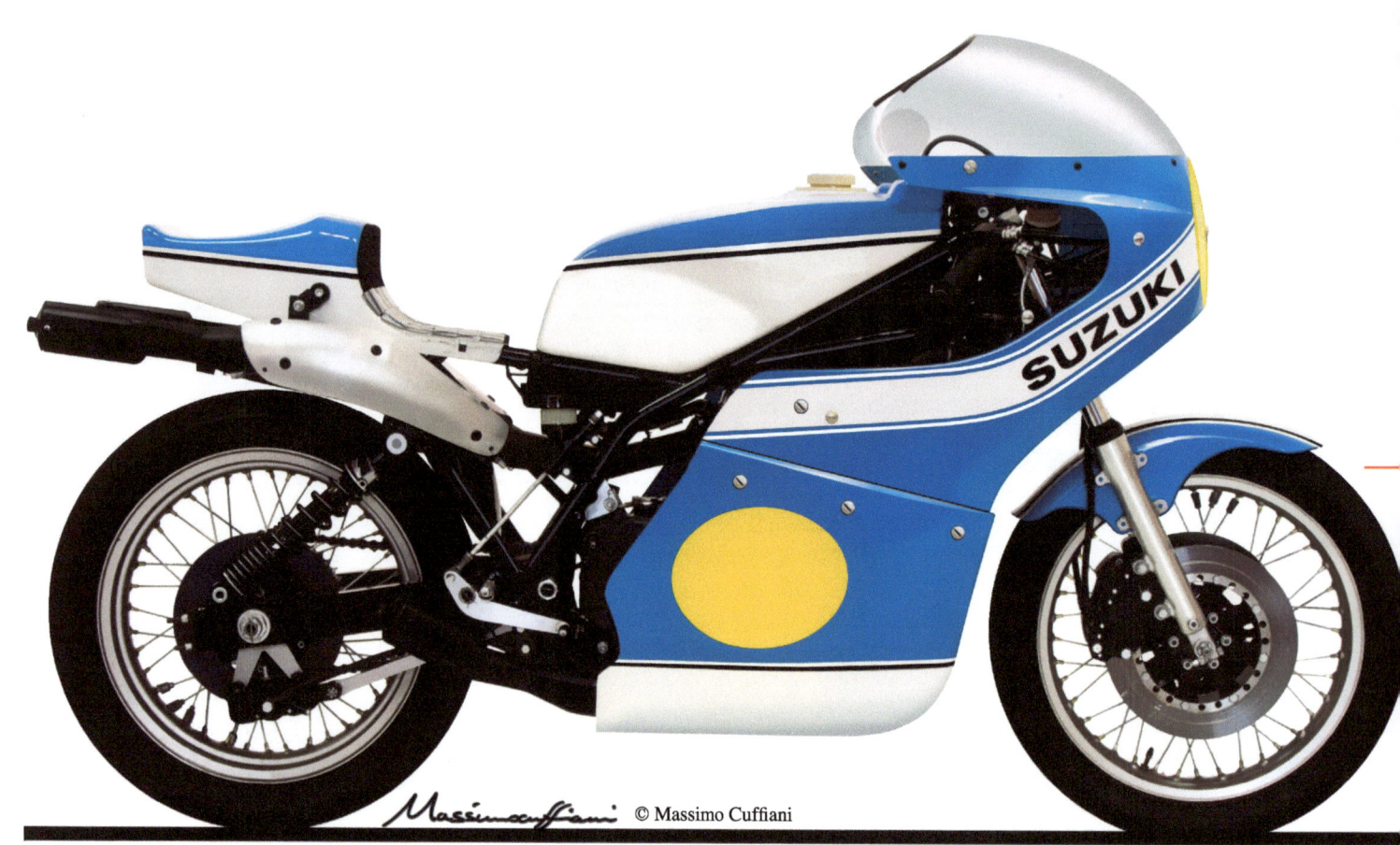

Year - 1976
Model - RG 500 MK I
Rider - Giacomo Agostini - Dutch TT Assen
Power - 100 HP
Max speed - 275 km/h

Year - **1976**
Model - **RG 500 MK I**
Rider - **Standard for privateer riders**
Power - **100 HP**
Max speed - **275 km/h**

© Massimo Cuffiani

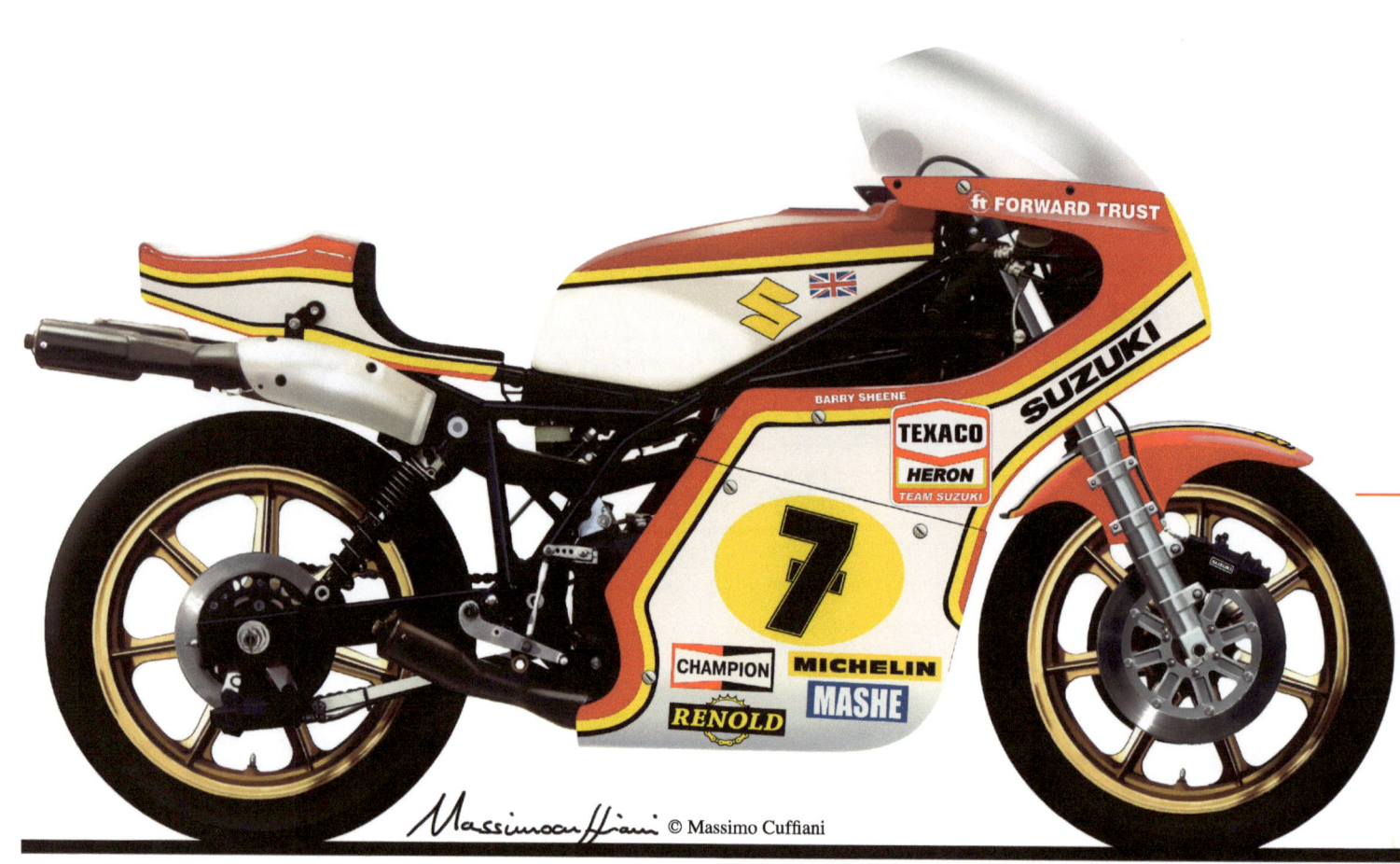

Year - 1977
Model - RG 500 XR14 - "Donald Duck 1"
Rider - Barry Sheene
Power - 119 HP
Max speed - 296 km/h

Year - **1976**
Model - **RG 500 XR14**
Rider - **Barry Sheene**
Power - **114 HP**
Max speed - **296 km/h**

© Massimo Cuffiani

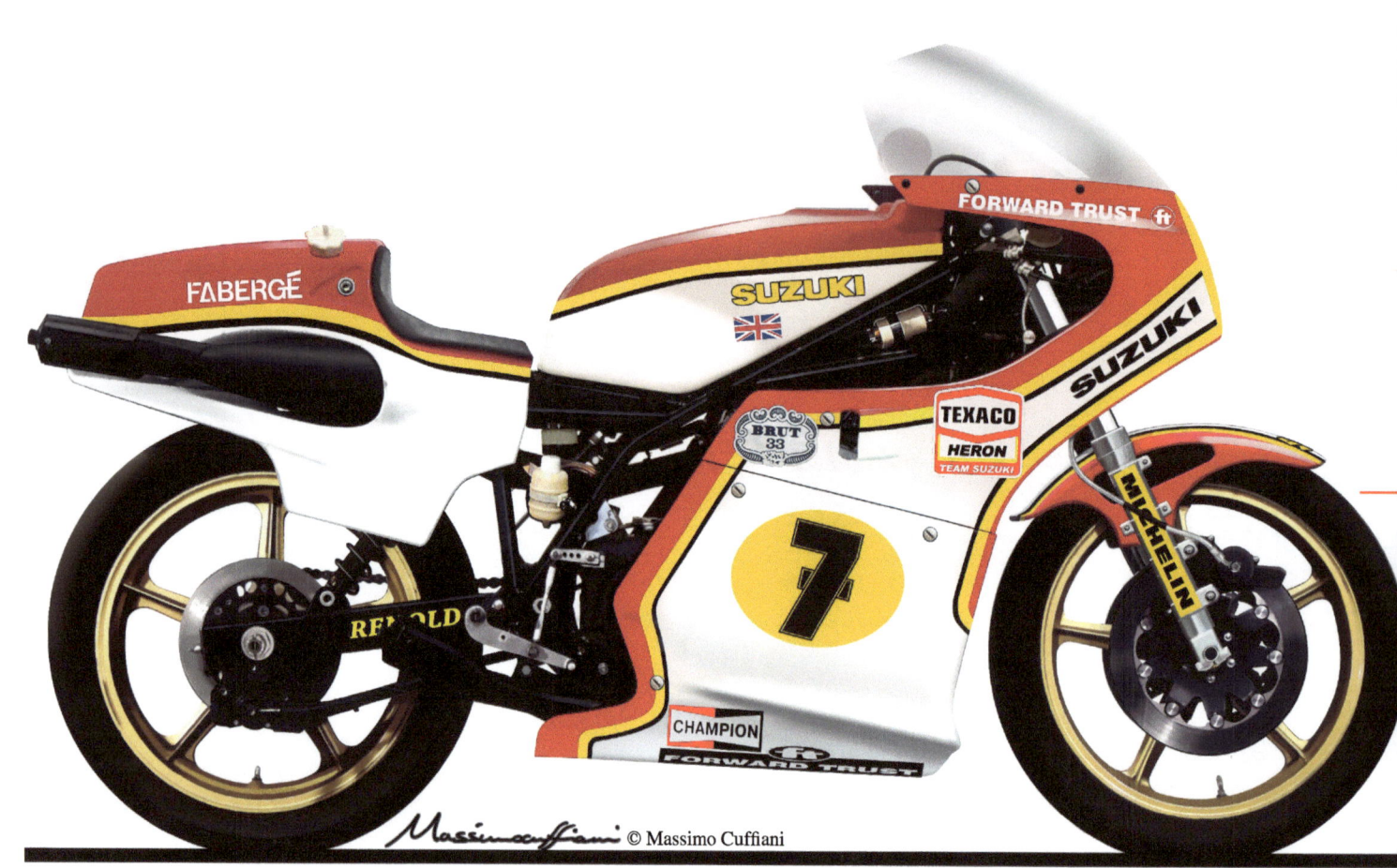

Year - 1977
Model - RG 500 XR14
Rider - Barry Sheene - GP Finland
Power - 119 HP
Max speed - 296 km/h

Year - 1977
Model - RG 500 XR14 - "Donald Duck 2"
Rider - Barry Sheene
Power - 119 HP
Max speed - 296 km/h

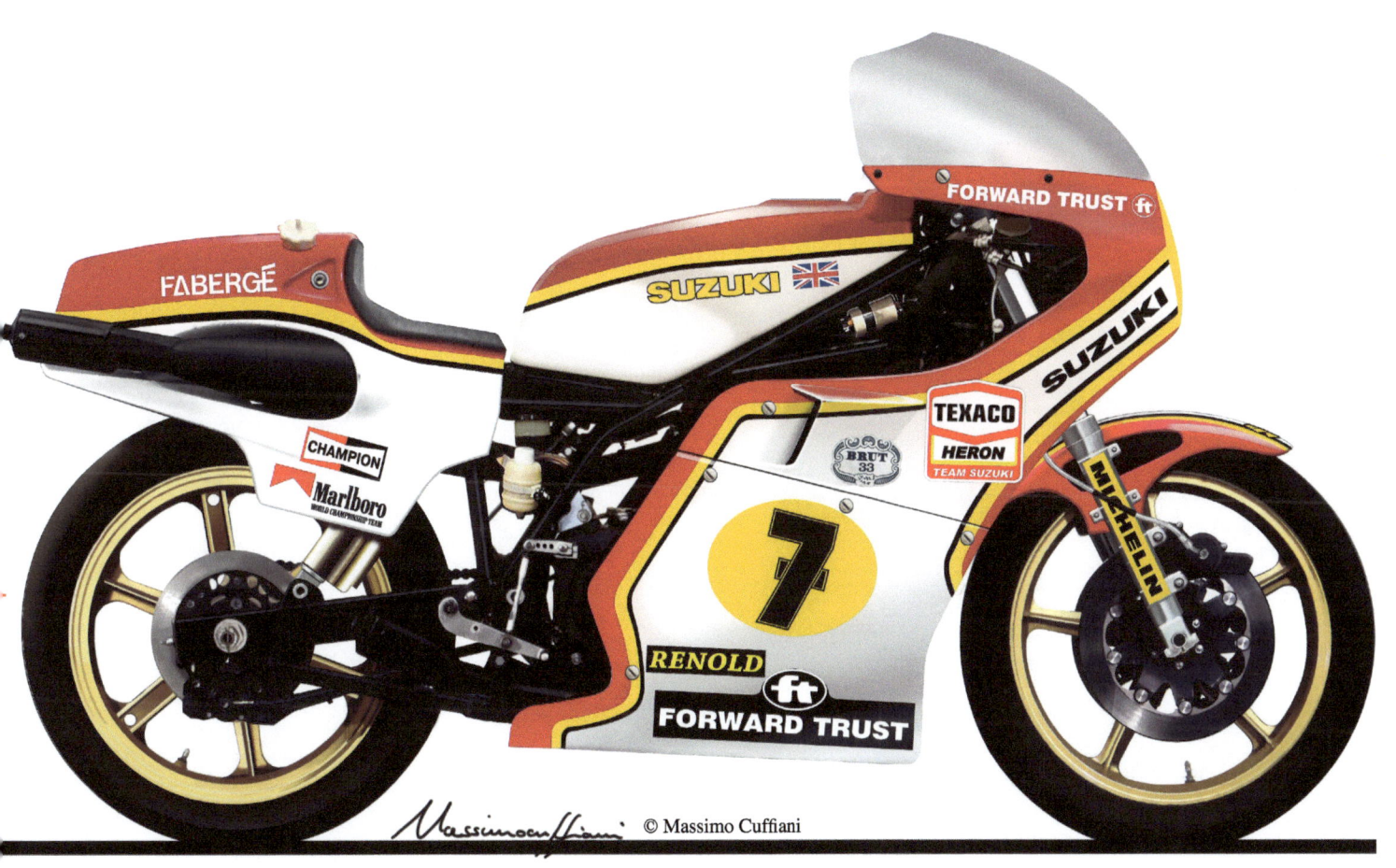

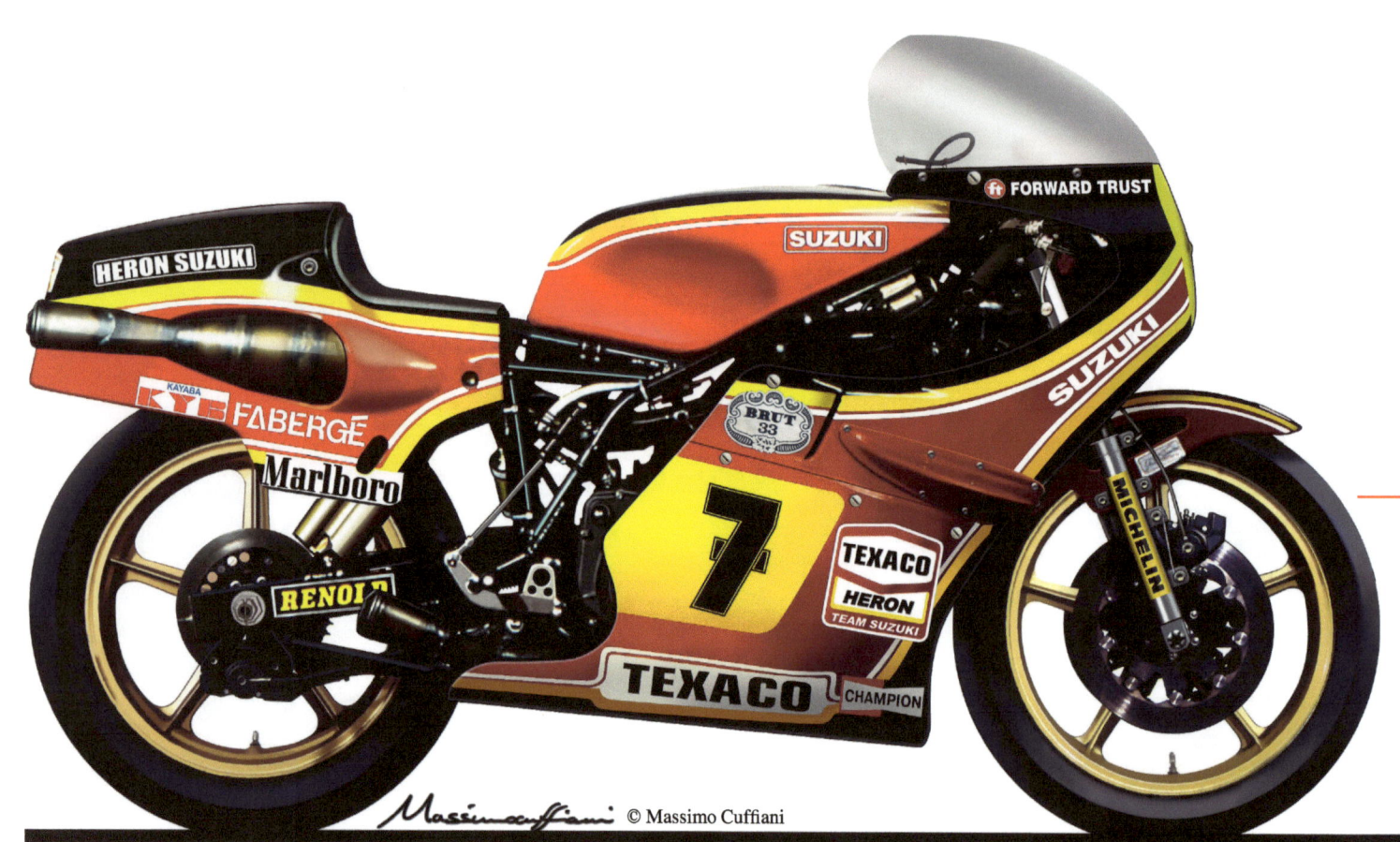

Year - 1979
Model - RGB 500 XR27B
Rider - Barry Sheene
Power - 124 HP
Max speed - 300 km/h

Year - **1978**
Model - **RGA 500 XR22**
Rider - **Barry Sheene - GP France**
Power - **122 HP**
Max speed - **300 km/h**

© Massimo Cuffiani

Year - 1980
Model - RGB 500 XR34
Rider - Graziano Rossi - GP West Germany
Power - 125 HP
Max speed - 309 km/h

Year - **1979**
Model - **RGB 500 XR27B**
Rider - **Wil Hartog - Dutch TT Assen**
Power - **124 HP**
Max speed - **300 km/h**

© Massimo Cuffiani

THE COLLECTION IMOLA CLASSIC
1976 - RG 500 MK I
GIACOMO AGOSTINI

RG 500
BIKES IN HISTORY

1976 - RG 500 MK I
GIACOMO AGOSTINI

1977 - RG 500 MK II BARRY SHEENE 76 tribute

archivio © F.Merzari

1977 - RG 500 MK II
BARRY SHEENE 76
tribute

1977 - RG 500 MK II
TEUVO LÄNSIVUORI

1977 - RG 500 MK II
TEUVO LÄNSIVUORI

1979 - RG 500 MK IV
FRANCO UNCINI

1979 - RG 500 MK IV
FRANCO UNCINI

1979 - RG 500 MK IV
TEAM NAVA GALLINA tribute

archivio © F.Merzari

1979 - RG 500 MK IV
TEAM NAVA GALLINA
tribute

1984 - RGB 500 III
VIRGINIO FERRARI
1982 XR40 tribute

1984 - RGB 500 III
VIRGINIO FERRARI
1982 XR40 tribute

**1976 - RG 500 MK I
GIACOMO AGOSTINI**

**1977 - RG 500 MK II
BARRY SHEENE 76
tribute**

**1977 - RG 500 MK II
TEUVO LÄNSIVUORI**

The bike, completely restored, is one of the two used by Agostini in 1976, here in the Nations GP version at Mugello where he obtained Pole Position.
Compared to a standard version, it is fitted with Ceriani Racing forks combined with brake calipers and Brembo discs and Veglia Borletti tachometer.

The idea of fit out a motorbike in its 1976 version started when a motorcycle with a particular numbering resembling the chassis used in the same year by Sheene came to light in a garage in Holland. Even the engine showed some details that suggested a past close to an official factory.

Motorcycle purchased for Read by the Life team in '77 and then brought in by Länsivuori and Lucchinelli. The bike had work done on the frame by the Cagiva team to keep it racing even in 1978 and 1979.
Its engine was found on a bike that the Gallina team used as a showbike in 1980.

1979 - RG 500 MK IV
FRANCO UNCINI

archivio © Massimo Cuffiani

1979 - RG 500 MK IV
TEAM NAVA
GALLINA

archivio © F.Merzari

1984 - RGB 500 III
VIRGINIO FERRARI
1982 XR40 tribute

archivio © F.Merzari

The bike is the only one used by Uncini in 1979.
Chassis No. 11302 and reserve engine, also by Uncini, No. 11340.
It should be noted that the motorcycle is fitted with the 1981 anti-dive fork, as well as the Brembo braking systems (calipers, front floating disc and rear disc) that Uncini used in 1981.
Livery of the GP of Belgium 1979.

The bike was used as a show bike by the Gallina team in the '80s and remained in a garage in La Spezia for many years.
Used in many historical Moto GP parades, in 2017 it was ridden around the track at SPA by Phil Read who commented: "very fast and good handling!"

Belonging to the Dutch team of Boet Van Dulmen who had enhanced it with the addition of many XR Factory parts. It lay dismantled for many years and for this reason it has safely remained preserved until the present day.
This is the 1982 version of Team HB UK, Virginio Ferrari rider.
The bike weighs only 123 kg because of the materials used such as magnesium, titanium and aluminium.

1976 - RG 500 MK I | **1977 - RG 500 MK II** | **1977 - RG 500 MK II**

1979 - RG 500 MK IV   **1979 - RG 500 MK IV**   **1984 - RGB 500 III**

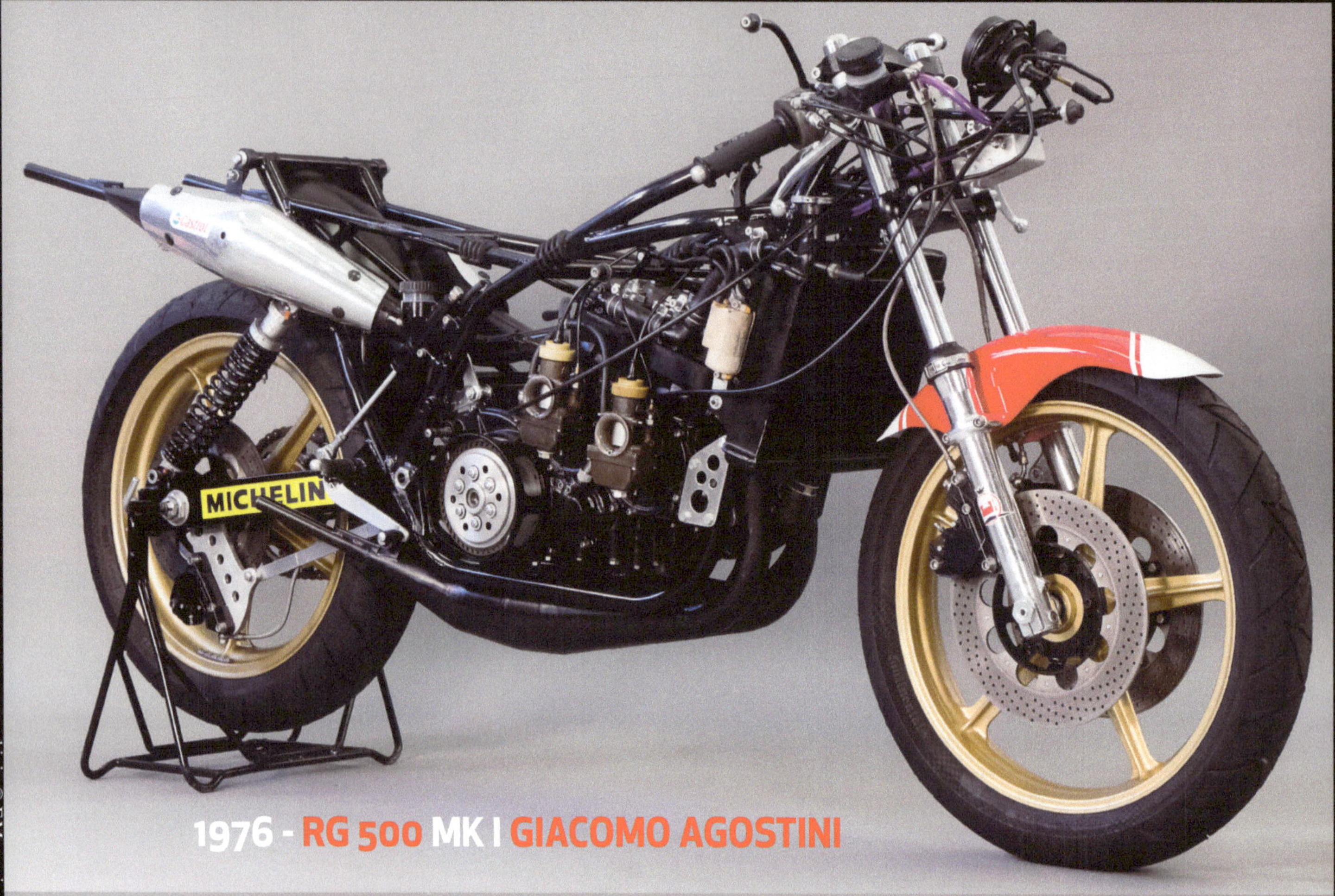

1976 - RG 500 MK I GIACOMO AGOSTINI

archivio © F.Merzari

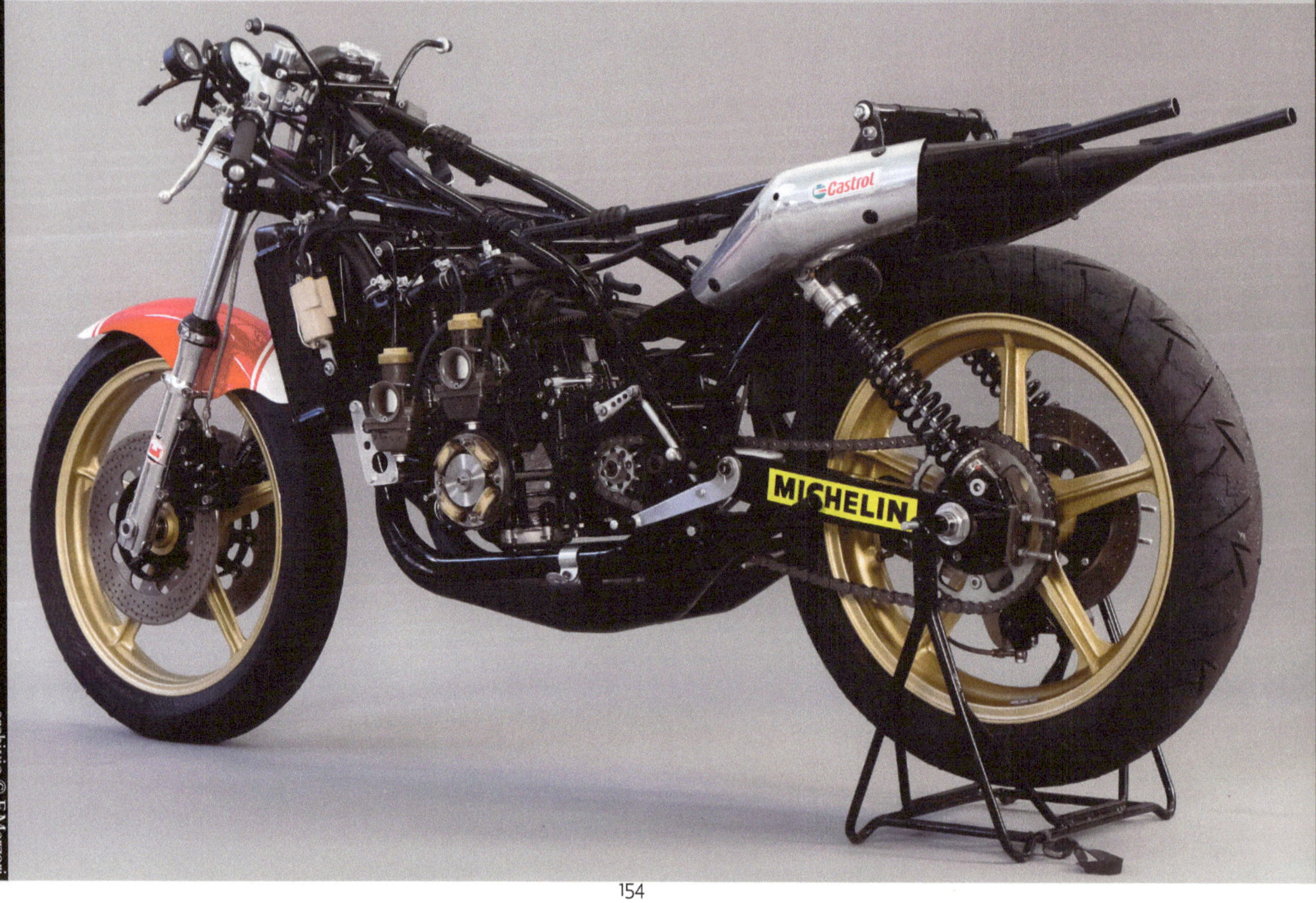

archivio © F.Merzari

1977 - RG 500 MK II TEUVO LÄNSIVUORI

1979 - RG 500 MK IV FRANCO UNCINI

1984 - RGB 500 III - VIRGINIO FERRARI 1982 XR40 tribute

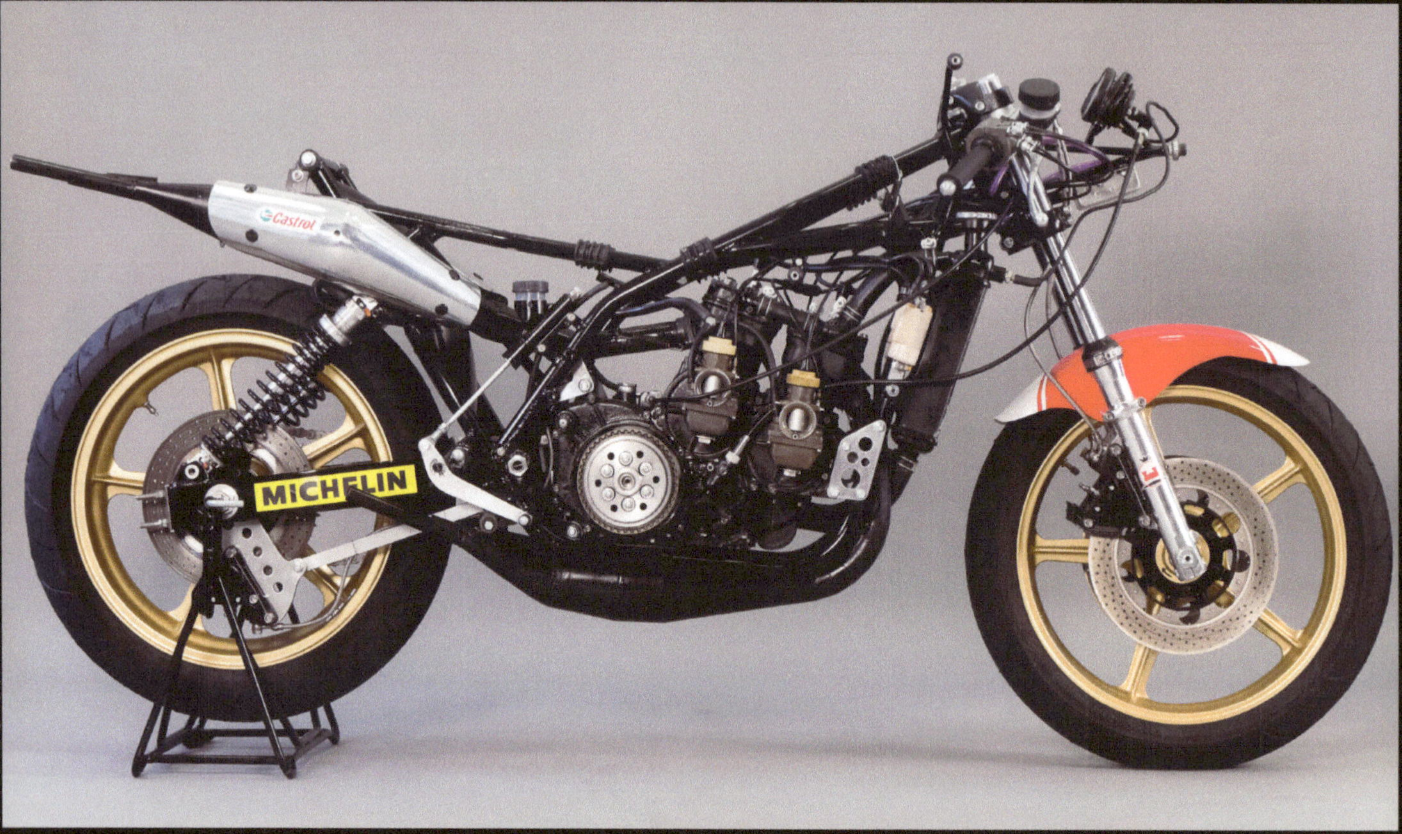

archivio © F.Merzari

1976 - RG 500 MK I GIACOMO AGOSTINI

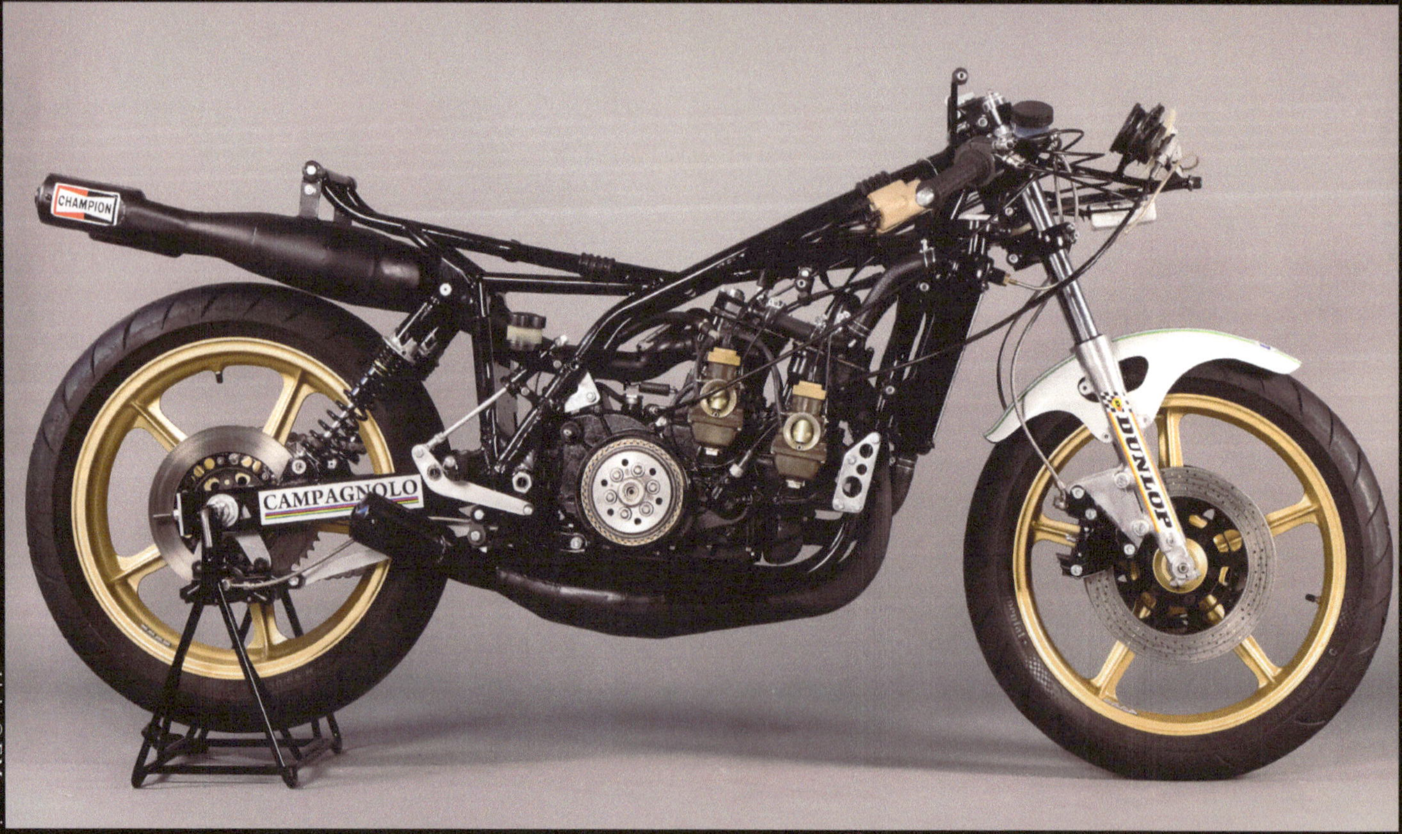

archivio © F.Merzari

1977 - RG 500 MK II TEUVO LÄNSIVUORI

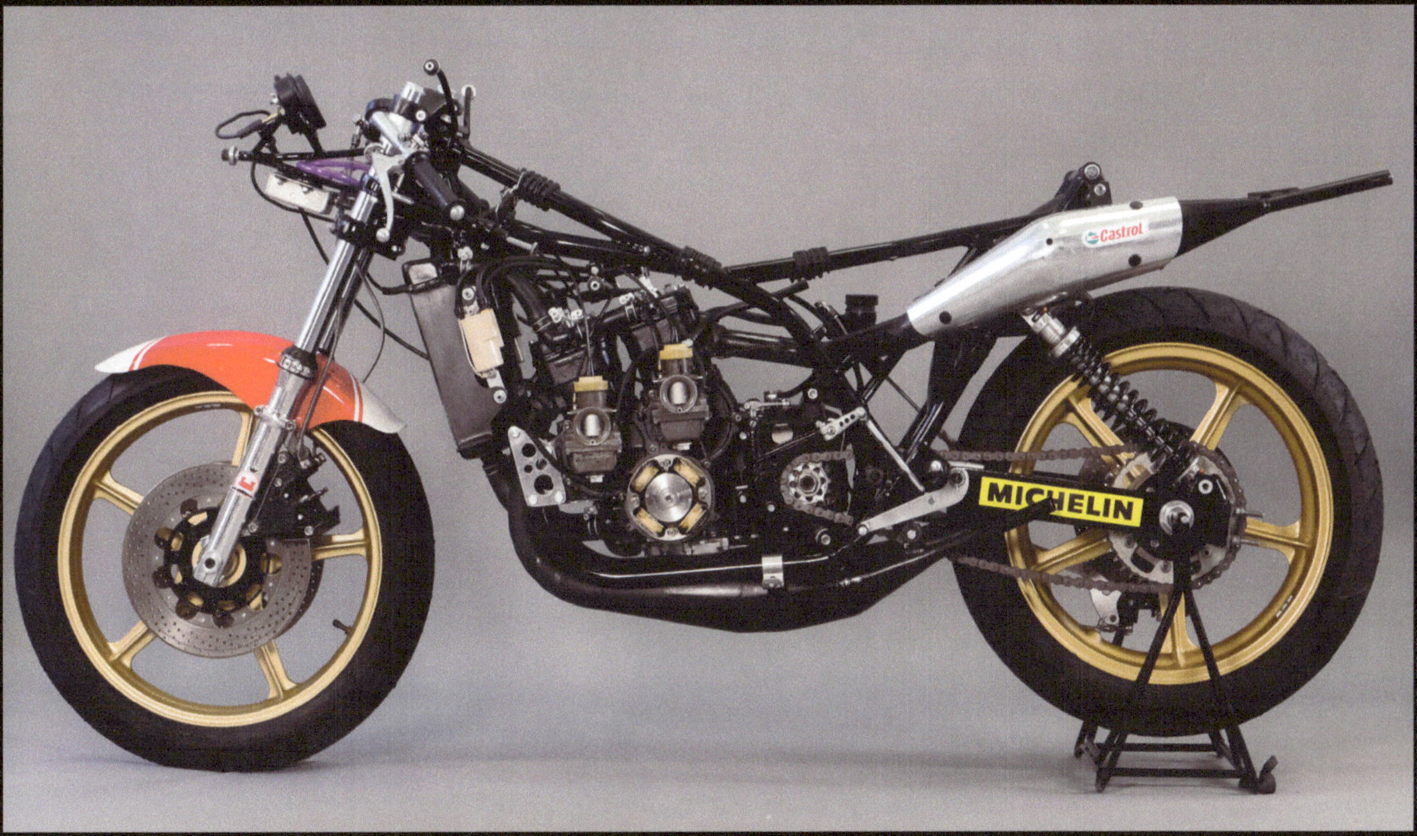

archivio © F.Merzari

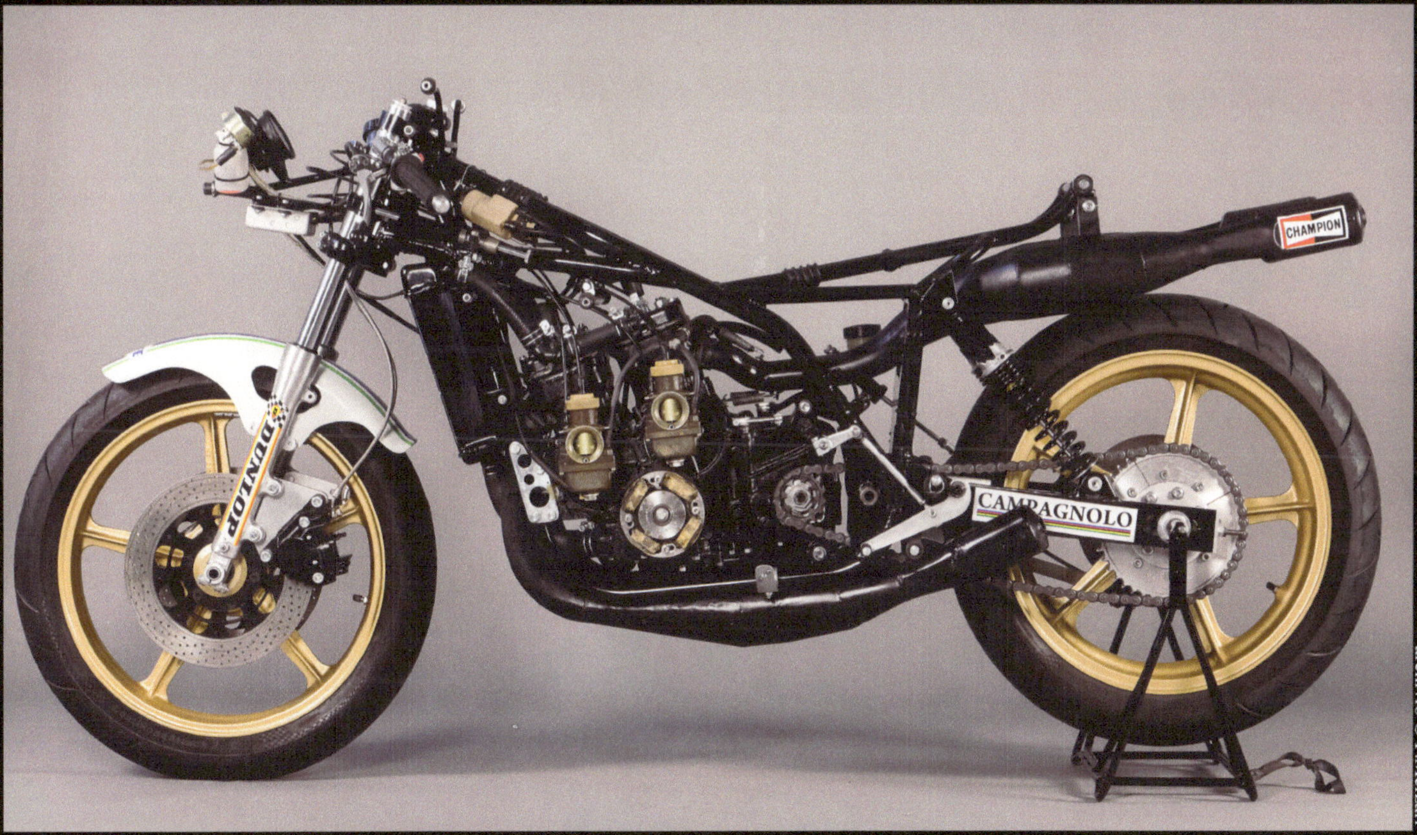

archivio © F.Merzari

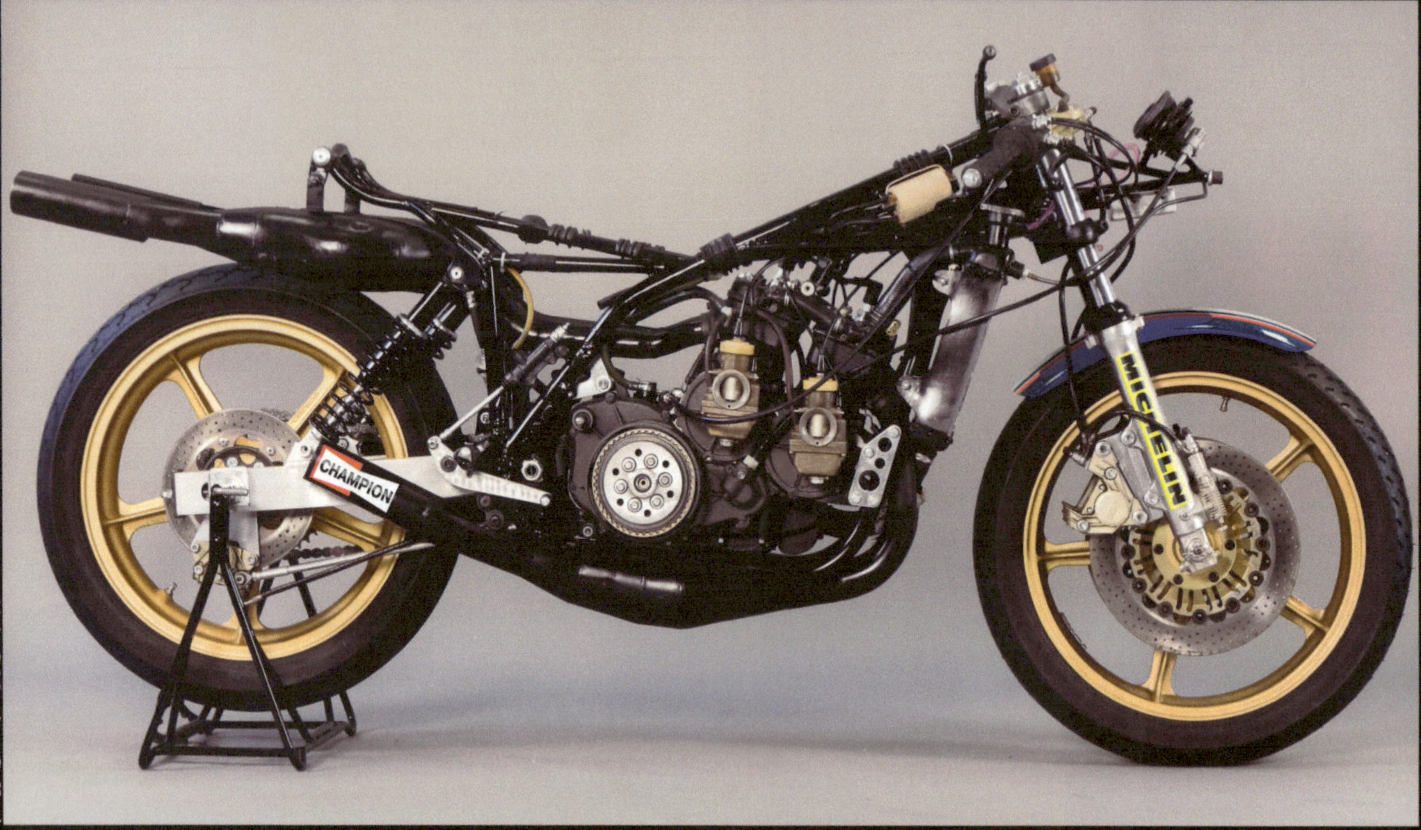

archivio © Massimo Curfiani

1979 - RG 500 MK IV FRANCO UNCINI

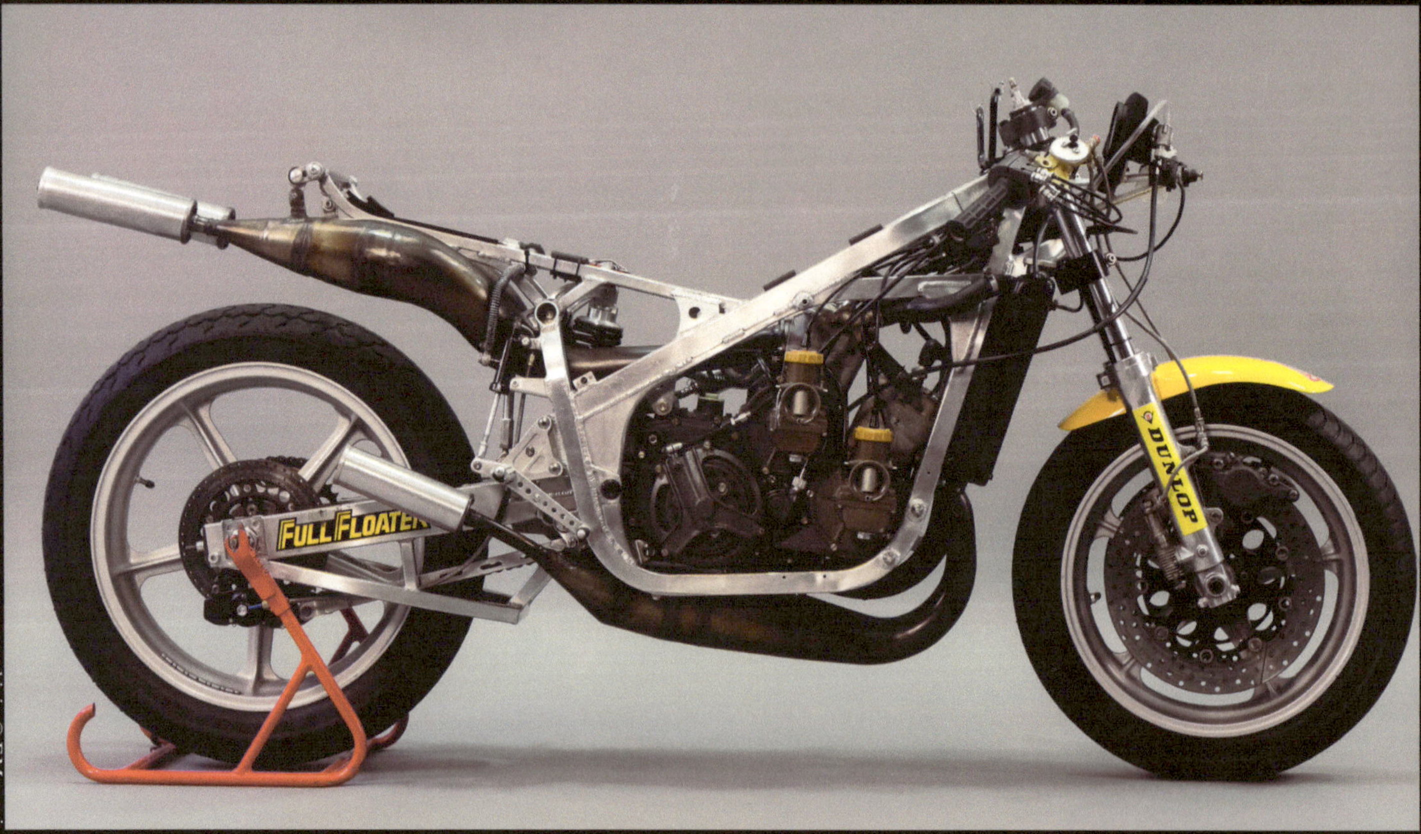

archivio © F.Merzari

1984 - RGB 500 III - VIRGINIO FERRARI 1982 XR40 tribute

archivio © Massimo Cuffiani

archivio © F.Merzari

1976 - RG 500 MK I
GIACOMO AGOSTINI

archivio © F.Merzari

164

archivio © F.Merzari

archivio © F.Merzari

archivio © Massimo Cuffiani

archivio © Massimo Cuffiani

archivio © Massimo Cuffiani

archivio © Massimo Cuffiani

archivio © F.Merzari

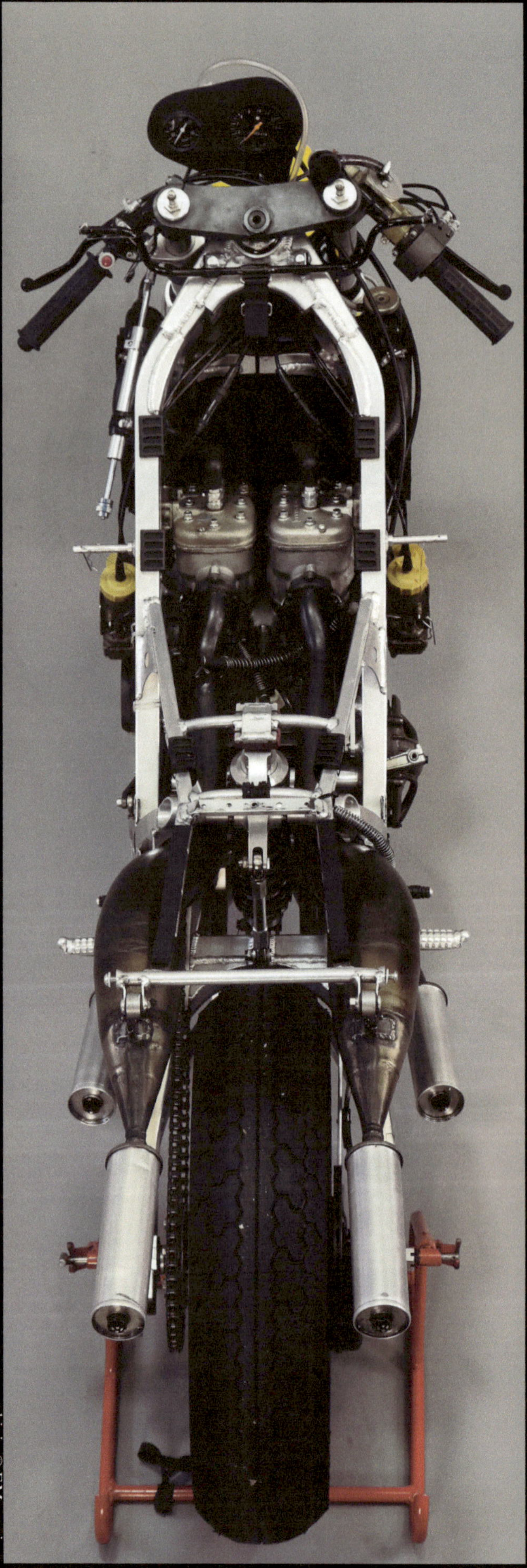

archivio © F.Merzari

168

1984 - RGB 500 III
VIRGINIO FERRARI
1982 XR40 tribute

archivio © F.Merzari

Ergal crown used by Team Gallina

VM36 MIKUNI carburettors

The anti-dive fork used in 1979 by the official factory RGB 500 XR27B

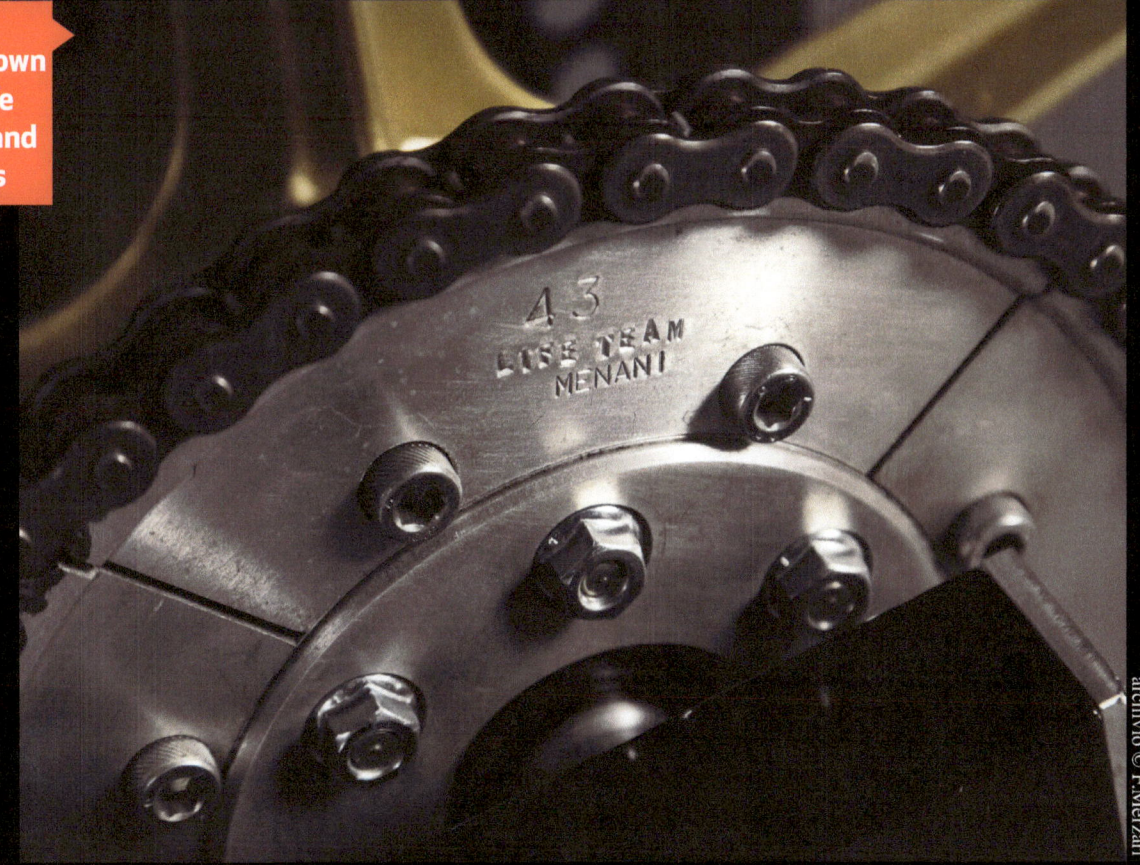

1977 Menani dismountable crown used by Team Life with Länsivuori and Lucchinelli riders

archivio © F.Merzari

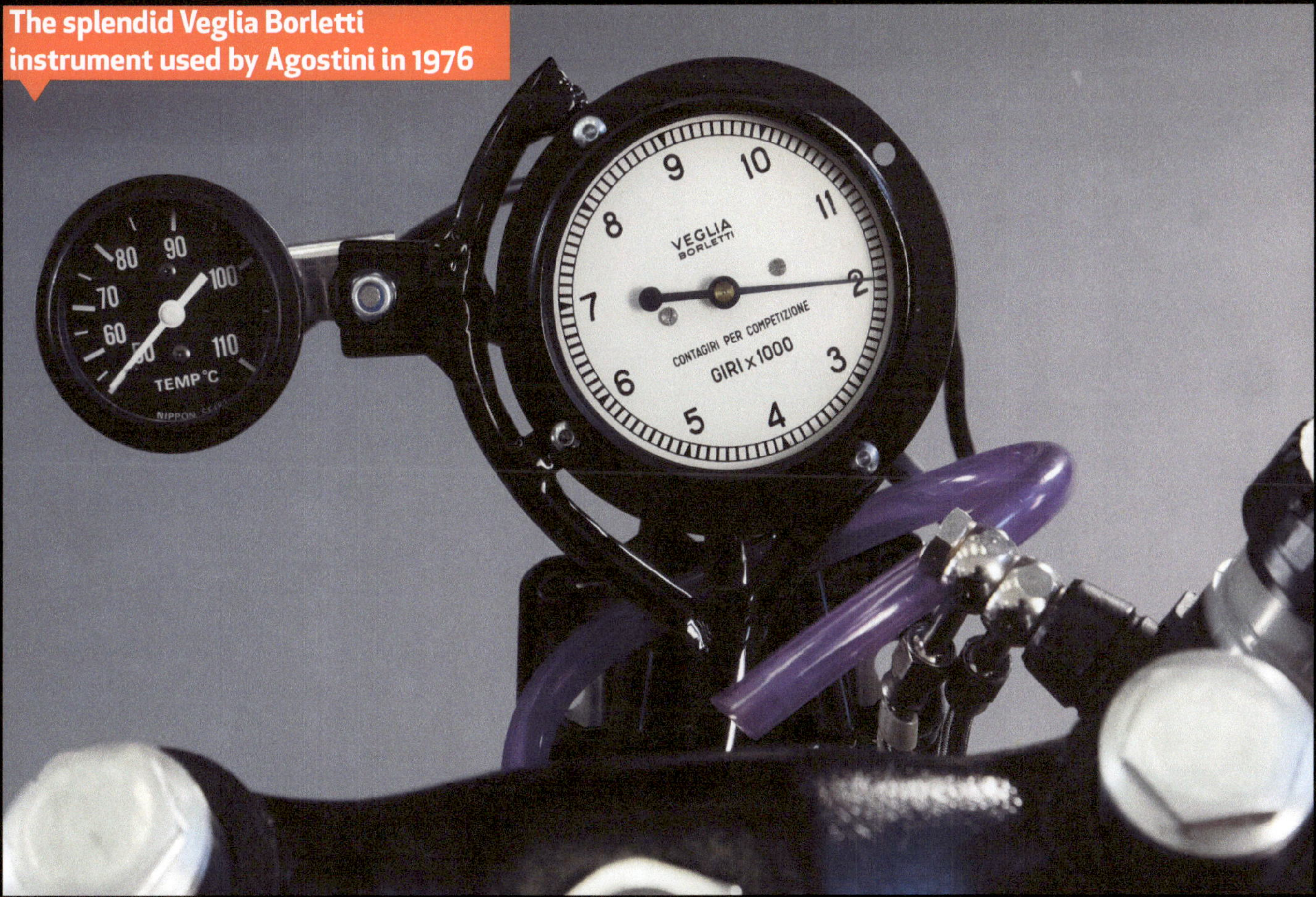

The splendid Veglia Borletti instrument used by Agostini in 1976

archivio © F.Merzari

ENGINE

The square four cylinders from above

archivio © Massimo Cuffiani

RG 500
THE TECNIC

In the first engine designed in 1973, the "square-four" lay-out made it possible to use rotary disc carburettors. In fact the engine consisted of 125 cm3 four cylinders and, considering that each cylinder had its own crankshaft and crankcase, this facilitated the engine tuning: testing the engine on the bench required no more that taking a single cylinder and measuring its results.

One of the initial criticisms was that of limiting weights because the magnesium castings were a problem in Japan, but the Project Manager, Eng. Makoto Hase, managed to find the Kobe-Seiko Company, able of producing the RG expensive castings.

The first engine came to light in November 1973 and it was tested throughout December and January.

The cylinders had a cast iron barrel and five port barrels, 4 main ones plus an additional washing fifth on which cooled the connecting rod. Pistons were cast and included space for the fifth port. They had two small holes in the piston liner (Ø 1.7 mm) that were used to cool and lubricate the exhaust port.

1976 The "Closed Deck" 5 - port cylinder

archivio © F.Merzari

1976 The piston with pin and roll cage. Note the housings next to the cage to keep the connecting rod guided and the two small holes on the skirt

archivio © F.Merzari

1976 The piston with the window for the fifth port

archivio © F.Merzari

The average mounting clearance in the barrel was 6/100, the same for the 54x54 mm bore and stroke version.
Two segments: the upper one with a trapezoidal section was 1.2 mm, the lower one with a cylindrical section was 0.63 mm.
Each of the four crankshaft cranks controlled the primary gear, but this led to some difficulties. To solve the initial problems of crankshaft gears unreliability, a forced lubrication system was created by means of an oil pump.

It was mounted under the frontal carburettors, with its own tank in the tail. After many tests and the use of better materials, the pump was no longer needed and it was eliminated from 1976 onwards.
Another important change in 1976 was the transition to a 54x54 mm bore and stroke for Sheene's engine purely in order to increase power at low and medium rpm. Maximum power was slightly increased too.
The unreliable primary shaft was also modified: from two pieces it became a single forged piece.

Two of the four drive shafts that drive the primary gear

In 1978 the 4 crankshafts were modified from pairs into one piece

1979 RG 500 MK IV - Manufacturing diagram of cylinder and cylinder head

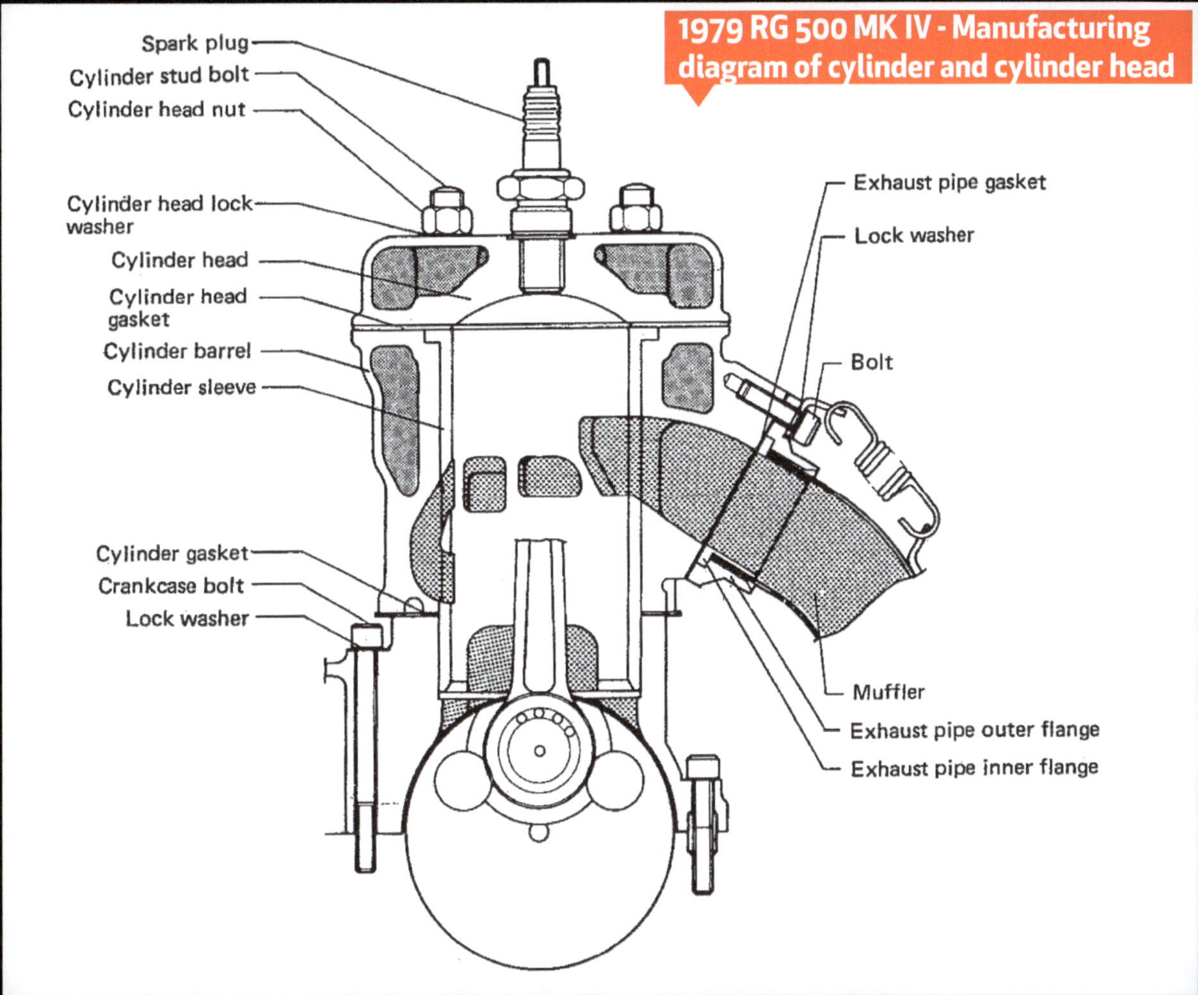

The head of the RG 500 cylinder from 1976 to 1978

archivio © F.Merzari

The head of the RG 500 cylinder from 1979 to 1981

archivio © F.Merzari

Cylinder with NIKASIL treatment still to be processed

Left cylinder used in the RG 500 from '76 to '78, right from '79 to '81

The ports in the cylinders became seven, ten holes totally: two connected as exhausts, two of the overlapping washing cycle and three per transfer side.

With the piston to the PMI, there are actually seven ports that transfer the mixture to the cylinder. This is due to the shape of the transfer holes; the wash port may be directly opposite to the open exhaust port, but being very angled upward, the swirling gases emitted by the wash effectively prevent the mixture from escaping from the exhaust port.

The bursts occurred simultaneously in the cylinders diagonally, because each cylinder had cranks out of phase 180° with respect to the nearby cylinder.

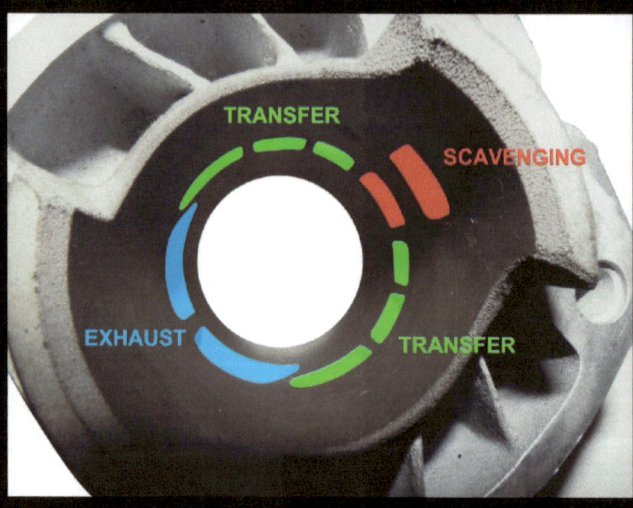

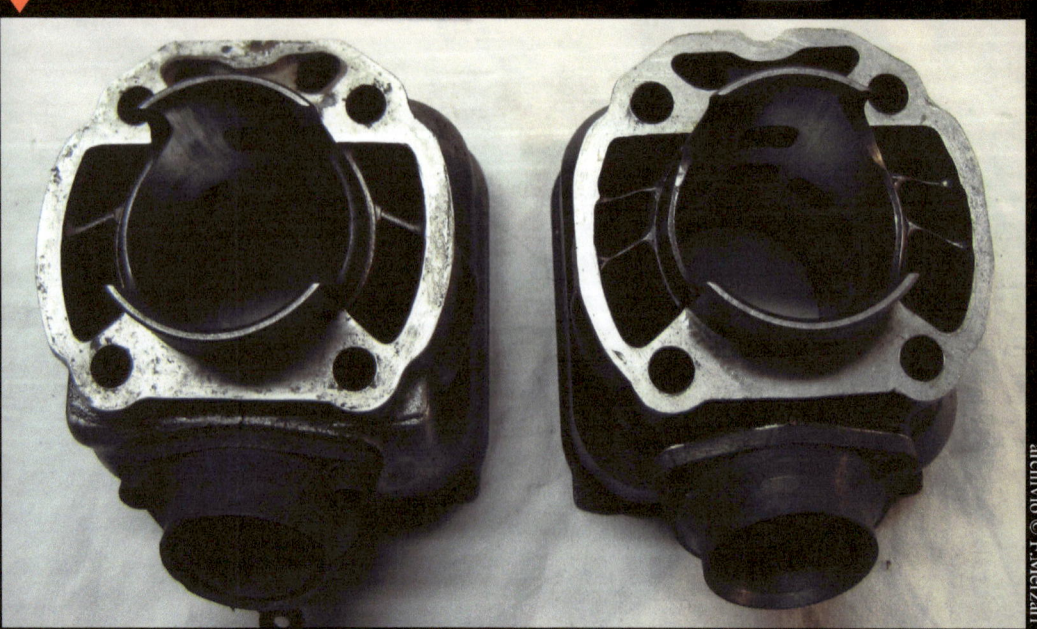

1974 - 1977 XR14

Evolution of the cylinder alignment

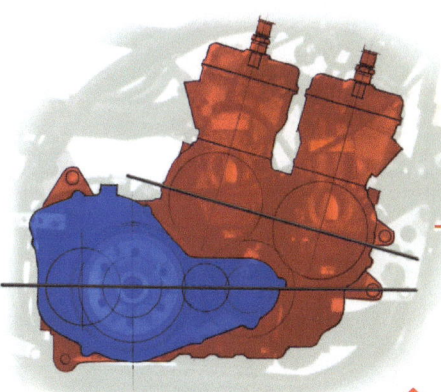

Power - 95 - 119 HP
Displacement - 497,5 - 494,4 cm³
Carter - 3 aluminium parts
Crankshafts - 4 crank + 4

1978 - 1980 XR22-34

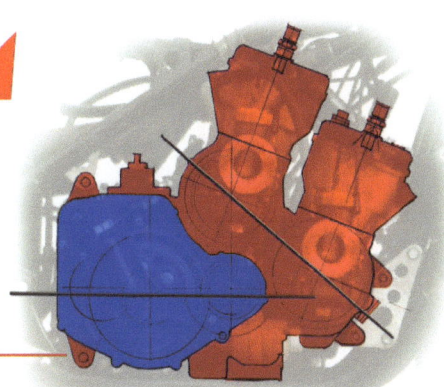

Power - 122 - 125 HP
Displacement - 494,4 cm³
Carter - '78 2 Al parts - from '79 2 Mg (magnesium) parts
Crankshafts - 2 crank + 3

1981-~ XR35-~

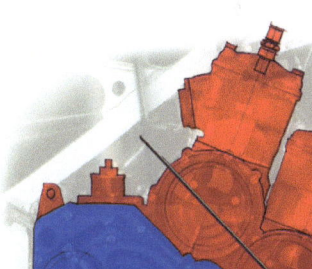

Power - 128 HP - ~
Displacement - 494,4 cm³
Carter - 2 Mg (magnesium) parts
Crankshafts - 2 crank + 3

© Massimo Cuffiani

The engine was divided into 3 parts, joined together by liquid sealing compound.
The official factory XR was in magnesium, while that of the customer version RG was in light alloy. Both were obtained by sand casting.
In the upper part, the 16-cylinder stud bolts were lightened, while the housing of the port on the carter was without a guide wall.

View of both sides of the lower carter

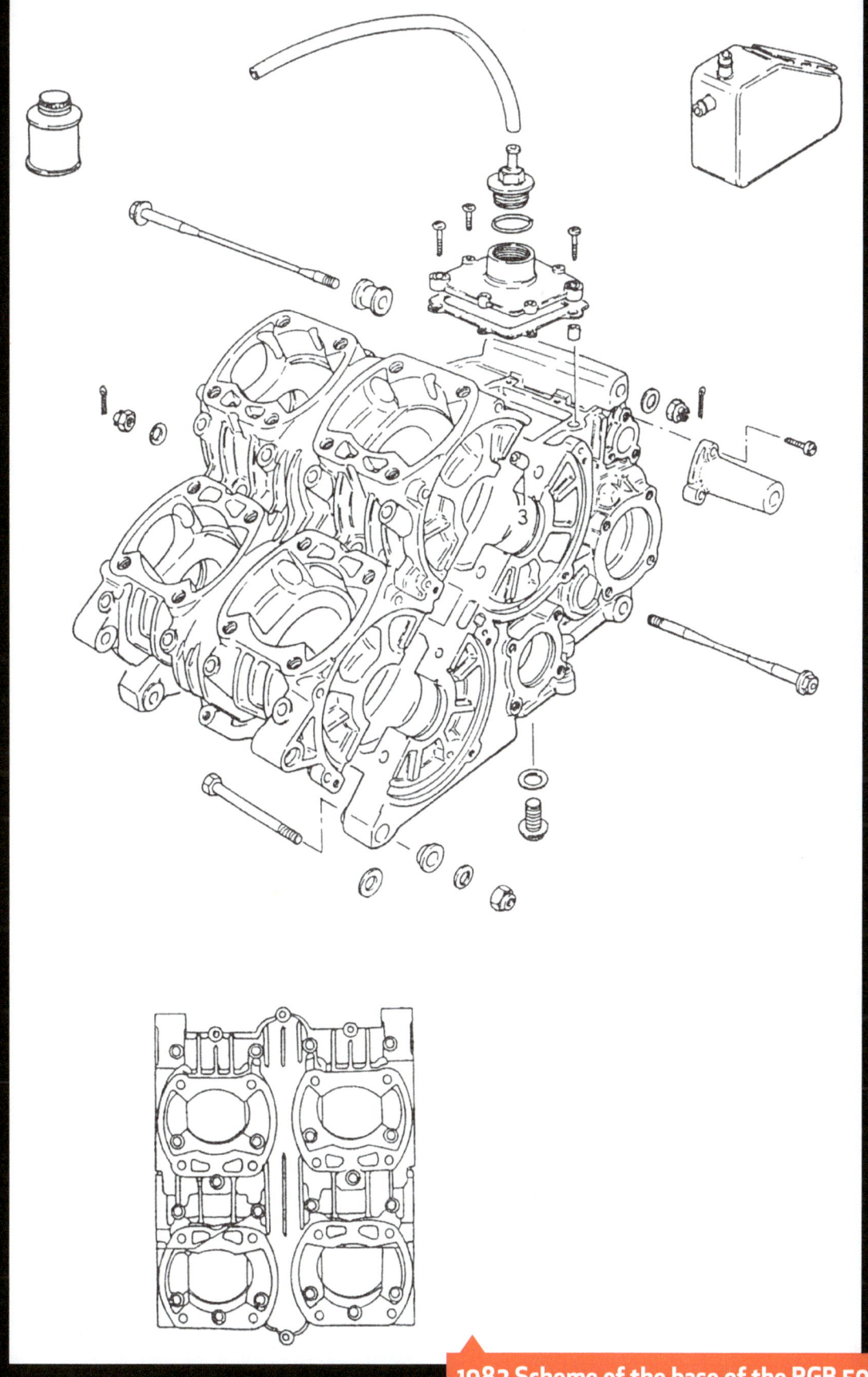

1982 Scheme of the base of the RGB 500 MK I

Bottom view of the upper casing

archivio © F.Merzari

In the lower carter, on the front side, the primary shaft was housed, whose toothed wheel was inserted on the gears' integral with the 4 individual drive shafts. At its left end there was the cone for the setting of the ignition rotor, on the right side instead there was the grip for the tachometer, while centrally there was the worm screw, which acting on the vertical shaft, controlled the water pump.

It should be noted that the latter from 1978 was extractable with its casings and supports.

Afterwards, after the primary there was the gear train that transmitted the bike to the six-speed gearbox, made up of the gearbox or idler and the primary and secondary gearbox shafts.

The crankcases of each crankshaft consisted of a ball bearing on the drive side and a needle bearing on the side on which the rotating disk was mounted. The connecting rods were mounted on needle roller cages, had a grooved foot, two holes and four notches for lubrication.

At the side of the crank chambers were the rotary disc housings with the inlet duct leading into one of the transfer channels. The rotating discs were made of steel and turned between two cheeks of synthetic material to reduce friction. The admission phase lasted 210°.

The subsequent versions, from the XR22 of 1978 onwards, also improved from the point of view of resistance and overall dimensions through the use of two crankshafts in one piece, instead of the four single units previously used (see picture pag.172).

Top view of the lower carter

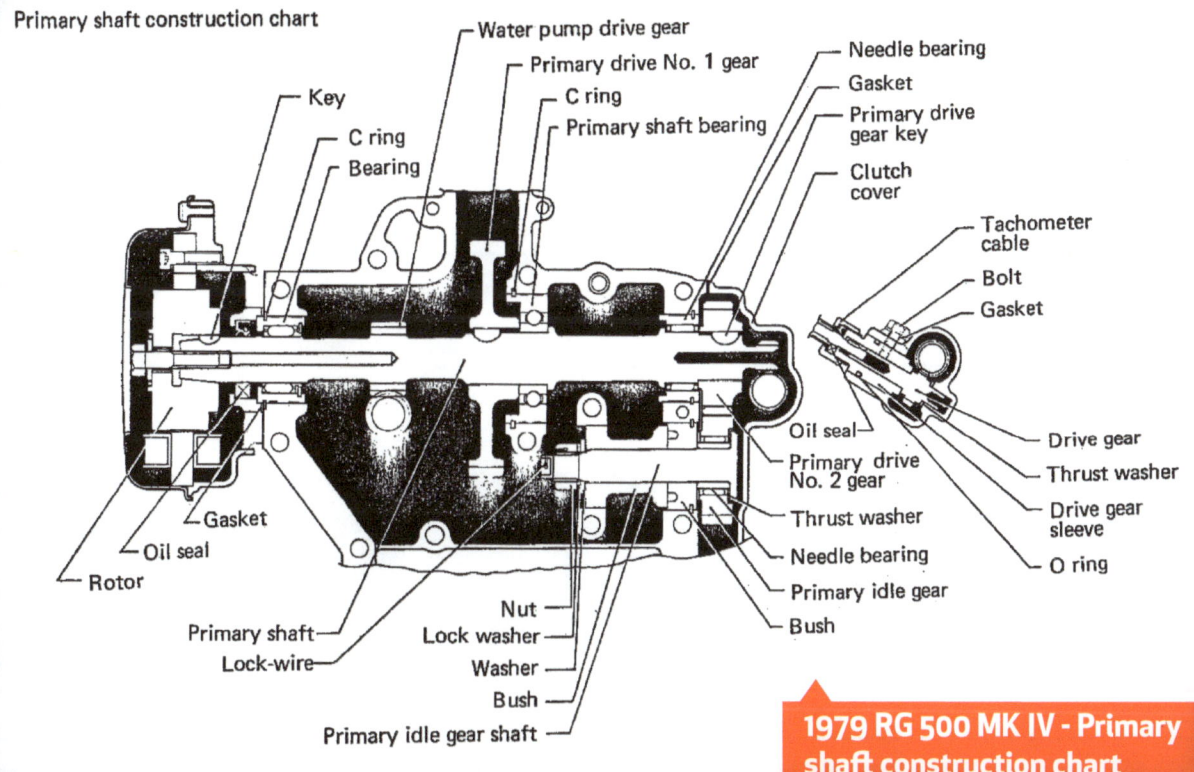

1979 RG 500 MK IV - Primary shaft construction chart

The direction of rotation of the primary shaft was also inverted and consequently the postponement was eliminated.
Another important new feature introduced in the XR22, derived from the XR23, was the removable gearbox.
In 1979, in the XR27B, some improvements were introduced deriving from the XR23A, such as the clutch mechanism, the cylinders with the "Nikasil" treatment and the MIKUNI "twin-float" carburettors.
In 1980 with the XR34 model only minor changes were carried out, such as the transition to larger carburettors, the MIKUNI VM36SS.

SUZUKI RG 500 - ENGINE SPECIFICATIONS

		1974	1975	1976	1977	1978	1979	1980	1981
MODEL		RG500	RG500	RG500	RG500	RGA500	RGB500	RGB500	RGr500
CODE		XR14	XR14	XR14	XR14	XR22	XR27	XR34	XR35
DISPLACEMENT		497,5 cc	←	494,4 cc	←	←	←	←	←
BORE & STROKE		56,0 x 50,5 mm	←	54,0 x 54,0 mm	←	←	←	←	←
COMPRESSION RATIO		8:0	←	8:2	8:3	←	←	8:5	←
POWER SUPPLY		4 Rotary valve Carburettor	←	←	←	←	←	←	←
CARBURETTOR		MIKUNI single float VM34 SS	←	←	←	←	MIKUNI 'funnel type' twin float VM34 SS	MIKUNI 'funnel type' twin float VM36 SS	MIKUNI 'funnel type' twin float VM37.5 SS
IGNITION		NIPPON-DENSO CDI Magnet	←	←	←	←	←	←	←
TRANSMISSION		Primary with gears, secondary with chain	←	←	←	←	←	←	←
CLUTCH		Multi-plate dry	←	←	←	←	Multi-plate dry, 'pull-type'	←	←
POWER SUPPLY		95 cv @ 11.200 rpm	100 cv @ 11.200 rpm	114 cv @ 11.000 rpm	119 cv @ 10.800 rpm	122 cv @ 11.000 rpm	124 cv @ 11.000 rpm	125 cv @ 10.800 rpm	126 cv @ 11.000 rpm
BURST INTERVAL		180°, 2 Cylinders together	←	←	←	←	←	←	←
SPARK PLUG ORDER		1&4 - 2&3	←	←	←	←	←	←	←
CYLINDER MATERIAL		Aluminum	←	←	←	←	←	←	←
CYLINDER PROCESSING		cast-iron liner	←	←	←	SCEM pressed-in liner	←	←	←
PISTON		Casted in AC8A	←	←	Forged in AC8A	←	←	←	←
CRANKCASE		3 Aluminum parts	←	←	←	2 Aluminum parts	2 Magnesium parts	←	←
CRANKSHAFTS		4 Crank + Primary, Primary idle, Gearbox main, Gearbox lay	←	←	←	2 Crank + Primary, Gearbox main, Gearbox lay	←	←	←
SPARK PLUG ORDER		Champion	←	←	←	←	←	←	←
GEAR SHIFT		6 speed	←	←	←	←	←	←	←
MAX SPEED		275 Km/h	284 Km/h	296 Km/h	←	300 Km/h	←	309 Km/h	313 Km/h
						"cassette" gearbox	←	←	←

SUZUKI RG 500 - CARBURETTOR SPECIFICATIONS

		1974	1975	1976	1977	1978	1979	1977/78/79
MODEL		RG 500	RG 500	RG 500	RG 500	RGA 500	RGB 500	RG 500 MK2/3/4
CODE		XR14	XR14	XR14	XR14	XR22	XR27B	
RIDER								
RACE								
CARBURETTOR		MIKUNI VM34	←	←	←	←	←	MIKUNI VM34SS
DIAMETER		Ø 34 mm	←	←	←	←	←	←
MAIN JET	MJ			340				320
JET NEEDLE	JN			6DP5-4				6DP5-4
NEEDLE JET	NJ			Q-6				Q-6
PILOT JET	PJ			35				35
AIR JET	AJ							0.5
CUTAWAY	CA			2.0				2.0
PILOT AIR ADJ.	AS			3/4				1 3/4
VALVE SEAT	VS			2.8				

Mikuni VM36 carburettors. On the left for official factory motorcycles and on the right those for over the counter bikes. Note the differences, especially in the lightened "official factory" pulveriser, which weighs 9 gr. instead of 13 gr.

archivio © Massimo Cuffiani

Functional diagram of MIKUNI carburettors

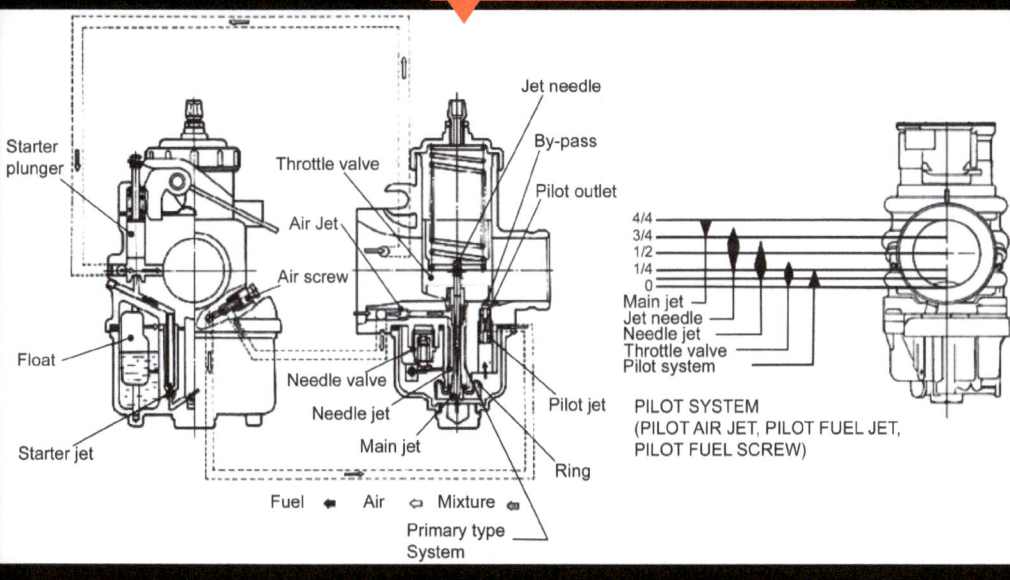

Since 1978 the water pump was extractable from below. In the picture, its housing case

archivio © Massimo Cuffiani

1980	1980	1980	1980	1980	1982	1981
RGB 500	RGB 500	RGB 500	RGB 500	RGB 500	RGB 500 MK1	RGr 500
XR34	XR34	XR34	XR34	XR34		XR35
ROSSI	CROSBY	HARTOG	MAMOLA	LUCCHINELLI		
GP GER	GP GER	GP GER	GP GER	GP GER		
MIKUNI VM37.5	MIKUNI VM36	←	←	←	MIKUNI VM36SS	MIKUNI VM37.5
Ø 37,5 mm	Ø 36 mm	Ø 36 mm	Ø 36 mm	Ø 36 mm	←	
330→330→330→330	310→300→300→310	310→310→310→310	320→320→310→320	300→300→310→310	360	
ff-3	←	←	←	←	ff-3	
Q-8	←	Q-6 / Q-8	Q-8	Q-8 / Q-9	Q-8	
35	←	←	←	←	←	
0.5	←	←	←	←	0.6	
2.25	←	←	←	←	←	
1 4/4	1 1/2	←	←	1/2	1 1/2	
					3.0	

FRAME

The XR14 project started in the summer of 1973, with Makoto Hase as director and Makoto Suzuki as his assistant. While the two Japanese engineers took care of the development of the engine, the frame part was under the control of another Japanese: Hisao Inagaki.

His initial goal was saving weight, so he designed an open cradle frame, similar to that of the small 125 RS67. It was not easy to immediately get an ideal frame and throughout 1974 various changes happened.

The initial layout, with the cradle open at the bottom, gave stability problems on bends, so provisional tubes were added. At the end of the season, with the third version of the frame, the cradle was completely closed, and the problems of handling were resolved.

Paul Smart's bike was the subject of further experiments and a particular chassis was tested with engine moved forward, at the limit with the front wheel, while the radiator, divided into two parts, was positioned behind the four cylinders.

The rear shock absorbers were in an almost vertical position with little possibility of adjustment. Suzuki worked extensively over the years to these components and already in 1975 changed its position and geometry. The upper attachment was moved forward, while the lower one was carried behind the rear wheel spindle.

The bike thus gained a more progressive action of rear cushioning. At the same time a new aluminium swingarm with a square section was inserted and no longer in round steel tubes.

In 1976, two of Sheene's three official factory bikes had a new chassis, with the advanced dampers in the swingarm attachment position, now in front of the wheel axle.

The Kayaba suspension supplier developed a new front air fork, charged it with Nitrogen up to 1.2 atmospheres, and this allowed further improvements in handling and an increase in adjustments. The outer tubes were 35 mm with an excursion of 150 mm.

In 1977, other innovations were introduced, such as the lower pipe truss reinforcement in the swingarm and the "Golden Shocks" shock absorbers. These were built by Kayaba completely by hand, with the cartridges obtained by milling an aluminium block.

The suspension was obtained only from the internal volume of the nitrogen, while the preload was obtained by modifying the gas pressure, usually 3.5 atmospheres. The damping was adjustable both through the viscosity of the oil and by acting on a knurled ring, which created progressively smaller and smaller holes inside the hydraulic track.

GOLDEN SHOCKS rear shock absorber - On the left the 1977 first version, on the right the 1978 version with the supplementary tank mounted on the top

RG 500
THE TECNIC

> Summary diagram of the evolution of the official factory RG 500 chassis from 1974 to 1980. Note the evolution of the attachment points of the shock absorbers and the relative manufacturing of the frame

© Massimo Cuffiani

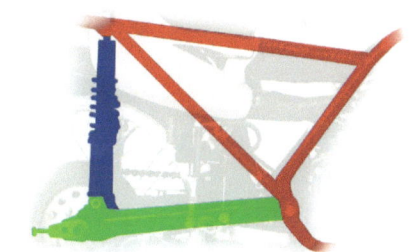
1974 - RG500 XR14

1975 - RG500 XR14

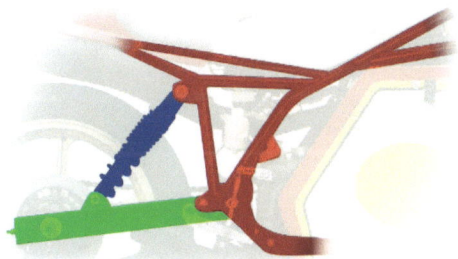
1976/77 - RG500 XR14

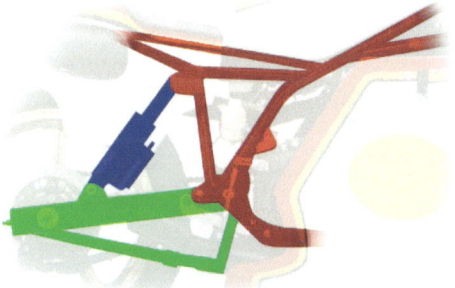
1977 - RG500 XR14 2°V

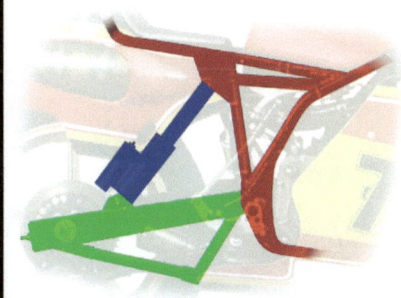
1978 - RGA500 XR22

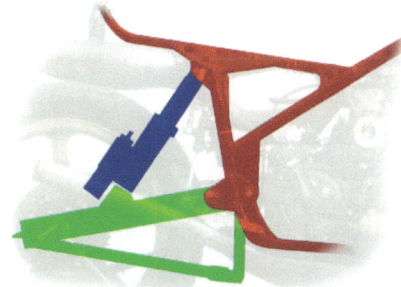
1979 - RGB500 XR27

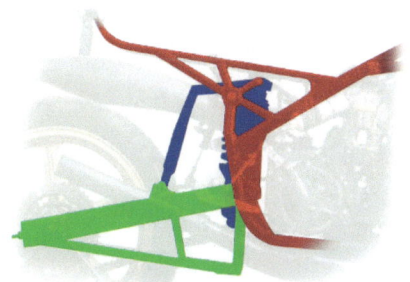
1980 - RGB500 XR34M

1978 RG 500 XR14 of Sheene in the paddock of Nürburgring

The trim of the bike was lowered by 10 mm, still modifying the front forks, which became 36 mm in diameter, with a 140 mm excursion.

These details underwent further refinements the following year. In fact, in 1978 the XR22 version was introduced, which fitted forks with a diameter of 37 mm and a further stroke reduced to 130 mm. The rear "Golden Shocks" was improved and mounted with the auxiliary tank above the main body, so as not to interfere with the swingarm.

Even the brake discs underwent changes in the various racing seasons and the general tendency was to increase the front discs and to reduce the rear ones. The front ones went from 270 mm in diameter in 1975 to 310 mm in 1979 and in the rear from 250 mm in 1974 to 220 mm in 1979.

In 1979 the great news was the introduction of anti-diving system on the front forks.

Initially it needed some tuning, but this system proved to be effective in braking, because it avoided the problematic change of attitude that compromised stability in the most violent breaks. The operating principle was that which was acting on a small piston opposed by a spring. This piston was connected to a needle jet which regulated the damping force of the forks.

The Gallina Team also developed the "squat", a rear diving system, connecting a "reaction" tube to the rear brake caliper with the frame over the swingarm pivot. This allowed the bike to lower itself completely during braking so as not to alter geometry.

That year a lot of work was done on the chassis and a version was tested, the XR27BFR (FR was for Front Radiator), with the radiator positioned in the front fairing in front of the steering plate.

his solution was chosen to avoid the annoying tendency to do wheelies. Other benefits were better cooling efficiency and the ability to use smaller and lighter radiators.

On the other hand, the centre of gravity was raised, worsening manoeuvrability and reduced the top speed due to the greater resistance forces.

Initially, it only pleased Sheene, who then switched to the standard version during the season.

The common problem that tormented all the official factories was their search for stability. From Sheene to Ferrari, many complained about it. In some GPs like Assen and Imola, the trucks of the various official factory teams were "full" of frames to be tested, looking for the optimal chassis that would have guaranteed the best timing.

They alternated XR27-1, XR27-2, XR22, RG MK IV (with related problems of engine coupling), often trying also the 16" rim in the case of Ferrari.

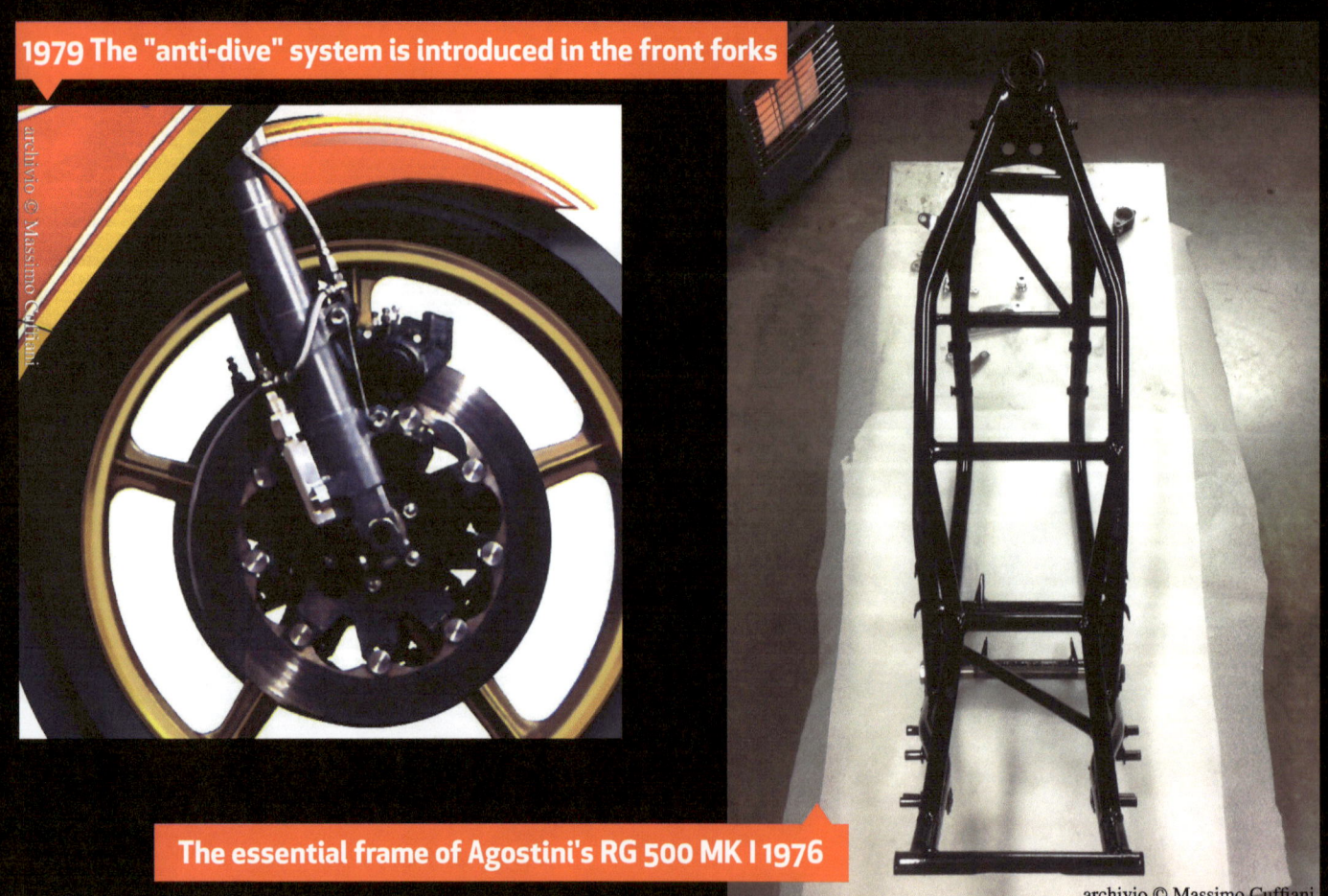

1979 The "anti-dive" system is introduced in the front forks

The essential frame of Agostini's RG 500 MK I 1976

archivio © Massimo Cuffiani

Bike power was increasing and a growing problem, in addition to driveability, was how to be able to discharge the power to the ground.
In 1980 a completely new rear suspension system was developed: the "Full Float" with a single shock absorber. In this system the shock absorber was not fixed rigidly to the frame, but through a bridge tube that acted on a connecting rod pivoted in the rear frame.
The geometry was completely adaptable, the system was more rigid and with better tyre ground contact than to the previous one.
The rear "squat" or "anti-lift" system was then perfected and this led, together with the full float, to a truly stable motion that "crouched" literally in braking.

The frame of Agostini's RG 500 MK I 1976 undergoing repair

Note the differences in chassis and in passing silencers between the MK I 1976 and on the right the MK IV 1979

archivio © Massimo Cuffiani

Team Gallina Nava Olio Fiat did some winter tests in Imola where two motorcycles were tested: the one used by Ferrari in 1979 and a prototype arrived from Japan with several new solutions, which would then be used in the 1980 World championship with a modified weight distribution, increased to the front to solve the slight sway of the front end.
The prototype still had Kayaba standard gas and oil shock absorbers, but with separate air tanks.
The season then started with the version called XR34H with double rear shocks.
This underwent a development during the season, the Suzuki in fact made three versions: XR3400, XR3402H, XR3403H, with the latter differing for the steering head set back by 20 mm and the swingarm lengthened by 20 mm.

1978 The Suzuki RGA 500 XR22 factory of Pat Hennen

The "Full Float" version, the XR34M1, was introduced by the Spanish GP, which was replaced by the XR34M2 from the British GP. The M2 version differed from the M1 substantially at the joining point of the connecting rod onto the frame tube, in the section of the upper "U" linkage of the swingarm and in the position of the small connecting pipe between the swingarm and the lower reinforcement.

The advantages of the M "Full Float" version compared to the conventional H were clear: less wear on the rear tyre, better ability to discharge the power to the ground, better traction, "squat" effect of constant lowering during braking and acceleration.

More refinements were done to the forks, with the diameter increasing from 38mm to 40mm, with the stroke decreased to 120mm. In this way it was possible to increase the stiffness by 50% and reducing the stroke by only 20%.

Regarding the RG 500 customer version, cycling refinements usually debuted the following year, or even after the official factory ones.

The front forks were not made from solid but obtained in die-cast. The diameters of the stems went from 35 mm in 1976 to 37 mm in 1979.

In 1980, fixing points were added to fix a plate that served as a stiffening bridge between the two outer tubes and a link for the front fender and a reinforcement truss inferior to the swingarm, as already seen in the official factory bikes in 1978. In 1981 the anti-dive system finally arrived for the privateers, while the Full Float system was introduced only on the RGB 500 MK I in 1982, which also had a frame completely redesigned compared to the previous RG 500 MK VI,1981.

The various riders refined their bikes with other components. Giacomo Agostini, for example, in 1976 on his RG 500 MK I, used two types of Ceriani front fork combined with Brembo and Lockheed front brakes. Franco Uncini on the other hand, from about the middle of the 1979 season, replaced calipers and discs with Brembo material and Girling rear shock absorbers.

SUZUKI RG 500 - FRAME SPECIFICATIONS

	1974	1975	1976	1977	1978	1979
MODEL	RG500	RG500	RG500	RG500	RGA500	RGB500
CODE	XR14	XR14	XR14	XR14	XR22	XR27
RIDER/TEAM	SHEENE	←	←	←	←	HERON SUZUKI
RACE	GP FRA					
FRONT RIM	2.50 - 18	←	←	←	←	←
REAR RIM	3.50 - 18	←	←	4.00 - 18	←	←
FRONT TYRE	DUNLOP 2.50 – 18	MICHELIN 2.50 – 18	MICHELIN VARIOUS DIMENSIONS	←	←	←
REAR TYRE	DUNLOP 3.50 – 18	MICHELIN 3.50 – 18	MICHELIN VARIOUS DIMENSIONS	←	←	←
FRONT BRAKE DISC	Ø 280 mm X 2	Ø 270 mm X 2	Ø 290 mm X 2	Ø 295 mm X 2	Ø 300 mm X 2	Ø 310 mm X 2
REAR BRAKE DISC	Ø 250 mm	←	Ø 240 mm	←	Ø 230 mm	Ø 220 mm
FRAME TYPE	OPEN - TUBES	DOUBLE SIDE PIPE	←	←	←	←
FRAME MATERIAL	HIGH STRENGTH STEEL ROUND TUBES	←	←	←	←	←
BACK SWING ARM	HIGH STRENGTH STEEL ROUND TUBES	ALUMINUM Z5D SQUARE TUBES	←	←	←	←
FRONT FORK	TELESCOPIC WITH SPRING	←	PNEUMATIC TELESCOPIC	←	←	←
FORK SUPPLIER	KAYABA	←	←	←	←	←
ANTI-DIVE SYSTEM	NONE	←	←	←	←	FRONT ANTI-DIVE SYSTEM
BACK SUSPENSION	DOUBLE DIRECT SPRING REAR-SHOCKS	←	←	DIRECT NITROGEN "GOLDEN SHOCK"	←	←
BACK SUSPENSION SUPPLIER	KAYABA	←	←	←	←	←
WEIGHT	137 Kg	135 Kg	132 Kg	135 Kg	136 Kg	←

Specific considerations must be made on the size of the rims since Suzuki experimented in 1975 with smaller diameter 17" rims. This did not go very far because there were problems with the tyres. They tried it again in 1979, when tyre manufacturers took an interest in the Honda NR 500 project, which fitted 16" wheels.

Roberto Gallina was also pursuing the same idea at this time. And, as confirmed by Ferrari, he was the first to debut the 16" rim in the Nava Olio Fiat Suzuki Team. Ferrari, for example, in their search for greater stability, put on the 16" Michelin 12/60 in the second round of tests at the Dutch TT at Assen. Initially, they started with the front wheel and in the next round also on the rear, but without getting any improvement on the 18".

In December 1979, tests continued at Misano and Imola with the Team Gallina riders Lucchinelli and Rossi, too. The tests which had started two years earlier and the occasional use by Virginio Ferrari in the 1979 World Championship had suffered from the lack of suitable covers. At these comparative tests, however, Michelin brought along several kinds of covers.

As Gallina explained at the time, the advantage of the 16" rim in the front and in the rear is multiple: with the traditional 18" rim you cannot go beyond a certain fork inclination, around 23 degrees. By decreasing the diameter, the angle of the steering head can be increased without affecting driveability.

It also decreases the gyroscopic moment of the rim around its axis, thus facilitating manoeuvrability. The bike is also lower and that improved centre of gravity and aerodynamics.

The new 16" Michelin tyres were also lighter as they were tubeless (i.e. without inner tube).

Lucchinelli and Rossi therefore used this measure on the front throughout the 1980 World championship, as well as Wil Hartog. The Heron Team with Mamola and Crosby, instead, preferred to continue with the classic 18" size.

1979	1980	1980	1980	1980	1980	1981
RGB500	RGB500	RGB500	RGB500	RGB500	RGB500	RGr500
XR27	XR34	XR34	XR34	XR34	XR34	XR35
GALLINA NAVA FIAT	ROSSI/GALLINA	CROSBY/HERON	HARTOG/NIMAG	MAMOLA/HERON	LUCCHINELLI/GALLINA	
	GP GERMANIA	GP GERMANIA	GP GERMANIA	GP GERMANIA	GP GERMANIA	
2.50-18 / 2.50-16	3.50 – 16	2.50 – 18	3.50 – 16	2.50 – 18	3.50 – 16	3.00-16/3.50-16/3.00-18
←	←	←	←	←	←	4.00-18/4.50-18
←	MICHELIN 813AB 3.75 – 16	DUNLOP KR108 2.50 – 18	MICHELIN 813AB 3.50 – 16	DUNLOP KR108 2.50 – 18	MICHELIN 813A 3.75 - 16	VARIOUS DIMENSIONS
←	MICHELIN 842NA 3.50 – 18	DUNLOP KR111 4.00 - 18	MICHELIN SB13 3.00 - 18	DUNLOP KR111 4.00 - 18	MICHELIN 842N 3.50 - 18	VARIOUS DIMENSIONS
←	←	←	←	←	←	←
←	←	←	←	←	←	←
←	←	←	←	←	←	←
←	←	←	←	←	←	ALUMINUM ROUND TUBES/ALUMINUM SQUARE TUBES
←	←	←	←	←	←	←
←	←	←	←	←	←	←
←	←	←	←	←	←	←
FRONT, REAR ANTI-DIVE SYSTEM	←	←	←	←	←	←
←	M=MONO-SHOCK. FULL FLOAT WITH LINK	H=DOUBLE DIRECT SPRING REAR-SHOCKS	M=MONO-SHOCK. FULL FLOAT WITH LINK	←	←	MONO-SHOCK. FULL FLOAT WITH LINK
←	←	ARAGOSTA	←	KAYABA	KONI	KAYABA
←	144 Kg	←	←	←	←	125 Kg

AERODYNAMICS

"Donald Duck" 1

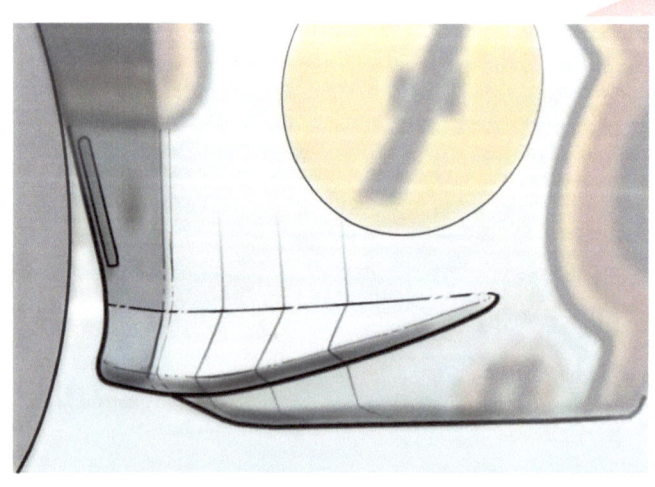

RG 500 THE TECNIC

For the whole duration of the RG 500 project, Suzuki heavily invested in improving aerodynamics.

In **1977** different fairing solutions were tested but without any satisfactory results, as demonstrated by **the Hennen's fall at Imola**, which was probably due to aerodynamic problems.

The season started with the small tail **XR23 653 type** and a fairing with an integrated baffle in the lower part.

This version was dubbed by the mechanics **"Donald Duck"** because it reminded people of a duck. Subsequently, other variants were introduced, such as a more enveloping "big tail" that incorporated silencers and various versions of fairings without deflectors and rounder front fairings.

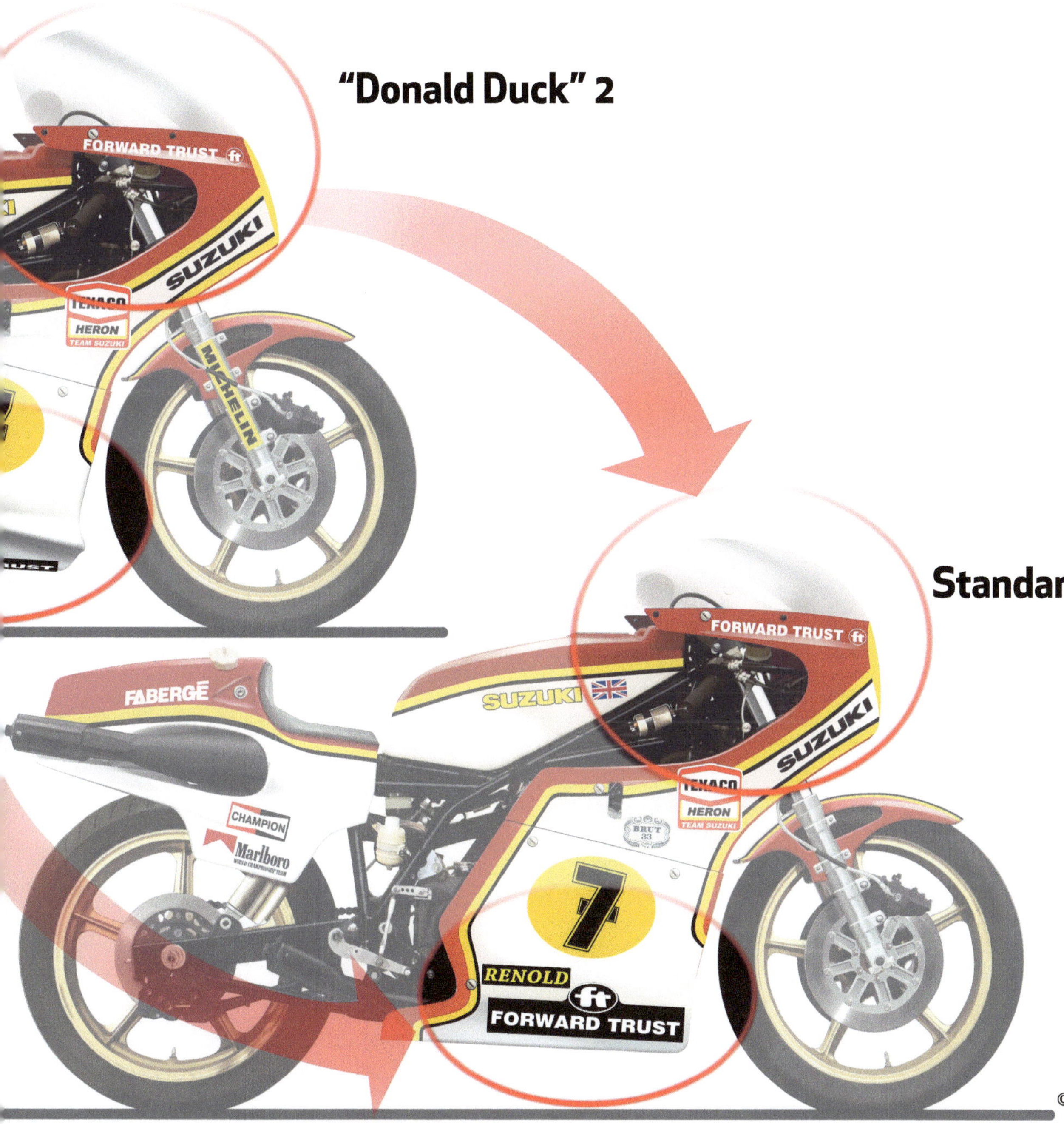

"Donald Duck" 2

Standard

© Massimo Cuffiani

In 1978, with the XR22, Suzuki introduced **two aerodynamic add-ons**, two real "wings", on the sides of the fairing.

The idea was not entirely original, not just because it was something that had been done in Formula 1 for years, but because in the 1970s, during the **tests at the 1974 Nürburgring GP**, two small profiles mounted as a moustache debuted on the small front fairing of **Giacomo Agostini's MV Agusta 500** - a solution he later abandoned during the race.

In **1976 Team Gallina** carried out further tests **on Lucchinelli's RG 500 MK I.**

He confirms that for the French GP at Le Mans they installed some fins that were subsequently put on again in 1978.

© Massimo Cuffiani

1974 MV AGUSTA 500 - GP WEST GERMANY - Agostini

1979 RGB 500 XR27B - GP FRANCE Le Mans - Ferrari

Team Gallina tried several alternative solutions instead but often gave up on these appendages.

The following year, the Italian team also made use of fins as for example in the **Austrian GP at Salzburgring or in the French GP at Le Mans in 1979.**

On those occasions, however, they placed the **"wings" on the upper part of the fairing** to limit the tendency to lift the front end of the Dunlop bridge, as confirmed personally by Virginio Ferrari.

This solution enabled them to use a "cleaner" aerodynamic flow, even if the fins were further from the centre of gravity of the bike than the classic position.

The "wings" adopted by Suzuki **in 1978 and in some races of 1979** were of two types: a simpler one that was **preferred by Sheene (A in the drawing)**, with a profile that was more evocative of the F1 ailerons, and others with vertical bulkheads **(B in the drawing)**, the latter preferred by **Hennen in 1978 and Tom Herron in 1979.** Even **Franco Uncini in 1983** used the fins on his **RG Gamma 500** in several races.

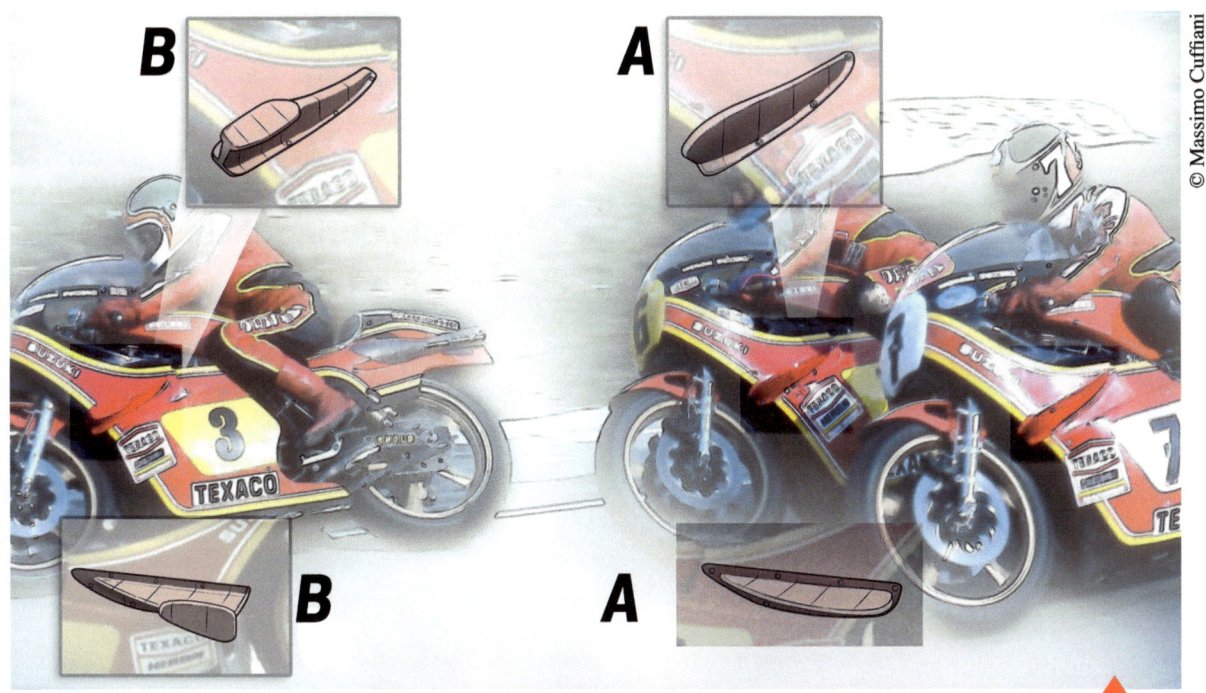

1979 RGB 500 XR27B - Herron (3), Parrish (6), Sheene (7)

We can find other examples of appendages many years later **in 1999 in Max Biaggi's Yamaha YZR500** and **in 2010, on the Ducati Desmosedici GP10**, used that year by **Casey Stoner and Nicky Hayden**.

The two Ducati top-rider were persuaded of the advantage of the two flaps for the **improvement in during the acceleration phase**.

Ducati continued with this solution initially **into 2011** on the **Desmosedici GP11** used **by Hayden and by Valentino Rossi**, who later rejected this solution.

© Massimo Cuffiani

B   **A**

In **2015 Ducati** again inserted aerodynamic flaps into **Andrea Dovizioso's and Andrea Iannone's Desmosedici GP15s** and, in the mid of the season, launched a "biplane" version with two horizontal wings (B in the drawing).

© Massimo Cuffiani

In the same year the **Yamaha M1**, introduced two 'appendages' for the **Misano GP tests** in positions more like those of the 1974 MV Agusta, which are placed just below the fairing and not in the side fairing as preferred by Suzuki and Ducati.
This solution was then **adopted for the race by Valentino Rossi, but dropped by Jorge Lorenzo.**

As an illustration of the research in this field, **Ducati** introduced a solution in the third to last race of the **2015** World Championship **at Phillip Island** - with **four appendages** - two in their usual position and two in the position used by Yamaha at Misano.

The search for higher performance led **Honda, Suzuki and Aprilia in 2016** to experiment with various versions of fins, until, in mid-season, **the Federation decided to ban any type of aerodynamic appendix from 2017.**
Research on two-wheelers therefore came to the same conclusion.
They considered fins of little value for performance, because it would be influenced by the human element too much.
The efficiency of these appendages has often been – and still continues to be – much discussed.
This innovation ensures more aerodynamic load during transitory periods by limiting the wheelie tendency during full acceleration at medium-high speed, thus ensuring better exploitation of available power, and faster steering correction.
Considering that the ailerons in question have very small extensions, this leads to their low efficiency at low speeds, while their deporting capacity is evident at higher speeds, to be clear, those in the straights.
Its greatest utility is probably that of reducing the many stresses on the handlebars, which on long straights, and especially with cross winds or holes in the asphalt, create problematic responses by the bike, and also of enabling the bike to reach maximum speed faster and to succeed in transmitting its full power faster than its competitors do.

RIDERS

TEUVO LÄNSIVUORI

09 Dec 1945
Lisalmi
FINLAND

RESULTS - 500 cc

Colors Code: 1° / 2° / 3° / other / Retired

Year	Races	Bike	Points	Pos.
1978	SPA AUT FRA NAT NED BEL SWE FIN GBR WGER	SUZUKI	39	8
1977	VEN WGER NAT FRA NED BEL SWE FIN TCH GBR	SUZUKI	35	9
1976	FRA AUT NAT NED BEL SWE FIN TCH	SUZUKI	48	2
1975	FRA AUT WGER NED BEL SWE FIN TCH	SUZUKI	40	4
1974	FRA AUT NAT NED BEL SWE FIN TCH	YAMAHA	67	3

RG 500
THE PROTAGONISTS

WIL HARTOG

28 May 1948
Abbekerk
NETHERLANDS

RESULTS - 500 cc   Colors Code: 1° | 2° | 3° | other | Retired

Year / Races	Bike	Points	Pos.
1981 AUT WGER	SUZUKI	2	23
1980 NAT SPA NED BEL FIN GBR WGER	SUZUKI	31	6
1979 VEN AUT WGER NAT SPA JUG NED SWE FIN GBR FRA	SUZUKI	66	4
1978 SPA AUT FRA NAT NED BEL SWE FIN GBR WGER	SUZUKI	65	4
1977 WGER NAT FRA NED BEL SWE FIN TCH GBR	SUZUKI	30	10
1976 AUT NED SWE	SUZUKI	10	21
1975 NED	SUZUKI	0	-
1973 NED	YAMAHA	8	24
1972 WGER NED	YAMAHA	0	-

BARRY SHEENE

11 Sep 1950 London
GREAT BRITAIN

10 Mar 2003 Sidney
AUSTRALIA

RESULTS - 500 cc   Colors Code: 1° | 2° | 3° | other | Retired

Year	Results	Bike	Points	Pos.
1984	RSA NAT SPA AUT WGER FRA JUG NED BEL GBR SWE RSM	SUZUKI	34	6
1983	RSA FRA NAT WGER AUT JUG NED GBR SWE RSM	SUZUKI	9	14
1982	ARG AUT SPA NAT NED BEL JUG	YAMAHA	68	4
1981	AUT WGER NAT FRA JUG NED BEL RSM GBR FIN SWE	YAMAHA	72	4
1980	NAT SPA FRA NED GBR BEL Did Not Qualify	YAMAHA	10	15
1979	VEN AUT WGER NAT SPA JUG NED SWE FIN GBR FRA	SUZUKI	87	3
1978	VEN SPA AUT FRA NAT NED BEL SWE FIN GBR WGER	SUZUKI	100	2
1977	VEN WGER NAT FRA NED BEL SWE FIN GBR	SUZUKI	107	①
1976	FRA AUT NAT NED BEL SWE	SUZUKI	72	①
1975	WGER NAT NED BEL SWE FIN TCH	SUZUKI	30	6
1974	FRA AUT NAT NED BEL SWE TCH	SUZUKI	30	6
1973	FIN	SUZUKI	0	-
1970	SPA	BULTACO	0	-

VIRGINIO FERRARI

19 Oct 1952
Pellegrino Parmense
ITALY

RESULTS - 500 cc   Colors Code: 1° | 2° | 3° | other | Retired

Year	Races	Bike	Points	Pos.
1985	RSM	CAGIVA	0	-
1984	RSA NAT SPA AUT WGER FRA JUG NED BEL GBR SWE RSM	YAMAHA	22	10
1983	RSA FRA NAT WGER AUT GBR RSM	CAGIVA	0	-
1982	ARG AUT NED JUG GBR SWE RSM WGER	SUZUKI	25	11
1981	WGER NAT JUG RSM	CAGIVA	0	-
1980	WGER	CAGIVA	0	-
1979	VEN AUT WGER NAT SPA JUG NED SWE FIN GBR FRA	SUZUKI	89	2
1978	VEN SPA AUT FRA NAT BEL SWE FIN GBR WGER	SUZUKI	22	9
1977	VEN AUT WGER NAT FRA NED BEL SWE FIN TCH	SUZUKI	21	12
1976	NAT FIN TCH WGER	SUZUKI	10	21
1975	NAT	PATON	0	-

MARCO LUCCHINELLI

26 Jun 1954
Ceparana
ITALY

RESULTS - 500 cc

Colors Code: 1º (green) | 2º (yellow) | 3º (blue) | other (grey) | Retired (orange)

Year	Races	Bike	Points	Pos.
1986	NAT	CAGIVA	0	-
1985	JUG NED BEL RSM	CAGIVA	0	-
1984	RSA NAT SPA AUT NED	CAGIVA	0	-
1983	RSA FRA NAT WGER SPA AUT JUG NED BEL GBR SWE RSM	HONDA	48	7
1982	ARG AUT SPA NAT NED BEL JUG GBR SWE RSM WGER	HONDA	43	8
1981	AUT WGER NAT FRA JUG NED BEL RSM GBR FIN SWE	SUZUKI	105	①
1980	NAT SPA FRA NED BEL FIN GBR WGER	SUZUKI	59	3
1979	AUT WGER NAT SPA JUG NED SWE FIN GBR FRA	SUZUKI	11	18
1978	SPA AUT FRA NAT NED BEL SWE FIN GBR WGER	SUZUKI	30	9
1977	VEN WGER NAT FRA NED BEL SWE FIN TCH	SUZUKI	25	11
1976	FRA AUT SWE FIN TCH WGER	SUZUKI	40	4

PAT HENNEN

27 Apr 1953
Phoenix
USA

RESULTS - 500 cc

Colors Code: 1° | 2° | 3° | other | Retired

		Points	Pos.
1978 VEN SPA AUT FRA NAT	SUZUKI	39	8
1977 VEN WGER NAT FRA NED BEL SWE FIN TCH GBR	SUZUKI	67	3
1976 FRA AUT NAT NED BEL SWE FIN TCH WGER	SUZUKI	46	3

GRAZIANO ROSSI

14 Mar 1954
Pesaro
ITALY

RESULTS - 500 cc

Colors Code 1° 2° 3° other Retired

		Points	Pos.
1982 ARG AUT SPA NED BEL JUG GBR SWE RSM	YAMAHA	0	-
1981 AUT NAT JUG NED BEL GBR FIN SWE	MORBIDELLI SUZUKI	0	-
1980 NAT SPA FRA NED BEL FIN GBR WGER	SUZUKI	38	5
1979 WGER NAT SPA JUG NED SWE FIN GBR FRA	MORBIDELLI	2	31
1978 FRA NAT NED BEL FIN GBR WGER	SUZUKI	7	16
1977 NAT FRA	SUZUKI	0	-

JACK MIDDELBURG

30 Apr 1952
Naaldwijk
NETHERLANDS

3 Apr 1984
Groninga
NETHERLANDS

RESULTS - 500 cc

Colors Code: 1° 2° 3° other Retired

		Points	Pos.
1983 FRA SPA AUT NED	HONDA	12	12
1982 ARG JUG RSM	SUZUKI	13	16
1981 AUT WGER NAT FRA NED BEL RSM GBR FIN SWE	SUZUKI	60	7
1980 NED GBR WGER	YAMAHA	20	9
1979 AUT WGER NAT SPA JUG NED SWE FIN	SUZUKI	36	7
1978 AUT NED SWE GBR WGER	SUZUKI	0	-
1977 NED	SUZUKI	0	-

FRANCO UNCINI

09 Mar 1955
Civitanova Marche
ITALY

RESULTS - 500 cc   Colors Code: 1° | 2° | 3° | other | Retired

Year	Races	Bike	Points	Pos.
1985	RSA WGER NAT AUT JUG NED BEL FRA GBR SWE RSM	SUZUKI	8	15
1984	RSA NAT SPA AUT WGER GBR SWE RSM	SUZUKI	14	14
1983	RSA FRA NAT WGER SPA AUT JUG NED	SUZUKI	31	9
1982	ARG AUT SPA NAT NED BEL JUG GBR SWE RSM WGER	SUZUKI	103	①
1981	AUT WGER NAT FRA JUG NED BEL RSM GBR FIN SWE	SUZUKI	12	13
1980	NAT SPA FRA NED BEL FIN GBR WGER	SUZUKI	50	4
1979	VEN AUT WGER NAT SPA JUG NED SWE FIN GBR FRA	SUZUKI	51	5

RANDY MAMOLA

10 Nov 1959
San Josè
USA

RESULTS - 500 cc   Colors Code: 1° / 2° / 3° / other / Retired

1992
| JAP | AUS | USA | SPA | ITA | EUR | NED | HUN | FRA | GBR | BRA | RSA | YAMAHA | 45 | 10 |

1990
| JAP | USA | NAT | GER | AUT | JUG | NED | BEL | FRA | GBR | SWE | TCH | HUN | CAGIVA | 55 | 13 |

1989
| JAP | AUS | USA | SPA | WGER | AUT | JUG | NED | BEL | FRA | TCH | BRA | CAGIVA | 33 | 18 |

1988
| JAP | NAT | WGER | AUT | NED | BEL | JUG | FRA | GBR | SWE | TCH | BRA | CAGIVA | 58 | 12 |

1987
| JAP | SPA | WGER | NAT | AUT | JUG | NED | FRA | GBR | SWE | TCH | RSM | POR | BRA | ARG | YAM | 158 | 2 |

1986
| SPA | NAT | WGER | AUT | JUG | NED | BEL | FRA | GBR | SWE | RSM | YAMAHA | 105 | 3 |

1985
| RSA | SPA | WGER | NAT | AUT | JUG | NED | BEL | FRA | GBR | SWE | RSM | HONDA | 72 | 6 |

1984
| SPA | AUT | WGER | FRA | JUG | NED | BEL | GBR | SWE | RSM | HONDA | 111 | 2 |

1983
| RSA | FRA | NAT | WGER | SPA | AUT | JUG | NED | BEL | GBR | SWE | RSM | SUZUKI | 89 | 3 |

1982
| ARG | AUT | SPA | NAT | NED | BEL | JUG | GBR | SWE | RSM | WGER | SUZUKI | 65 | 6 |

1981
| AUT | WGER | NAT | FRA | JUG | NED | BEL | RSM | GBR | FIN | SWE | SUZUKI | 94 | 2 |

1980
| NAT | SPA | FRA | NED | BEL | FIN | GBR | WGER | SUZUKI | 72 | 2 |

1979
| NED | SWE | FIN | GBR | FRA | SUZUKI | 29 | 8 |

INTERVIEWS

Graziano Rossi — 16-09-2015

Your first RG 500?
It was 1976 and it was the first version, the one with the highly inclined rear shocks. I raced in the Italian Championship with Focarini's OECE Team. When I did a great overtake of Agostini at the Brutapela (Misano Track, Ed.), I became famous and I entered the doors of the World Championship (1977, Ed.).

Your first impression when driving the RG 500?
Amazing! I was just not used to that level of performance. And it was a completely new bike – I would even say like magic. Nothing like previous bikes.

And the RG 500's strong point?
Definitely engine performance, and fantastic power. In addition, the 1980 official factory version (the RGB500 XR34, Ed.) had an excellent frame. Truly unbeatable!

And the RG 500's weak point?
Frankly, nothing at all.

You have used both the RG 500s, both official factory and over the counter. Did you notice any difference?
Yes, I did. Many differences. To give you an idea in numerical terms, there was 1 sec gap in a track like Imola's. And also, as usually happens, the official factory bikes got updates during the season while customer version bikes didn't.

In your GP500 career you have also driven Morbidelli and Yamaha bikes. Differences with Suzuki?
I drove the official factory Yamaha only in the last race of the Italian Championship in 1982. As far as I was concerned, it was just as good as the Suzuki. Morbidelli was a little more complicated.
It was a bike with huge potential, theoretically capable of winning in the same way as the GP125 and GP250, which wiped out their competition. But the bike was completely dependent on Giancarlo Morbidelli and if he had continued to develop it, I'm sure it would have become competitive. This did not happen because, at the same time, his son Gianni had a fast-growing career in car racing and so, as often happens, the father focused on his son.

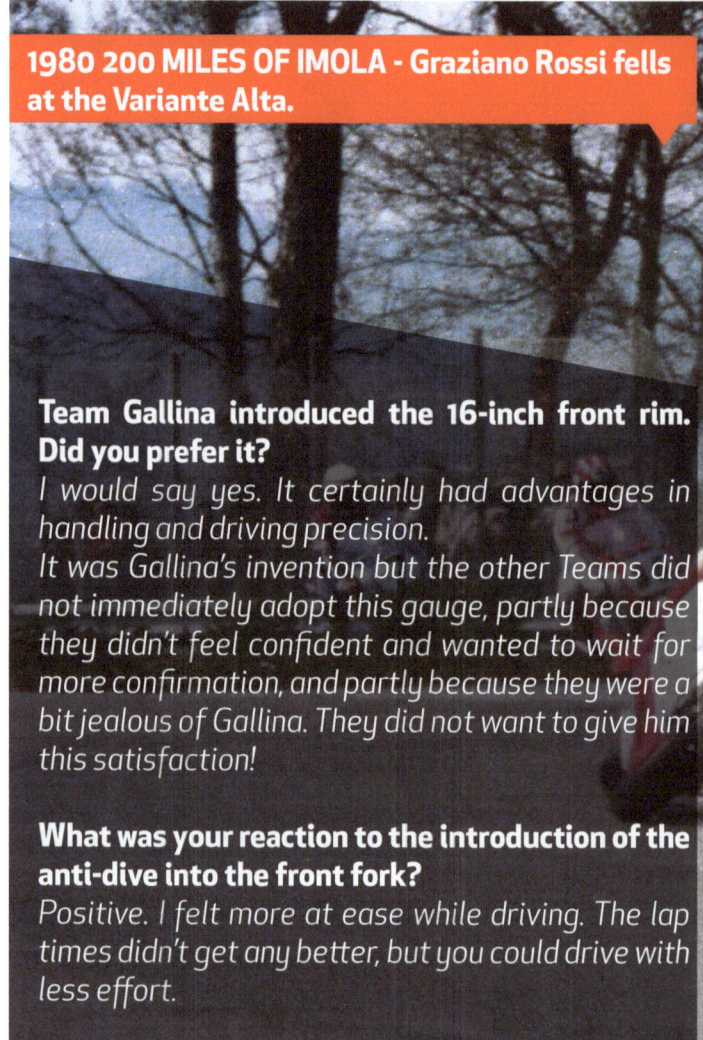

1980 200 MILES OF IMOLA - Graziano Rossi fells at the Variante Alta.

Team Gallina introduced the 16-inch front rim. Did you prefer it?
I would say yes. It certainly had advantages in handling and driving precision.
It was Gallina's invention but the other Teams did not immediately adopt this gauge, partly because they didn't feel confident and wanted to wait for more confirmation, and partly because they were a bit jealous of Gallina. They did not want to give him this satisfaction!

What was your reaction to the introduction of the anti-dive into the front fork?
Positive. I felt more at ease while driving. The lap times didn't get any better, but you could drive with less effort.

What was your best race on the RG 500?
In 1979 at an International competition at Imola, the Nations Cup (6 laps mini-races were held, each time the riders of two nations faced each other, Ed.). I was second in the final points standings for the riders, but I drove really fast! (He won 3 sets out of 4, beating Roberts in the last one with Yamaha, Ed.).

RG 500
THE PROTAGONISTS

What was your worst race on the RG 500?
In 1980, on the saddle of a 653 (RG700 XR23, Ed.), at the 200Mile race in Imola. I got the Pole Position, but on the first lap of the Variante Alta I flew off onto the ground...

Who was the strongest rider you ever met?
Kenny Roberts, without a doubt! You hardly ever saw him around. He used to come to the track with his helmet already on, race, and then leave.
A very particular kind of person. Also Lucky (Marco Lucchinelli, Ed.) and Barry Sheene.

archivio © Claudio Ghini

Tell me an anecdote about the RG 500...
In 1976, I had to run my RG 500's engine in. My mechanic Carlino Molinelli from Fano came up with an idea to run it in on the Fano-Rome highway! Lupo, a friend from Fano, accompanied me with his Laverda 1000 3-cylinder motorcycle. The problem was that while the Laverda was at full speed I was 8000 rpm, under torque and the engine was empty.
As soon as I accelerated to 8200 rpm, I passed it as if it were still! Other than that, it was all right... they did not stop me!

Virginio Ferrari

22-10-15

What was your first Suzuki RG 500?
The first RG was the MK I given to me by Suzuki Italy in 1976 for the Nations GP at Mugello, where I came third behind the winner Sheene and Read.

What was your first impression driving the RG 500?
Extreme ease of engine delivery, I found it particularly easy. I previously drove a four-stroke two-cylinder and a Paton, a four-cylinder four-stroke that was definitely grumpy and more abrupt than the Suzuki.
The RG 500 surprised me because of its flexibility.

The RG 500's strengths?
The RG had many strengths but the main one was that it was simple to set up. And it was not complicated to get the most out of the frame.

Weak points?
Its weak point was its power output coming out of a bend when compared to the Kenny's (Roberts, Ed.) and Cecotto's Yamaha.
We really paid the price when it was time to roll on the gas, then second, third gear, where you could take advantage of three or four meters.
As regards maximum power, on the other hand, we were the same as the others.

You have used both the RG 500s, both official factory and over the counter, did you notice any difference?
There was only a slight difference and I noticed it right here at Imola (1977 Nations GP disputed with an RG 500 MK II – Ed.). I can say even today that I made a mistake when I was in the lead and Barry Sheene was half a second behind me (driving an official factory RG 500 XR14 - Ed.) and I let him get past me after the Variante Alta.

> 1979 Virginio Ferrari with his RG 500 XR27B

As I was following him, I could see that he wasn't holding back and was actually pushing his bike to its limit.
I shadowed him for the first half of the race and I noticed that there was not much difference between our bikes. Barry was in first place, I was in second and Armando Toracca third. Maybe Barry had a bit more acceleration on that occasion and gained few meters on you coming out of the bend. Maybe they had a different rotating disc that gave a bit more oomph coming out of the bend, but the top speed was the same.

Differences between the first engine with its 56 x 50.5 stroke ratio and the subsequent 54 x 54 introduced with the XR14 in 1977?

The square engine (54 x 54 - Ed.) was more developed, but it was a bit more "twitchy", while the oversquare (56 x 50.5 - Ed.) had ampler power delivery and you could feel the acceleration better. In fact, some time later we came back to that bore and stroke as we placed more importance on engine delivery.

Team Gallina introduced the 16-inch front rim. Was it an advantage?

Credit where credit's due, Roberto Gallina didn't introduce the 16-inch rim. He merely thought up the idea but got Campagnolo's Roberto Marchesini to make it a reality. Being a Gallina rider I was the first to carry out all the tests, including on Michelin. We tested several sections, along with tyres, and also the power steering which, again, was thought up by Gallina. We were the Team that developed this solution.
The 16" wheel gave you a different feeling with the bike and, just by looking at it, you immediately felt that it was definitely going to be an advantage in the hurly burly on the chicanes and fast bends; but when you actually entered a fast bend, just before the bend tangent, you could feel that the bike was much more unstable, so it was at that point there that you were losing out compared to 18-inch wheels.

What were your thoughts on the anti-dive system in the front fork?

With the anti-dive I had fun like crazy, because with Roberto (Gallina - Ed.), we achieved something perfect - perfect for the technology at that time, for my way of braking and feeling the rear in the "squat", i.e. linked to the anchor of the rear brake caliper to lower down the bike. So, by combining the front anti-dive and the rear "squat", I did some really great braking. It felt really great and I was braking effectively.

In 1979 Suzuki made the XR27BFR, a version with front radiator in the fairing. What did you think of this solution?

I never wanted it! I tried it in Japan (the new RGB 500 XR27B in pre-championship tests – Ed.) and I made the track record, but I firmly refused the version with the front radiator and in fact the championship confirmed I was right. Everyone remembers when I overtook Barry in Assen, but I also did it to Karlskoga (GP of Sweden 1979 - Ed.) and in some other tracks.

In 1979, did you use multiple versions of frames, even some old ones, to solve configuration problems?

No, during that year two versions were available, the one chosen by Sheene, with engine in front, and the other chosen by me, with the engine, as I recall, 24 millimetres further back, without the radiator under the front fairing. I used that frame for the whole season, adjusting different aspects for each specific track.

In your career you also rode for Cagiva and Yamaha. How were they different from Suzuki?

I found something that surprised me positively, because during duels I saw Kenny Roberts following certain racing lines more easily, but I explained this to myself as being because he used Goodyears (tyres used by Roberts - Ed.), when I looked at him from just behind - because you can study a rider easily when you're just behind him and not when you're thirty meters behind or ahead of him - I saw him perform certain manoeuvres with a narrower bend radius, with a less widened radius after the bend. But when mounted the Yamaha 500 from Team Zago, for that short and unfortunate period, I remember that the bike was able to withstand incredible banking. I remember when in Monza, during an Italian championship race (I have some pictures!), I reached incredible inclination angles and I think I've never banked so much! In my opinion the engine was so large and abundant that it caused the gyroscopic effect, so the longer the crankshaft and the more it gives this flywheel effect that prevents you from changing your straight motion when you have to go into a bend; in short, I believe that this type of Yamaha engine/frame combination could give you such a self-stability of the bike in the bend that I did not feel with the Suzuki RG 500.

Absurdly, to really understand it, you would have had to have simultaneously got on the four-cylinder in-line parallel Yamaha and the square four cylinder Suzuki with its two narrow shafts but at the same time Kenny Roberts had a train of tyres of another brand and you could see that his tyres were more pear-shaped than ours.

We had what could be considered to be the current system with a very wide rim and with the profile of the rubber that falls in fact on the total width of the rim. Remember that, at that time, we had narrow rims of 3.50 inches, so the Michelin tyre had a very short side profile, while on the Dunlop, which I tried in 1982 and experienced the big tyre tried by Kenny at Donington, when you were really going around a bend you could feel your elbows and ears on the floor, but manoeuvring took so long that you lost time turning right/left.

On the other hand, the Cagiva, I refer to it as it was, had one big flaw: its frame. In 1983, however, the bike improved slightly and I remember one small problem at Le Mans due, when braking, to the pressure of the tank against the frame.

A microfracture was created with a consequent fuel oozing and when I started braking, it felt as if the rear wheel was being blocked. I thought it might be the start of a seizure and so I returned to the pits.

Then, after disassembling the engine, we saw that it had no problems. It was a real shame because we were at that point fourth after 7/8 laps. The bike had started to run pretty well and so I put my heart and soul into it and perhaps never gone so fast with a racing bike like that season, but we were really held back by the limitations of the frame.

We also tried Nico Bakker's frames, but now, in hindsight, the engine was positioned too low; that is my technical opinion.

The effect remains inside your head, like the first time you get on a bike when you're a child and it sears your memory, and I remember that the effect of the Cagiva 500 in the various versions was that we had unfortunately made that kind of mistake: with the low centre of gravity at a certain point you create, as I call it, "the bulb effect of the sailboat", instead of helping you, it goes the other way and leads you to widen the trajectories and this was our problem.

Which was your best race on the RG 500?
The GP des Nations at Imola in 1979 is especially close to my heart, after the fall of the day before at the Tamburello Bend, because it was a sort of rebirth.

Before falling, when I felt the bike going away, I thought it was over and I had time to think about this detail.

During the race, the next day, I continued to feel a vibration on the front area, which was the cause of the fall, and so I lost positions at the Tamburello… I was twelfth, then thirteenth and I was going back. At that point I said to myself: either you keep gas open or you stop, so I started to recover positions and I reached Kenny who was first.

I was very close and maybe if I had reacted four, five laps earlier, maybe the race would have ended differently!

Which was the worst contest?
The worst? I must say Le Mans (GP of France 1979, last decisive race in the World Championship- Ed.), because I touched Barry (Sheene - Ed.), I went off the track and I made an unforgivable mistake when I went straight due to this "contact".

Afterwards I did a little bit of "cross" off the track, where the surface was a bit bumpy and when I came back to the track, I did not pump the brake to purge the pads.

At the first sharp braking behind Cecotto, the "S" one, I got confused and I was about to rear-end him, so I decided to go on the embankment at the edge of the track... and I pulled the bike onto my head, after skidding for hundreds of meters with the front tyre on the asphalt and the rear on the dirt road.

If I had worked on the brakes, who knows, maybe I could have recovered my position, but my goal was to get back behind Barry and the red mist just descended…

The strongest rider you met?
I met so many, from Kenny Roberts to Marco Lucchinelli, but there was one, as I always say, that impressed me most and that was Jack Middelburg. He impressed me because he overtook me and Gianfranco Bonera on a bend in a street track. We had just entered the track, which we didn't know very well: it was in the north of Belgium and had unpronounceable name: Sint-Joris-ten-Distel. It was an "upon invitation" race in a void week between two GP races and we saw this Yamaha 500 leaning on a bush after the checks, literally bound and held together by the wire, dirty, rusty: it was Jack Middelburg's bike.
On Sunday I found him on the highest step of the podium. We did not give our 100%, but that way he drove was just so terrifying!
So, I was particularly impressed by that overtake on the bend and from then on I always supported Jack Middelburg. Unfortunately, he lost his life on just one of those road tracks where he was particularly strong.
I definitely put him on the top step of the podium, along with Phil Read, Kenny Roberts, Steve Baker, Marco Lucchinelli, and many others.
There has never been a better rider, because there is no such thing as a better rider, there is only the driver has got things right setting things up better than the others, and doing it all with a big heart and full throttle.

1979 Virginio Ferrari with his RG 500 XR27B

Marco Lucchinelli

03-02-16

What was your first Suzuki RG 500?
In 1976. Two of them arrived in Italy, one for Cereghini and the one that Armando Toracca and I tossed a coin for to decide who would use it in the first race. We had a 4-cylinder and a twin-cylinder Titan 500 available. I won the toss for the debut at Misano, but due to snow I did not compete and lost my chance.
The following Sunday in Modena with the twin-cylinder I made the whole race in front of Agostini and I won again the RG for my debut in the world championship at Le Mans, where I won a third place!

What was your first impression when driving the RG 500?
It was like going with the perfect bike... I came from the 250, air-cooled and drum brakes and for once on a Bimota 350 with disc brakes, then the Laverda 1000 4-stroke endurance. Getting on the RG 500 was truly exciting. A real racing bike and no messing around. The others were street running bikes.

RG 500's strength?
I don't know... because I have not driven the others, it's a difficult question. Of course, when I started racing in the World Championship our bike was a customer version, while Barry Sheene, Roberts and the others had official factory bikes. But it wasn't so very different, maybe because I had some very good technicians like Gallina. At Le Mans I started in the front row, for the next race I was second behind Phil Read, in the wet I was almost always in front, at least during the tests. As the race progressed, the suspension got better; it was a different engine that worked better with its gears and new features.

You have used both the RG 500s, both official factory and private. Did you notice any difference?
There was a slight difference but as I said before, I was lucky enough to work with Gallina, who had a test bench. At that time, we could get inside the engine. Today it would be impossible with the four-stroke engine as the engines already come out optimized by the manufacturers' engineers. In the past, after polishing a cylinder, creating ports, removing a crossbar, lowering the head a little, making the muffler, in short, you could make a good running bike, if you were capable.
It was important to have the right technicians, because when we had the removable gearbox, making a good change was difficult.
I lost a race in Rjeka in 1980 against Mamola, because the fifth and the sixth gear had too much distance. On the straight I was shifting from the fifth to the sixth gear as he sped away from me, and then

I overtook him again on the inside later... all the laps where like that, but yet he still came up ahead of me.
I was a friend of Barry Sheene, a true friend, not just jokes. He leant me a hand, gave me some advice. We never had any problems. I won the race at Imola (1981 - ed.) thanks to him.
If you look at the film recordings of the time, after we arrived from the warm-up, Barry comes up and speaks in my ear. I had the intermediate tyre in the front and slick behind because the weather was lousy and he tells me: "Marcolino, change the front tyre; if it rains, they'll call off the race!"
In fact, we could see the mechanics turning my bike sideways and taking it into the box to change the front tyre with a slick.
In the end, I won the race ahead of him ... today these things do not happen ... I'm proud of my time."

1981 Lucchinelli with the RGΓ 500 before Roberts

Differences between the first engine with bore and stroke 56 x 50.5 and the next 54 x 54 introduced with the XR14 in 1977?
The next engine had more torque, it was more drivable, because at that time silencers were included into the mufflers. In the end it was like a four-stroke, with more torque at low speed and easier to drive despite having more horsepower.

Team Gallina introduced the 16-inch front rim. Was it an advantage?
It was something that had already been considered in 1976 with Tamburini. He wanted to try the power steering, but it was made with gears and had a bit of slack. We used the rear wheel of a 250 as a front wheel to be able to brake closer to the bend and steer faster. No one believed in the 16" except the Team Gallina and I developed it with a lot of commitment... in Brazil, in South Africa. I won the World Championship with it and the year after Dunlop included it in its product catalogue. That meant that it was the right choice.

How did you find the anti-dive system in the front fork?
I felt immediately at ease with the anti-dive on the front. We had done it on the rear and it worked well together. It was a simple aluminium splint that started from the rear brake anchor and went to the top of the frame. When you braked, the anchor pulled and lowered the bike in the rear part too. When I went to Honda, I brought the idea to them, but they did it with linkages whose effectiveness depended on how you positioned them. In the end there were just so many possible settings, but also just as many chances of making mistakes. Since we were not so great at doing the maths calculations needed, I just flipped.

In 1980, the models were the XR34 H and M. Initially you used the H version with two shock absorbers and then from the Finnish GP, the M2 Full Float. Differences and preferences?
I do not really remember the technical details, but it did give you that something extra. We never reversed any of the changes we made.
When anything new turned up during the winter tests, Mamola tried them first on his own, then Barry or whichever British rider happened to be there, and then I tried it out for three or four days. The difference between Gallina and the rest was that he always brought something down; some ideas; he never arrived empty-handed. Others usually tried it out first and then it was our turn give it a good going over. Maybe we didn't need everything, but there was always something that worked because Roberto (Gallina - Ed.) was a great man.

Was the 1981 RG Gamma XR35 a leap forward compared to the 1980 XR34M2?
Yes, it was a fascinating leap forward, especially in front. I take it as a reference to how good it was to 'go for it', because it was difficult for it to skid from under from you and you would only come off your bike because you had seized up or something broke. It was a great leap in quality and then it was easy to ride on any track. You did not have any more than the others, but it was in that moment that we took them all by surprise. However, in the 1980s it was already good and we should have won the World championship. In 1981 I won, Franco (Uncini - ed.) the year after.

Your best season with Suzuki?
Definitely 1980! Although the year after with the RG Gamma I won the World Cup. I have fewer successes, but I went like a rocket. At Misano I was first when I broke the bike, in the UK we overtook each other at least six times at every lap and after the race, the rear tyre was so worn-out that you could put your hand inside. I would have won there too! Then in Finland I was ahead of Graziano Rossi on Suzuki by 12 seconds. I broke the head gasket two laps from the end, then even Graziano broke the seal. In Holland I was first, I was way ahead of everyone, my visor fogged over, so I went into the pits and got a mechanic's glasses. I went back onto the track without a visor, but it was not possible to race in that condition and so I retired. Eventually in Suzuki they understood my worth and kept me for the following year. In 1980, at Paul Ricard, I recorded such good timings that the year after, despite winning, I could not repeat them.

In your career you also ran with Cagiva and Honda. Differences with Suzuki?
Suzuki was a big family and I think it is now too. When I went to Japan it was like going home. You asked for something and they did it for you: pedals, handlebars. It was the same at Honda, but they always tried to improve things, adding something more, although sometimes they could complicate your life.

When I took the Honda in 1982, they said we would not qualify. We went to the first debut race in Argentina and I got the best timing. Engineers like Gallina, Agostini, Moeller said that I had left only for the money and I would not have qualified! I was fifth in the race. At the second race in Austria if I had not come off on the last lap I would have won the World Championship again. But that fall changed everything.

Differences? I really enjoyed the Suzuki. I liked it and it suited me perfectly. On it, I had a really nice driving style, even as I look at myself all these years later. On the corners I was quite impressive - the 3-cylinder Honda was a smaller bike with problems on the front. So many riders - from Frutschi to Paci – ended up dead. I managed to control the front and go fast, but not as I wanted. But it was a fascinating bike, it was like a 250 compared to the Suzuki 500. In the end, I didn't enjoy riding it and didn't trust it. Then Spencer came and he was fast, he could ride it in his way and he was better than us.

Cagiva? After you get off a Honda... I really believed in it! In my mind I was the first Italian with an Italian bike. I had left it in 1979. I had given it that name when they took the bikes from Life in 1976. Then I came back. Can you imagine it? The bike's gears started with reverse. When you push-started it, sometimes the engine started but the tachometer did not move because the engine was going backwards! After three races I got tired and I stopped for almost a year. Then I persuaded myself to go back, I think in 1985, by which time they had also taken on Garriga. I thought definitely "the bike must have changed". I raced in Monza and on the Ascari bend I found myself with no front brakes; that really terrified me and I flew off onto the ground during tests! I stopped, Castiglioni bought the Ducati and I went on to race the Superbike.

Tell me who really won the Silverstone GP under the rain in 1978...
Without any doubt I won it! Not because I say it but because they say it; at the time everything was written in the notebook; those who kept the rounds for Barry Sheene say it; and he actually complained because they pulled me off the podium. Also, Roberts' team (who was eventually declared winner - Ed.) and other competitors, too. Unfortunately, there was no technology!

They immediately gave me the winner's cup and then they took it away five minutes later! I jokingly always say that maybe there was a reason: Gianni Rolando was third, according to his calculations. Probably even the management thought there was a mistake: Rolando standing and third! I always tell him this.

This happened to me too, in a race where you must show bravery, where everyone stopped to change the tyres and I went ahead with two slick tyres. Why? Firstly, if I had stopped in the pits there would have been nothing left to use, because we had to leave the race in two hours, so the mechanics had only left out the bare minimum and had packed everything else away. Secondly, at that time the tyre change was not so fast, it seemed to me that the others took two laps to change them: I remember that I kept going round and for two laps I saw them stopped in the pits. After they passed me once and when I arrived I was sure I had won. But you see, we did not stop to make a complaint, we had to leave and catch a plane!

Your best race with the RG 500?
I don't know. That's because there are races that I have not won, but which I thought I did, including the 1976 Nurburgring race where I reached second, because there was a psychological subjection to Giacomo Agostini. He was 15 times world champion, so who the hell was Lucchinelli? He fell, he drank, who was this? But at the Nürburgring I had the best time during tests. Agostini carried out tests with both and had understood that if it had been wet the MV would have been better.

On the Saturday evening, he would have to choose between Suzuki and MV, but the choice was made on the day of the race. However, in 1980 I got my own back and won my first race!

Your worst race with the RG 500?
The last race of 1981, as World Champion, because I lost the whole winter. It was a race by invitation organized by F1 rider Jody Schechter at Donington Park, because he wanted to do the World Series with a whole category of champions. It was a race that I had as good as already won with one hand, but they caught me up because I wanted to pass them where I could be seen by everyone, in the corner after the pits. Instead, I went past them high - very high! I broke two arms and two legs. I took it very badly because it ruined my winter and, plus, I was meant to go to meet President Pertini of Italy and I couldn't go! I often used to withdraw, but almost always because of engine seizure and at the end I always broke my clavicles ... eight times in the end – four times on each side, so it was evens.

What was the strongest rider you met?
There were so many for me, even if they did not win the World Cup. For example, Mamola, who got so many second positions. He was a young talent and he had a spectacular driving style. He was an opponent of the bad ones. Spencer changed driving styles; he was a "Martian" who did the incredible by winning 2 categories in a year plus the 200 Miles and made records in his own way. But he was not my kind of rider. Roberts was a true Martian because he hardly ever complained. I really liked him for that. He would swerve the bike and blow out tyres, but he never bothered people. He had calluses in his hand and he was a real 'rough diamond'. I liked Barry, because he had fun on motorbikes, we had fun on motorbikes and we always got on well. I've been to his home in England, he really was a great guy.
Some were even less famous, but they were very fast, like Carlos Lavado who was terrifying. I liked people who were a bit off-the-wall, I was a fan of Hailwood when everyone was for Agostini. Now that I'm older, I can re-evaluate Agostini, you cannot avoid considering his merits. If he won 15 World Cups, he was able to make choices, he was able to stay in the world… that could be also luck, but he did the same races as the others did.
He won 10 TTs, so he had been there and done that! The difference between him and the others that he was cultured; he knew English, which made things easier. Everyone said that he had only one rival and that was one of his own team mates, but it only takes one!
I like those who invented something. Barry was the first to do the opposite of Agostini, that is, everything that was bad for you: the cigarettes, and then whisky with "Sambuca con la mosca", and luxury cars. That was how we were.
I discovered drinking on Saturday night.

1977 DUTCH TT Assen - "Lucky" behind Sheene

If I made pole position then we would celebrate immediately, because tomorrow maybe I am going to crash!

Tell me an anecdote about the RG 500...
When we made the changes, we did them at the test bench. But it was the track that gave you the true result. I lived in Liguria and it was not easy to test. So, I waited until 5 pm in the evening when the traffic had died down and I took the coast road from La Spezia to Rio Maggiore. We wore a helmet because we had one, but generally you wouldn't. We did four stages, saw how well engine took the revolutions and then we finished and put the bike back on the trailer. Or when I was in Cagiva, the year after LIFE, we went to a road near Malpensa airport on the fire brigade road and we raced faster and faster. In the past we had fewer possessions, but we had more fun and you always looked forward to doing something great.

Franco Uncini

14-01-16

What was your first Suzuki RG 500?
It was in 1979, bought with our own money from Suzuki Italia. It was really exciting to buy it, but above all to get on it. In 1976 I started among the seniors with a Yamaha 350, so in 1977 I had the opportunity to race with the Harley Davidson. In 1978 I was identified as a good rider for the 250 and 350 and I had a proposal from Venemotos to race with them.

So I raced from 1976 to 1978 included in those two championships, but I dreamed of the 500! In 1978, after a not-so-good experience (Imola 200 Miles Ed.), I decided to ride in the 500 category and the only possibility was buying a customer version RG 500. So a team was made here in Recanati with my brother Henry as Team Manager, my mother as cook of the Team, and Mario Ciamberlini as my mechanic.

What was your first impression driving the RG 500?
Really exciting... except that I felt suited mentally to the 500 although little less so physically, as I was perhaps ideal for smaller-displacement engines. I felt the 500 was well suited to me also as regards driving style and experience, because I had done my first two years of career with production bikes, the Laverda SFC 750 and the Ducati 750, bikes that weighed over 200 kg. Although I weighed 53/54 kg., I managed to handle them well and so their weight and the power didn't worry me. On the contrary they attracted me even more.

While 250 and 350 require more meticulous driving and I was a bit more "bizarre", I liked riding with a little roughness, strength, and determination and the 500 was the ideal class and so it was. In 1979, in fact, I came fifth in the World Championship and so I was the fastest privateer rider in the world.

The strength of the RG 500?
Its drivability! It was a very drivable bike; it was not too cantankerous; it was well suited to all the different tracks; and it did not have any major drawbacks. It was not outstanding in terms of power, but the real secret of Mario Ciamberlini, who was my chief mechanic and to whom I give all the credit for the set-up, is that he understood the importance of not over-elaborating, but rather of keeping it in perfect order.

That way, we had a bike that was always 100% on every occasion, without creating major upheavals for ourselves, without changing the suspension, springs, or exhaust pipes. Mario always kept it in the immaculate condition that we had purchased it in and the bike was really a perfect compromise.

Weaknesses?
Weaknesses? Clearly compared to the official factory RG, it lacked something in terms of performance...

So, that leads us to the following question... you have used both the RG 500, both official factory and customer versions. Was there a difference?
Overall, the customer versions ones were not much different from the official factory models. The official factory engine was more advanced, more aggressive, but they were also slightly lighter and therefore were not so well modulated in braking, while my bike was perfectly modulated and on many occasions I managed to gain to the official factory bikes when braking, because I noticed that my bike was balanced.

Team Gallina introduced the 16-inch front rim. Was it an advantage?
It was Gallina, but it was also the Michelin who had a fascinating front tyre. It certainly gave me extra strength, because I had a lot of confidence in front tyre and my strong point was braking. I could even get into the middle of the bend with caliper well pulled and therefore very fast. Most overtakings happened right at the beginning of a bend. I had a faster speed going into the bend, I reached fold and very confident. The 16" rim and that tyre were common, but perhaps my real advantage was my confidence.

How did you find the anti-dive system in the front fork?
It was not something you felt very much, it was there, but it was not so obvious.

In 1981 from the GP of Yugoslavia you used the official factory XR34 Wil Hartog. How did it go?
It was a disaster! I had it in 1981 because Hartog stopped racing, then the Suzuki, since I had been the fastest rider in 1979 and 1980, he entrusted me with the bike.

I went to get this Suzuki in Holland two days before my wedding, I decided to get married on May 23rd, 1981, so on the 21st I left with Okamoto of Suzuki for Holland, I still remember, with a Volvo 240 Station Wagon diesel. I had this bike loaded on a pickup truck and I returned around midnight to Italy on my wedding day. Remember that at that time there were no cell phones and so as to hurry up, I did not even stop on the way to call my future wife. I know that she thought at a certain point: "He's run off". Anyway, I got married. Okamoto was also at my wedding, and the next day we left for Rjeka for the GP of Yugoslavia. This was my honeymoon! In Rjeka, as soon as I put my ring on, I went onto the track but I couldn't put on my gloves because of the ring, so I took it off again and gave it to my wife. And since that day on I have never worn it.

USAG

Going back to the bike, it was a disaster. It was difficult to develop it and in the end I did not know if you could fix it.
We had this bike with some spare parts, but with few instructions and no possibility of changing anything. That was the year I got my worst result, thirteenth in the World Championship. The following year, in the 1982 World Championship I changed number several times, because they gave the fixed number from the first to the tenth of the previous year, while from the tenth to the fifteenth, they gave different numbers if they were available, but I got thirteenth and some tracks thinking that 13 brought bad luck, they did not give it. Then I used 10, 13, 14, 15, 18, 41.

1981 Uncini with his RG 500 MK VI

1981 Uncini with Hartog's XR34M2

In your 500 career, have you raced with other bikes besides Suzuki?
No

Was the RG Gamma XR40 of the 1982 a big leap forward compared to the XR34 of the 1980 and the over the counter RG? In what particular?
It was a beautiful development. The engine was more powerful, but the frame was the real leap forward. It was as if it had been built especially for me and I actually did well with it.

What was your best race on the RG 500?
As a privateer, I remember the very good debut in Hockenheim (1979 GP Germany - Ed.). I made the second fastest time during tests, even though it was a very tough track. Then I remember a wonderful race in Rjeka in 1979 where I reached third.

Which one is the worst contest?
None in particular, perhaps those where I had technical problems.

The strongest rider you met?
I'm a little undecided between Kenny Roberts and Freddie Spencer. Spencer's real strength came out during the first two laps when he used to leave us all 3 or 4 seconds behind him and then stayed more or less at the same distance. I saw him from behind, at his speed in the bends in the first two laps it was impossible to follow him; when you brake you noticed that your bike was not gripping the ground. Roberts instead was solid, unwavering, and consistently strong in every race; beating Roberts was hard, tiring and you had to give a lot of thought before finding the right spot to overtake him.

One last thought on the RG 500
I am in love with the RG 500, I have always been in love with the RG 500, and I have always thanked Suzuki for this. I'm just so grateful and happy to have had this experience.

Mario Ciamberlini   01-10-16

Mario was the long-time mechanic of Franco Uncini, but also the discoverer of Marche talent!
He is the one who prepared the fastest customer version RG 500 in the world in 1979 and 1980.
So why not interview him and ask him about the secret of making the Uncini's Suzuki so reliable and performant, and a bit of history of that era?

archivio © Massimo Cuffiani

What was your first feeling when you saw a Suzuki RG 500?
The first time I saw the Suzuki RG 500 on Motosprint (Italian Magazine - Ed.), I immediately though that adjusting it would make people crazy! It had an engine like the Yamaha of Bill Ivy and Phil Read, i.e. with the four cylinders in the square and the carburettors on the sides. Yamaha then abandoned this system with the rotary valves and Suzuki took it back and built the most beautiful bike that ever existed, because it allowed a privateer rider, with just 8 million lire, to successfully compete in the World Championship! By accumulating 3 or 4 years' experience, you could also win the World Championship, by working on it and understanding the importance of tyres and suspensions, which were difficult to regulate. And it was necessary to dedicate time both to the chassis and to the engine of the motorcycle at the same time. At the end of the day, all this work is crucial because you can make a flying engine, but if the rest is not well set up you won't win. The Suzuki, however, gave you a bike that, with a phenomenal rider like Uncini, you could get a good impression, even if the bike was ordinary.

Was Franco Uncini immediately comfortable with the RG or changes were necessary to adapt it to his driving style?
He was born with the bike! I saw him the first time in front of the Coffee Bar, because it was where we held most discussions about the riders of the time like Agostini and Pasolini. Some backed the former, others the latter. One day Franco went by with a fifty and he pulled into a narrow street nearby in a way that neither Agostini nor Pasolini could have done. Then I said to those who had gathered to chat, 'Did you see that? Uncini can beat Agostini whenever he wants!'. They were all baffled by this and if I hadn't got away quickly they might have punched me. I saw immediately that he had something more than the others. I bumped into him wandering around Recanati and I advised him to go on the track avoiding the risks of traffic. It took a short time to see him in Misano. We tried the Laverda SFC, after 3 or 4 laps he set the track record, which was the prerogative of the riders of the series derived motorcycles like Cereghini or Gallina. After this first taste of track racing with the Laverda derivative series, Franco moved to Team Spaggiari in 1975 and subsequently to Harley-Davidson and Yamaha of Team Venemotos. In 1979 the RG Standard arrived and our couple was back together. I think Franco was an exceptional rider; adjusting the bike for him was never difficult and he adjusted easily. I think if we had had a few more years of experience we would have won the World Championship with the standard bike too! Moreover, thanks to his body, we always had 3 or 4 km/h more speed.

archivio © Massimo Cuffiani

What were the differences between your Suzuki and the others?
Our bike had 116 hp on one version and 130 on another. The one with 116 hp had very good torque, and the one with 130 hp included torque at high rmps. We tried both versions at Borghi Severi, but the one with 130 hp has never been used in the track because the delivery bend was too steep and this was, a priori, a negative characteristic. Meanwhile at Borghi Severi, Biliotti's bike came with 104 hp at the bench, but I don't know what condition it was in.

Were there any differences in performance between over the counter and official factory RGs?
In my opinion, in 1979 and 1980 there was not much difference. When they introduced the staggered cylinders into the over the counter bikes, the performance gap with the official factory ranges increased.

Were the RGs difficult to set up?
These 2-stroke bikes could be easily set up, as long as they did not have any particular design problems. Wil Hartog's prototype used in 1981 included an unbalanced thermal system with the expansion chambers: it was a disaster!

What kind of works had to be done on the engine?
At that time, the engine had to be dismantled, because when Suzuki supplied it to you, it was never set up properly; lots of things, the port barrels for example, had to be checked out. Furthermore, the first and third pistons had to come up together and, at 180°, the other two pistons, second and fourth, had to be aligned. After having tightened up the engine, a special key was inserted, with an integrated gauge as a clock, on the crankshaft. It was used to check the pressure kilos needed to make the latter turn. Then it was increased about 5° to the closing of the intake valves and the ports were set by widening them on the base of the cylinder.
The most important change, however, was carried out on the crankshaft bearings because they included Teflon which, if it exceeded "draft" by 5 hundredths, the bearing ring nut tightened the crankshaft too much with consequent seizing of the main bearings. All those who did not work on the bike and who wanted to buy it new and immediately race with it ended up with engine seizure. But it didn't have to be that way and, to avoid this problem, I had built a tool (which I still keep in my official factory hop) to give the right draft and thickness to the Teflon bearings.

Ciamberlini with Uncini in Recanati

It was also important that all valves closed and opened with the same degrees. Good carburation made the difference. Of course, if you were going to Salzburg you had to keep a special discharge port, while if you were running in a tortuous circuit or at sea level, you needed another setting. The atmospheric pressure of the track also influenced the compression ratio set up. However, we made no substantial replacements and we tried some new aluminium cylinders with a Nikasil bath (the original ones included internal cast-iron liner) which were not original or complete, but without getting any improvement. We then proceeded with the originals. Today these things are all gone!

During those years, Roberts with Yamaha and Spencer with Honda were your rivals. Were these bikes superior to the Suzuki?

Here, however, we are talking about official factory motorcycles that came out after 1982, when Suzuki invested less in racing! Initially, Spencer had the three-cylinder Honda and I think that it was better on a track Montjuïc-style with lots of accelerations, because it had a very low torque and as soon as I opened gas it "took off". I do not know the advantages of the frame, but the three-cylinder engine was certainly better in twisty tracks. During those times I felt Yamaha was not so fast, however they had the official factory tyre service and Kenny Roberts on the bike! Let's say that I preferred Suzuki more.

How were the 1980 and 1981 seasons?

1980 was a great year! Franco (Uncini Ed.) was third in the World Championship before Suzuki Team Gallina official factory bikes, until the last race. Then Lucchinelli won at Nürburgring and overtook us. The year 1981 was hell! Above all for Franco as a rider. But he had some joy at Mugello, at the end of the season, in the Italian championship: he finished ahead of the World Champion Lucchinelli. All of this thanks to that "disgusting" bike inherited from Hartog (the official factory XR34 used the year before, Ed.). Finally, we raised an exhaust port, lowered something there, changed something else over there, and finally some good came of it. Maybe it was just because Marco didn't care so much any longer about winning that race. He had a great bike that year (RG Gamma 500 XR35 - Ed.)! Someone, called Polese, set it up. He was a guy who had cut his teeth working for Gallina and after three or four seasons had learned how to do it.

What was Uncini like as a rider?
You didn't have to keep asking Franco to do things because he would take care of everything himself! Franco was truly talented! I remember for example that we managed to fit the Girling rear shock absorbers, instead of the original Kayaba. We didn't think the original ones were so good because, after two or three laps, they became too soft.

That choice enabled us to get fourth place in the World Championship and those Girlings helped us a lot. Even in Venezuela in the first 1979 race, from behind the pits I saw them going down and, near a street hollow, I realized that the bike was swinging too much. The shock absorbers had already seized up. While the other official factory bikes did not swing at all.

Can you tell us a particular anecdote?
(now Uncini intervenes and tells an anecdote about Ciamberlini - Ed.)

I will tell something about Mario, just to give you an idea of what he was like.

There was a friend of ours, an engineer in the team, who helped us on various research into temperature, gasoline and so on. It happened that he was doing the calculation of the fuel in the tank, which held about 30 litres.

He said, "Mario, according to my calculations, we can easily do the race on 21 litres"; and Mario replied, "21 litres, plus two more for safety, plus two for another doubt. Let's call it six and that's it!"
He just didn't trust anyone. Mario was like that.
"Hey, Franco!" - Ciamberlini answers again – "Your anecdote is a bit over the top. At Misano, we went around with the van and the bike inside and suddenly some people came up to us, took a look inside and asked, "Is that an official factory Laverda?" And I replied, "No, that is the winning Laverda!"
Actually, the official factory bike belonged to Augusto Brettoni - a really nice guy, by the way.

archivio © Massimo Cuffiani

RACES FINAL RESULTS

1974

Round 1 — GP France - Clermont Ferrand 21/04
1	Phil Read	GB	MV
2	Barry Sheene	GB	Suzuki
3	Gianfranco Bonera	ITA	MV
4	Teuvo Lansivuori	FIN	Yamaha
5	Michel Rougerie	FRA	H-D
6	Billie Nelson	GB	Yamaha
7	John Williams	GB	Yamaha
8	Chas Mortimer	GB	Yamaha
9	Ramon Jimenez	FRA	Yamaha
10	Philipp Gerard	FRA	Yamaha

Round 2 — GP W.Germany - Nurburgring 28/04
1	Edmund Czihak	GER	Yamaha
2	Horst Kassner	GER	Yamaha
3	Walter Kaletsch	GER	Yamaha
4	Udo Kochanski	GER	Köning

Round 3 — GP Austria - Salzburgring 05/05
1	Giacomo Agostini	ITA	Yamaha
2	Gianfranco Bonera	ITA	MV
3	Barry Sheene	GB	Suzuki
4	Jack Findlay	AUS	Suzuki
5	Dieter Braun	GER	Yamaha
6	Karl Auer	AUT	Yamaha
7	Billie Nelson	GB	Yamaha
8	John Williams	GB	Yamaha
9	Paul Eickelberg	GER	Köning
10	Jean-Paul Boinet	FRA	Yamaha

Round 4 — GP Nations - Imola 19/05
1	Gianfranco Bonera	ITA	MV
2	Teuvo Lansivuori	FIN	Yamaha
3	Phil Read	GB	MV
4	Jack Findlay	AUS	Suzuki
5	Michele Gallina	ITA	Yamaha
6	Karl Auer	AUT	Yamaha
7	Werner Giger	SWI	Yamaha
8	Billie Nelson	GB	Yamaha
9	Christian Léon	FRA	Kawasaki
10	Geoff Barry	GB	Matchless

Round 5 — TT - Isle of Man 06/06
1	Phil Carpenter	GB	Yamaha
2	Charlie Williams	GB	Yamaha
3	Tony Rutter	GB	Yamaha
4	Billie Guthrie	IRL	Yamaha
5	Paul Cott	GB	Yamaha
6	Helmut Kassner	GER	Yamaha
7	Billie Nelson	GB	Yamaha
8	Pete McKinley	GB	Yamaha
9	Selwyn Griffiths	GB	Matchless
10	Geoff Barry	GB	Matchless

Round 6 — Dutch TT - Assen 29/06
1	Giacomo Agostini	ITA	Yamaha
2	Teuvo Lansivuori	FIN	Yamaha
3	Phil Read	GB	MV
4	Gianfranco Bonera	ITA	MV
5	Charlie Williams	GB	Yamaha
6	Karl Auer	AUT	Yamaha
7	Pentti Korhonen	FIN	Yamaha
8	Victor Palomo	SPA	Yamaha
9	Werner Giger	SWI	Yamaha
10	John Williams	GB	Yamaha

Round 7 — GP Belgium - Spa 07/07
1	Phil Read	GB	MV
2	Giacomo Agostini	ITA	Yamaha
3	Dieter Braun	GER	Yamaha
4	Patrick Pons	FRA	Yamaha
5	Jack Findlay	AUS	Suzuki
6	Michel Rougerie	FRA	H-D
7	John Williams	GB	Yamaha
8	Christian Léon	FRA	Kawasaki
9	Paul Eickelberg	GER	Köning
10	Gianfranco Bonera	ITA	MV

Round 8 — GP Sweden - Anderstorp 21/07
1	Teuvo Lansivuori	FIN	Yamaha
2	Phil Read	GB	MV
3	Pentti Korhonen	FIN	Yamaha
4	Gianfranco Bonera	ITA	MV
5	Karl Auer	AUT	Yamaha
6	Billie Nelson	GB	Yamaha
7	Werner Giger	SWI	Yamaha
8	Victor Palomo	SPA	Yamaha
9	Tom Herron	IRL	Yamaha
10	John Williams	GB	Yamaha

Round 9 — GP Finland - Imatra 28/07
1	Phil Read	GB	MV
2	Gianfranco Bonera	ITA	MV
3	Teuvo Lansivuori	FIN	Yamaha
4	Jack Findlay	AUS	Suzuki
5	Pentti Korhonen	FIN	Yamaha
6	John Williams	GB	Yamaha
7	Christian Léon	FRA	Kawasaki
8	Werner Giger	SWI	Yamaha
9	Philippe Coulon	SWI	Yamaha
10	Karl Auer	AUT	Yamaha

Round 10 — GP Czech Rep. - Brno 25/08
1	Phil Read	GB	MV
2	Gianfranco Bonera	ITA	MV
3	Teuvo Lansivuori	FIN	Yamaha
4	Barry Sheene	GB	Suzuki
5	Dieter Braun	GER	Yamaha
6	Giacomo Agostini	ITA	Yamaha
7	Jack Findlay	AUS	Suzuki
8	Michel Rougerie	FRA	H-D
9	Pentti Korhonen	FIN	Yamaha
10	Chas Mortimer	GB	Yamaha

1974 Riders' 500 World Championship
1	Phil Read	GB	MV	82(92) pt
2	Gianfranco Bonera	ITA	MV	69(78) pt
3	Teuvo Lansivuori	FIN	Yamaha	67 pt
4	Giacomo Agostini	ITA	Yamaha	47 pt
5	Jack Findlay	AUS	Suzuki	34 pt
6	Barry Sheene	GB	Suzuki	30 pt
7	Dieter Braun	GER	Yamaha	22 pt
8	Pentti Korhonen	FIN	Yamaha	22 pt
9	Billie Nelson	GB	Yamaha	21 pt
10	Charlie Williams	GB	Yamaha	18 pt

1974 Manufacturers' 500 World Championship
1	Yamaha	87(127) pt
2	MV Agusta	87(109) pt
3	Suzuki	52 pt
4	Dugdale Maxton Yamaha	18 pt
5	Harley Davidson	14 pt

1975

Round 1 — GP France - Le Castellet 30/03
1	Giacomo Agostini	ITA	Yamaha
2	Hideo Kanaya	JAP	Yamaha
3	Phil Read	GB	MV
4	Armando Toracca	ITA	MV
5	Patrick Pons	FRA	Yamaha
6	Pete McKinley	GB	Yamaha
7	Michel Rougerie	FRA	H-D
8	Karl Auer	AUT	Yamaha
9	Alex George	GB	Yamaha
10	Kjell Solberg	NOR	Yamaha

Round 2 — GP Austria - Salzburgring 04/05
1	Hideo Kanaya	JAP	Yamaha
2	Teuvo Lansivuori	FIN	Suzuki
3	Phil Read	GB	MV
4	Armando Toracca	ITA	MV
5	Horst Lahfield	GER	Köning
6	Dieter Braun	GER	Yamaha
7	Karl Auer	AUT	Yamaha
8	Tom Herron	IRL	Yamaha
9	Alex George	GB	Yamaha
10	Thierry Tchemine	FRA	Yamaha

Round 3 — GP W. Germany - Hockenheim 11/05
1	Giacomo Agostini	ITA	Yamaha
2	Phil Read	GB	MV
3	Teuvo Lansivuori	FIN	Suzuki
4	Hideo Kanaya	JAP	Yamaha
5	Stan Woods	GB	Suzuki
6	Dieter Braun	GER	Yamaha
7	Christian Léon	FRA	Köning
8	Alex George	GB	Yamaha
9	Adu Celso-Santos	BRA	Yamaha
10	Jack Findlay	AUS	Yamaha

Round 4 — GP Nations - Imola 18/05
1	Giacomo Agostini	ITA	Yamaha
2	Phil Read	GB	MV
3	Hideo Kanaya	JAP	Yamaha
4	Armando Toracca	ITA	MV
5	Stan Woods	GB	Suzuki
6	Alex George	GB	Yamaha
7	John Newbold	GB	Suzuki
8	Thierry Tchemine	FRA	Yamaha
9	Bernard Fau	FRA	Yamaha
10	Rudolph Keller	SWI	Yamaha

Round 5 — TT - Isle of Man 04/06
1	Mike Grant	GB	Yamaha
2	John Williams	GB	Yamaha
3	Chas Mortimer	GB	Yamaha
4	Billie Guthrie	IRL	Yamaha
5	Steve Tonkin	GB	Yamaha
6	Geoff Barry	GB	Yamaha
7	Charlie Williams	GB	Yamaha
8	Tony Rutter	GB	Yamaha
9	Helmut Kassner	GER	Yamaha
10	Les Kenny	AUS	Yamaha

Round 6 — Dutch TT - Assen 28/06
1	Barry Sheene	GB	Suzuki
2	Giacomo Agostini	ITA	Yamaha
3	Phil Read	GB	MV
4	John Newbold	GB	Suzuki
5	Teuvo Lansivuori	FIN	Suzuki
6	Gianfranco Bonera	ITA	MV
7	John Williams	GB	Yamaha
8	Hans Stadelmann	SWI	Yamaha
9	Karl Auer	AUT	Yamaha
10	Piet van der Wal	NL	Yamaha

Round 7 — GP Belgium - Spa 06/07
1	Phil Read	GB	MV
2	John Newbold	GB	Suzuki
3	Jack Findlay	AUS	Yamaha
4	Alex George	GB	Yamaha
5	John Williams	GB	Yamaha
6	Christian Léon	FRA	Köning
7	Alan North	SA	H-D
8	Francis Hollebecq	BEL	Yamaha
9	Thierry Tchemine	FRA	Yamaha
10	Jean-Francois Baldé	FRA	Yamaha

Round 8 — GP Sweden - Anderstorp 20/07
1	Barry Sheene	GB	Suzuki
2	Phil Read	GB	MV
3	John Williams	GB	Yamaha
4	Gianfranco Bonera	ITA	MV
5	Dieter Braun	GER	Yamaha
6	Pentti Korhonen	FIN	Yamaha
7	Gérard Choukroun	FRA	Yamaha
8	Edmar Ferreira	BRA	Yamaha
9	Jack Findlay	AUS	Yamaha
10	Pekka Nurmi	FIN	Yamaha

Round 9 — GP Finland - Imatra 27/07
1	Giacomo Agostini	ITA	Yamaha
2	Teuvo Lansivuori	FIN	Suzuki
3	Jack Findlay	AUS	Yamaha
4	Chas Mortimer	GB	Yamaha
5	Steve Ellis	GB	Yamaha
6	Horst Lahfield	GER	Köning
7	Thierry van der Veken	BEL	Yamaha
8	Johnny Bengtsson	SWE	Yamaha
9	Björn Hasli	NOR	Yamaha
10	Seppo Kangasniemi	FIN	Yamaha

Round 10 — GP Czech Rep. - Brno 24/08
1	Phil Read	GB	MV
2	Giacomo Agostini	ITA	Yamaha
3	Alex George	GB	Yamaha
4	Karl Auer	AUT	Yamaha
5	Olivier Chevallier	FRA	Yamaha
6	Chas Mortimer	GB	Yamaha
7	Marcel Ankoné	NL	Suzuki
8	Hans Braumandl	AUT	Yamaha
9	Börge Nielsen	DEN	Yamaha
10	Anssi Resko	FIN	Yamaha

1975 Riders' 500 World Championship
1	Giacomo Agostini	ITA	Yamaha	84
2	Phil Read	GB	MV	76 (96)
3	Hideo Kanaya	JAP	Yamaha	45
4	Teuvo Lansivuori	FIN	Suzuki	40
5	John Williams	GB	Yamaha	32
6	Barry Sheene	GB	Suzuki	30
7	Alex George	GB	Yamaha	30
8	John Newbold	GB	Suzuki	24
9	Armando Toracca	ITA	MV	24
10	Jack Findlay	AUS	Yamaha	23

1975 Manufacturers' 500 World Championship
1	Yamaha	87 (131)
2	MV Agusta	78 (98)
3	Suzuki	76 (86)
4	Köning	20
5	Kawasaki	15

1975 Länsivuori was fourth in the World Championship

1976 Phil Read was tenth in the World Championship

1976

Round 1 — GP France - Le Mans 25/04
#	Rider	Country	Bike
1	Barry Sheene	GB	Suzuki
2	Johnny Cecotto	VEN	Yamaha
3	Marco Lucchinelli	ITA	Suzuki
4	Teuvo Lansivuori	FIN	Suzuki
5	Giacomo Agostini	ITA	MV Agusta
6	Victor Palomo	SPA	Yamaha
7	Stuart Avant	NZ	Suzuki
8	Dieter Braun	GER	Suzuki
9	Karl Auer	AUT	Yamaha
10	Boet van Dulmen	NL	Yamaha

Round 2 — GP Austria - Salzburgring 02/05
#	Rider	Country	Bike
1	Barry Sheene	GB	Suzuki
2	Marco Lucchinelli	ITA	Suzuki
3	Phil Read	GB	Suzuki
4	Michel Rougerie	FRA	Suzuki
5	Stuart Avant	NZ	Suzuki
6	Giacomo Agostini	ITA	MV Agusta
7	Victor Palomo	SPA	Yamaha
8	Jack Findlay	AUS	Suzuki
9	Karl Auer	AUT	Yamaha
10	Alex George	GB	Hermetite

Round 3 — GP Nations - Mugello 16/05
#	Rider	Country	Bike
1	Barry Sheene	GB	Suzuki
2	Phil Read	GB	Suzuki
3	Virginio Ferrari	ITA	Suzuki
4	Teuvo Lansivuori	FIN	Suzuki
5	Pat Hennen	USA	Suzuki
6	Marcel Ankoné	NL	Suzuki
7	Stuart Avant	NZ	Suzuki
8	Philippe Coulon	SWI	Suzuki
9	Dieter Braun	GER	Suzuki
10	Börge Nielsen	DEN	Yamaha

Round 4 — TT - Isle of Man 10/06
#	Rider	Country	Bike
1	Tom Herron	IRL	Yamaha
2	Ian F. Richards	GB	Yamaha
3	Billie Guthrie	IRL	Yamaha
4	Takazumi Katayama	JAP	Yamaha
5	Roger Nicholls	GB	Yamaha
6	John Ekerold	SA	Yamaha
7	John Williams	GB	Suzuki
8	Gordon Pantall	GB	Yamaha
9	John Weeden	GB	Yamaha
10	William A. Smith	GB	Yamaha

Round 5 — Dutch TT - Assen 26/06
#	Rider	Country	Bike
1	Barry Sheene	GB	Suzuki
2	Pat Hennen	USA	Suzuki
3	Wil Hartog	NL	Suzuki
4	Alex George	GB	Suzuki
5	Jack Findlay	AUS	Suzuki
6	John Williams	GB	Suzuki
7	Bernard Fau	FRA	Yamaha
8	Rob Bron	NL	Yamaha
9	Helmut Kassner	GER	Suzuki
10	Dave Potter	GB	Yamaha

Round 6 — GP Belgium - Spa 04/07
#	Rider	Country	Bike
1	John Williams	GB	Yamaha
2	Barry Sheene	GB	Suzuki
3	Marcel Ankoné	NL	Suzuki
4	Michel Rougerie	FRA	Suzuki
5	Teuvo Lansivuori	FIN	Suzuki
6	Dieter Braun	GER	Suzuki
7	Chas Mortimer	GB	Suzuki
8	Pat Hennen	USA	Suzuki
9	John Newbold	GB	Suzuki
10	Helmut Kassner	GER	Suzuki

Round 7 — GP Sweden - Anderstorp 25/07
#	Rider	Country	Bike
1	Barry Sheene	GB	Suzuki
2	Jack Findlay	AUS	Suzuki
3	Chas Mortimer	GB	Suzuki
4	Teuvo Lansivuori	FIN	Suzuki
5	Stuart Avant	NZ	Suzuki
6	Philippe Coulon	SWI	Suzuki
7	Victor Palomo	SPA	Yamaha
8	Karl Auer	AUT	Yamaha
9	Tom Herron	IRL	Yamaha
10	John Newbold	GB	Suzuki

Round 8 — GP Finland - Imatra 01/08
#	Rider	Country	Bike
1	Pat Hennen	USA	Suzuki
2	Teuvo Lansivuori	FIN	Suzuki
3	Philippe Coulon	SWI	Suzuki
4	John Newbold	GB	Suzuki
5	Marco Lucchinelli	ITA	Suzuki
6	Dieter Braun	GER	Suzuki
7	Jack Findlay	AUS	Suzuki
8	Christian Estrosi	FRA	Suzuki
9	Pekka Nurmi	FIN	Yamaha
10	Karl Auer	AUT	Yamaha

Round 9 — GP Czech Rep. - Brno 24/08
#	Rider	Country	Bike
1	John Newbold	GB	Suzuki
2	Teuvo Lansivuori	FIN	Suzuki
3	Philippe Coulon	SWI	Suzuki
4	Karl Auer	AUT	Yamaha
5	Max Wiener	AUT	Yamaha
6	Olivier Chevallier	FRA	Yamaha
7	Bernd Tüngenthal	GER	Yamaha
8	Boet van Dulmen	NL	Suzuki
9	Chas Mortimer	GB	Suzuki
10	Edmar Ferreira	BRA	Yamaha

Round 10 — GP W. Germany - Hockenheim 29/08
#	Rider	Country	Bike
1	Giacomo Agostini	ITA	MV Agusta
2	Marco Lucchinelli	ITA	Suzuki
3	Pat Hennen	USA	Suzuki
4	John Newbold	GB	Suzuki
5	Marcel Ankoné	NL	Suzuki
6	Boet van Dulmen	NL	Yamaha
7	Alan North	SA	Suzuki
8	Christian Bourgeois	FRA	Yamaha
9	Chas Mortimer	GB	Suzuki
10	Egid Schwemmer	GER	Nava

1976 Riders' 500 World Championship
#	Rider	Country	Bike	Points
1	Barry Sheene	GB	Suzuki	72 (87)
2	Teuvo Lansivuori	FIN	Suzuki	48 (54)
3	Pat Hennen	USA	Suzuki	46
4	Marco Lucchinelli	ITA	Suzuki	40
5	John Newbold	GB	Suzuki	31 (34)
6	Philippe Coulon	SWI	Suzuki	28
7	Giacomo Agostini	ITA	MV/Suzuki	26
8	Jack Findlay	AUS	Suzuki	25
9	John Williams	GB	Suzuki	24
10	Phil Read	GB	Suzuki	22

1976 Manufacturers' 500 World Championship
#	Make	Points
1	Suzuki	90 (136)
2	Yamaha	48 (55)
3	MV Agusta	26
4	Hermetite	1
4	Nava	1

1977

Round 1 — GP Venezuela - San Carlos 20/03
#	Rider	Country	Bike
1	Barry Sheene	GB	Suzuki
2	Steve Baker	USA	Yamaha
3	Pat Hennen	USA	Suzuki
4	Johnny Cecotto	VEN	Yamaha
5	Philippe Coulon	SWI	Suzuki
6	Virginio Ferrari	ITA	Suzuki
7	Marco Lucchinelli	ITA	Suzuki
8	Christian Estrosi	FRA	Suzuki
9	Steve Parrish	GB	Suzuki
10	Alan North	SA	Yamaha

Round 2 — GP Austria - Salzburgring 01/05
#	Rider	Country	Bike
1	Jack Findlay	AUS	Suzuki
2	Max Wiener	AUT	Suzuki
3	Alex George	GB	Suzuki
4	Helmut Kassner	GER	Suzuki
5	Franz Heller	GER	Suzuki
6	Michael Schmid	AUT	Suzuki

Round 3 — GP W. Germany - Hockenheim 08/05
#	Rider	Country	Bike
1	Barry Sheene	GB	Suzuki
2	Pat Hennen	USA	Suzuki
3	Steve Baker	USA	Yamaha
4	Steve Parrish	GB	Suzuki
5	Philippe Coulon	SWI	Suzuki
6	Wil Hartog	NL	Suzuki
7	Marco Lucchinelli	ITA	Suzuki
8	Anton Mang	GER	Suzuki
9	Max Wiener	AUT	Suzuki
10	Boet van Dulmen	NL	Suzuki

Round 4 — GP Nations - Imola 15/05
#	Rider	Country	Bike
1	Barry Sheene	GB	Suzuki
2	Virginio Ferrari	ITA	Suzuki
3	Armando Toracca	ITA	Suzuki
4	Steve Baker	USA	Yamaha
5	Giacomo Agostini	ITA	Yamaha
6	Philippe Coulon	SWI	Suzuki
7	John Newbold	GB	Suzuki
8	Christian Estrosi	FRA	Suzuki
9	Boet van Dulmen	NL	Suzuki
10	Anton Mang	GER	Suzuki

Round 5 — GP France - Le Castellet 29/05
#	Rider	Country	Bike
1	Barry Sheene	GB	Suzuki
2	Giacomo Agostini	ITA	Yamaha
3	Steve Baker	USA	Yamaha
4	Gianfranco Bonera	ITA	Suzuki
5	Philippe Coulon	SWI	Suzuki
6	Steve Parrish	GB	Suzuki
7	Teuvo Lansivuori	FIN	Suzuki
8	Virginio Ferrari	ITA	Suzuki
9	Armando Toracca	ITA	Suzuki
10	Pat Hennen	USA	Suzuki

Round 6 — Dutch TT - Assen 25/06
#	Rider	Country	Bike
1	Wil Hartog	NL	Suzuki
2	Barry Sheene	GB	Suzuki
3	Pat Hennen	USA	Suzuki
4	Philippe Coulon	SWI	Suzuki
5	Steve Baker	USA	Yamaha
6	Marco Lucchinelli	ITA	Suzuki
7	Teuvo Lansivuori	FIN	Suzuki
8	Michel Rougerie	FRA	Suzuki
9	Armando Toracca	ITA	Suzuki
10	Virginio Ferrari	ITA	Suzuki

Round 7 — GP Belgium - Spa 03/07
#	Rider	Country	Bike
1	Barry Sheene	GB	Suzuki
2	Steve Baker	USA	Yamaha
3	Pat Hennen	USA	Suzuki
4	Teuvo Lansivuori	FIN	Suzuki
5	Steve Parrish	GB	Suzuki
6	Philippe Coulon	SWI	Suzuki
7	Wil Hartog	NL	Suzuki
8	Giacomo Agostini	ITA	Yamaha
9	Jack Findlay	AUS	Suzuki
10	John Williams	GB	Suzuki

Round 8 — GP Sweden - Anderstorp 24/07
#	Rider	Country	Bike
1	Barry Sheene	GB	Suzuki
2	Johnny Cecotto	VEN	Yamaha
3	Steve Baker	USA	Yamaha
4	Steve Parrish	GB	Suzuki
5	Wil Hartog	NL	Suzuki
6	Gianfranco Bonera	ITA	Suzuki
7	Armando Toracca	ITA	Suzuki
8	John Williams	GB	Suzuki
9	Giacomo Agostini	ITA	Yamaha
10	Pat Hennen	USA	Suzuki

Round 9 — GP Finland - Imatra 31/07
#	Rider	Country	Bike
1	Johnny Cecotto	VEN	Yamaha
2	Marco Lucchinelli	ITA	Suzuki
3	Gianfranco Bonera	ITA	Suzuki
4	Michel Rougerie	FRA	Suzuki
5	Steve Parrish	GB	Suzuki
6	Barry Sheene	GB	Suzuki
7	Teuvo Lansivuori	FIN	Suzuki
8	Armando Toracca	ITA	Suzuki
9	Jean P. Orban	BEL	Suzuki
10	Karl Auer	AUT	Yamaha

Round 10 — GP Czech Rep. - Brno 07/08
#	Rider	Country	Bike
1	Johnny Cecotto	VEN	Yamaha
2	Giacomo Agostini	ITA	Yamaha
3	Michel Rougerie	FRA	Suzuki
4	Pat Hennen	USA	Suzuki
5	Gianfranco Bonera	ITA	Suzuki
6	Teuvo Lansivuori	FIN	Suzuki
7	Steve Parrish	GB	Suzuki
8	Max Wiener	AUT	Suzuki
9	Franz Rau	GER	Suzuki
10	Helmut Kassner	GER	Suzuki

Round 11 — GP Great Britain - Silverstone 14/08
#	Rider	Country	Bike
1	Pat Hennen	USA	Suzuki
2	Steve Baker	USA	Yamaha
3	Teuvo Lansivuori	FIN	Suzuki
4	Gianfranco Bonera	ITA	Suzuki
5	Steve Wright	GB	Suzuki
6	Alex George	GB	Suzuki
7	Derek Chatterton	GB	Suzuki
8	Max Wiener	AUT	Suzuki
9	Giacomo Agostini	ITA	Yamaha
10	Kevin Wrettom	GB	Suzuki

1977 Riders' 500 World Championship
#	Rider	Country	Bike	Pts
1	Barry Sheene	GB	Suzuki	107
2	Steve Baker	USA	Yamaha	80
3	Pat Hennen	USA	Suzuki	67
4	Johnny Cecotto	VEN	Yamaha	50
5	Steve Parrish	GB	Suzuki	39
6	Giacomo Agostini	ITA	Yamaha	37
6	Gianfranco Bonera	ITA	Suzuki	37
8	Philippe Coulon	SWI	Suzuki	36
9	Teuvo Lansivuori	FIN	Suzuki	35
10	Wil Hartog	NL	Suzuki	30

1977 Manufacturers' 500 World Championship
#	Manufacturer	Pts
1	Suzuki	157
2	Yamaha	114

1978

Round 1 — GP Venezuela - San Carlos 19/03
#	Rider	Country	Bike
1	Barry Sheene	GB	Suzuki
2	Pat Hennen	USA	Suzuki
3	Steve Baker	USA	Suzuki
4	Steve Parrish	GB	Suzuki
5	Roberto Pietri	VEN	Yamaha
6	Gerhard Vogt	GER	Yamaha
7	Leandro Becheroni	ITA	Suzuki

Round 2 — GP Spain - Jarama 16/04
#	Rider	Country	Bike
1	Pat Hennen	USA	Suzuki
2	Kenny Roberts	USA	Yamaha
3	Takazumi Katayama	JAP	Yamaha
4	Johnny Cecotto	VEN	Yamaha
5	Barry Sheene	GB	Suzuki
6	Steve Baker	USA	Suzuki
7	Teuvo Lansivuori	FIN	Suzuki
8	Christian Estrosi	FRA	Suzuki
9	Wil Hartog	NL	Suzuki
10	Steve Parrish	GB	Suzuki

Round 3 — GP Austria - Salzburgring 30/04
#	Rider	Country	Bike
1	Kenny Roberts	USA	Yamaha
2	Johnny Cecotto	VEN	Yamaha
3	Barry Sheene	GB	Suzuki
4	Marco Lucchinelli	ITA	Suzuki-Ca
5	Teuvo Lansivuori	FIN	Suzuki
6	Michel Rougerie	FRA	Suzuki
7	Wil Hartog	NL	Suzuki
8	Boet van Dulmen	NL	Suzuki
9	Gianfranco Bonera	ITA	Suzuki
10	Steve Parrish	GB	Suzuki

Round 4 — GP France - Nogaro 07/05
#	Rider	Country	Bike
1	Kenny Roberts	USA	Yamaha
2	Pat Hennen	USA	Suzuki
3	Barry Sheene	GB	Suzuki
4	Christian Estrosi	FRA	Suzuki
5	Wil Hartog	NL	Suzuki
6	Graziano Rossi	ITA	Suzuki
7	Steve Parrish	GB	Suzuki
8	Jean P. Orban	FRA	Suzuki
9	Carlo Perugini	ITA	Suzuki
10	Kenny Blake	AUS	Yamaha

Round 5 — GP Nations - Mugello 14/05
#	Rider	Country	Bike
1	Kenny Roberts	USA	Yamaha
2	Pat Hennen	USA	Suzuki
3	Marco Lucchinelli	ITA	Suzuki-Ca
4	Steve Baker	USA	Suzuki
5	Barry Sheene	GB	Suzuki
6	Wil Hartog	NL	Suzuki
7	Teuvo Lansivuori	FIN	Suzuki
8	Philippe Coulon	SWI	Suzuki
9	Boet van Dulmen	NL	Suzuki
10	Gianni Rolando	ITA	Suzuki

Round 6 — Dutch TT - Assen 24/06
#	Rider	Country	Bike
1	Johnny Cecotto	VEN	Yamaha
2	Kenny Roberts	USA	Yamaha
3	Barry Sheene	GB	Suzuki
4	Takazumi Katayama	JAP	Yamaha
5	Wil Hartog	NL	Suzuki
6	Michel Rougerie	FRA	Suzuki
7	John Newbold	GB	Suzuki
8	Boet van Dulmen	NL	Suzuki
9	Steve Baker	USA	Suzuki
10	Steve Parrish	GB	Suzuki

Round 7 — GP Belgium - Spa 02/07
#	Rider	Country	Bike
1	Wil Hartog	NL	Suzuki
2	Kenny Roberts	USA	Yamaha
3	Barry Sheene	GB	Suzuki
4	Michel Rougerie	FRA	Suzuki
5	Teuvo Lansivuori	FIN	Suzuki
6	Takazumi Katayama	JAP	Yamaha
7	Marco Lucchinelli	ITA	Suzuki-Ca
8	Alex George	GB	Suzuki
9	Tom Herron	IRL	Suzuki
10	Dennis Ireland	NZ	Suzuki

Round 8 — GP Sweden - Karlskoga 23/07
#	Rider	Country	Bike
1	Barry Sheene	GB	Suzuki
2	Wil Hartog	NL	Suzuki
3	Takazumi Katayama	JAP	Yamaha
4	Steve Baker	USA	Suzuki
5	Virginio Ferrari	ITA	Suzuki
6	Johnny Cecotto	VEN	Yamaha
7	Kenny Roberts	USA	Yamaha
8	Teuvo Lansivuori	FIN	Suzuki
9	Philippe Coulon	SWI	Suzuki
10	Alex George	GB	Suzuki

Round 9 — GP Finland - Imatra 30/07
#	Rider	Country	Bike
1	Wil Hartog	NL	Suzuki
2	Takazumi Katayama	JAP	Yamaha
3	Johnny Cecotto	VEN	Yamaha
4	Teuvo Lansivuori	FIN	Suzuki
5	Steve Parrish	GB	Suzuki
6	Steve Baker	USA	Suzuki
7	Boet van Dulmen	NL	Suzuki
8	Jürgen Steiner	GER	Suzuki
9	Graziano Rossi	ITA	Suzuki
10	Bruno Kneubühler	SWI	Suzuki

Round 10 — GP Great Britain - Silverstone 06/08
#	Rider	Country	Bike
1	Kenny Roberts	USA	Yamaha
2	Steve Manship	GB	Suzuki
3	Barry Sheene	GB	Suzuki
4	Marco Lucchinelli	ITA	Suzuki-Ca
5	Teuvo Lansivuori	FIN	Suzuki
6	Gianni Rolando	ITA	Suzuki
7	Johnny Cecotto	VEN	Yamaha
8	John Newbold	GB	Suzuki
9	Takazumi Katayama	JAP	Yamaha
10	Virginio Ferrari	ITA	Suzuki

Round 11 — GP W. Germany - Nürburgring 20/08
#	Rider	Country	Bike
1	Virginio Ferrari	ITA	Suzuki
2	Johnny Cecotto	VEN	Yamaha
3	Kenny Roberts	USA	Yamaha
4	Barry Sheene	GB	Suzuki
5	Takazumi Katayama	JAP	Yamaha
6	Michel Rougerie	FRA	Suzuki
7	Steve Baker	USA	Suzuki
8	Boet van Dulmen	NL	Suzuki
9	Teuvo Lansivuori	FIN	Suzuki
10	Jürgen Steiner	GER	Suzuki

1978 Riders' 500 World Championship
#	Rider	Country	Bike	Pts
1	Kenny Roberts	USA	Yamaha	110
2	Barry Sheene	GB	Suzuki	100
3	Johnny Cecotto	VEN	Yamaha	66
4	Wil Hartog	NL	Suzuki	65
5	Takazumi Katayama	JAP	Yamaha	53
6	Pat Hennen	USA	Suzuki	51
7	Steve Baker	USA	Suzuki	42
8	Teuvo Lansivuori	FIN	Suzuki	39
9	Marco Lucchinelli	ITA	Suzuki-Cagiva	30
10	Michel Rougerie	FRA	Suzuki	23

1978 Manufacturers' 500 World Championship
#	Make	Pts
1	Suzuki	146
2	Yamaha	139

1977 GP France - 3° Baker, 1° Sheene, 2° Agostini

1978 Estrosi leads a group of over the counter RG 500

archivio © Claudio Ghini

1979

Round 1 — GP Venezuela - San Carlos 18/03
#	Rider	Country	Bike
1	Barry Sheene	GB	Suzuki
2	Virginio Ferrari	ITA	Suzuki
3	Tom Herron	IRL	Suzuki
4	Franco Uncini	ITA	Suzuki
5	Michel Rougerie	FRA	Suzuki
6	Roberto Pietri	VEN	Suzuki
7	Christian Sarron	FRA	Yamaha
8	Gerhart Vogt	GER	Yamaha
9	Sergio Pellandini	SWI	Suzuki
10	Dennis Ireland	NZ	Suzuki

Round 2 — GP Austria - Salzburgring 29/04
#	Rider	Country	Bike
1	Kenny Roberts	USA	Yamaha
2	Virginio Ferrari	ITA	Suzuki
3	Wil Hartog	NL	Suzuki
4	Tom Herron	IRL	Suzuki
5	Hiroyuki Kawasaki	JAP	Suzuki
6	Franco Uncini	ITA	Suzuki
7	Steve Parrish	GB	Suzuki
8	Max Wiener	AUT	Suzuki
9	Marco Lucchinelli	ITA	Suzuki
10	Mick Grant	GB	Suzuki

Round 3 — GP W. Germany - Hockenheim 06/05
#	Rider	Country	Bike
1	Wil Hartog	NL	Suzuki
2	Kenny Roberts	USA	Yamaha
3	Virginio Ferrari	ITA	Suzuki
4	Bernard Fau	FRA	Suzuki
5	Philippe Coulon	SWI	Suzuki
6	Franco Uncini	ITA	Suzuki
7	Jack Middelburg	NL	Suzuki
8	Christian Sarron	FRA	Yamaha
9	Steve Parrish	GB	Suzuki
10	Mike Baldwin	USA	Suzuki

Round 4 — GP Nations - Imola 13/05
#	Rider	Country	Bike
1	Kenny Roberts	USA	Yamaha
2	Virginio Ferrari	ITA	Suzuki
3	Tom Herron	IRL	Suzuki
4	Barry Sheene	GB	Suzuki
5	Mike Baldwin	USA	Suzuki
6	Bernard Fau	FRA	Suzuki
7	Jack Middelburg	NL	Suzuki
8	Philippe Coulon	SWI	Suzuki
9	Graziano Rossi	ITA	Morbidelli
10	Giovanni Pelletier	ITA	Suzuki

Round 5 — GP Spain - Jarama 20/05
#	Rider	Country	Bike
1	Kenny Roberts	USA	Yamaha
2	Wil Hartog	NL	Suzuki
3	Mike Baldwin	USA	Suzuki
4	Virginio Ferrari	ITA	Suzuki
5	Franco Uncini	ITA	Suzuki
6	Boet van Dulmen	NL	Suzuki
7	Jack Middelburg	NL	Suzuki
8	Philippe Coulon	SWI	Suzuki
9	Michel Rougerie	FRA	Suzuki
10	Marco Lucchinelli	ITA	Suzuki

Round 6 — GP Yugoslavia - Rijeka 17/06
#	Rider	Country	Bike
1	Kenny Roberts	USA	Yamaha
2	Virginio Ferrari	ITA	Suzuki
3	Franco Uncini	ITA	Suzuki
4	Wil Hartog	NL	Suzuki
5	Boet van Dulmen	NL	Suzuki
6	Michel Rougerie	FRA	Suzuki
7	Christian Sarron	FRA	Yamaha
8	Carlo Perugini	ITA	Suzuki
9	Steve Parrish	GB	Suzuki
10	Max Wiener	AUT	Suzuki

Round 7 — Dutch TT - Assen 23/06
#	Rider	Country	Bike
1	Virginio Ferrari	ITA	Suzuki
2	Barry Sheene	GB	Suzuki
3	Wil Hartog	NL	Suzuki
4	Boet van Dulmen	NL	Suzuki
5	Philippe Coulon	SWI	Suzuki
6	Franco Uncini	ITA	Suzuki
7	Jack Middelburg	NL	Suzuki
8	Kenny Roberts	USA	Yamaha
9	Christian Sarron	FRA	Yamaha
10	Steve Parrish	GB	Suzuki

Round 8 — GP Belgium - Spa 01/07
#	Rider	Country	Bike
1	Dennis Ireland	NZ	Suzuki
2	Kenny Blake	AUS	Yamaha
3	Gary Lingham	GB	Suzuki
4	Gustav Reiner	GER	Suzuki
5	Henk de Vries	NL	Suzuki
6	Josef Hage	GER	Suzuki
7	Jacky Matagne	BEL	Suzuki
8	Gerhardt Vogt	GER	Suzuki
9	Guy Cooremans	BEL	Suzuki
10	Dieter Heinen	BEL	Suzuki

Round 9 — GP Sweden - Karlskoga 22/07
#	Rider	Country	Bike
1	Barry Sheene	GB	Suzuki
2	Jack Middelburg	NL	Suzuki
3	Boet van Dulmen	NL	Suzuki
4	Kenny Roberts	USA	Yamaha
5	Steve Parrish	GB	Suzuki
6	Randy Mamola	USA	Suzuki
7	Marco Lucchinelli	ITA	Suzuki
8	Ikujiro Takai	JAP	Yamaha
9	Christian Sarron	FRA	Yamaha
10	Seppo Rossi	FIN	Suzuki

Round 10 — GP Finland - Imatra 29/07
#	Rider	Country	Bike
1	Boet van Dulmen	NL	Suzuki
2	Randy Mamola	USA	Suzuki
3	Barry Sheene	GB	Suzuki
4	Jack Middelburg	NL	Suzuki
5	Christian Sarron	FRA	Yamaha
6	Kenny Roberts	USA	Yamaha
7	Johnny Cecotto	VEN	Yamaha
8	Philippe Coulon	SWI	Suzuki
9	Marco Lucchinelli	ITA	Suzuki
10	Wil Hartog	NL	Suzuki

Round 11 — GP Great Britain - Silverstone 12/08
#	Rider	Country	Bike
1	Kenny Roberts	USA	Yamaha
2	Barry Sheene	GB	Suzuki
3	Wil Hartog	NL	Suzuki
4	Virginio Ferrari	ITA	Suzuki
5	Boet van Dulmen	NL	Suzuki
6	Christian Sarron	FRA	Yamaha
7	Franco Uncini	ITA	Suzuki
8	Philippe Coulon	SWI	Suzuki
9	Marco Lucchinelli	ITA	Suzuki
10	John Newbold	GB	Suzuki

Round 12 — GP France - Le Mans 02/09
#	Rider	Country	Bike
1	Barry Sheene	GB	Suzuki
2	Randy Mamola	USA	Suzuki
3	Kenny Roberts	USA	Yamaha
4	Franco Uncini	ITA	Suzuki
5	Johnny Cecotto	VEN	Yamaha
6	Philippe Coulon	SWI	Suzuki
7	Steve Parrish	GB	Suzuki
8	Michel Rougerie	FRA	Suzuki
9	John Woodley	NZ	Suzuki
10	Peter Sjöström	SWE	Suzuki

1979 Riders' 500 World Championship
#	Rider	Country	Bike	Pts
1	Kenny Roberts	USA	Yamaha	113
2	Virginio Ferrari	ITA	Suzuki	89
3	Barry Sheene	GB	Suzuki	87
4	Wil Hartog	NL	Suzuki	66
5	Franco Uncini	ITA	Suzuki	51
6	Boet van Dulmen	NL	Suzuki	50
7	Jack Middelburg	NL	Suzuki	36
8	Randy Mamola	USA	Suzuki	29
8	Philippe Coulon	SWI	Suzuki	29
10	Tom Herron	IRL	Suzuki	28

1979 Manufacturers' 500 World Championship
#	Manufacturer	Pts
1	Suzuki	165
2	Yamaha	138
3	Morbidelli	2

1979 Uncini was the best privateer

1980 Randy Mamola was second behind Roberts in the World Championship

archivio © Claudio Ghini

1980

Round 1 — GP Nations - Misano 11/05
#	Rider	Country	Bike
1	Kenny Roberts	USA	Yamaha
2	Franco Uncini	ITA	Suzuki
3	Graziano Rossi	ITA	Suzuki
4	Johnny Cecotto	VEN	Yamaha
5	Carlo Perugini	ITA	Suzuki
6	Takazumi Katayama	JAP	Suzuki
7	Barry Sheene	GB	Yamaha
8	Christian Estrosi	FRA	Suzuki
9	Philippe Coulon	SWI	Suzuki
10	Sergio Pellandini	SWI	Suzuki

Round 2 — GP Spain - Jarama 18/05
#	Rider	Country	Bike
1	Kenny Roberts	USA	Yamaha
2	Marco Lucchinelli	ITA	Suzuki
3	Randy Mamola	USA	Suzuki
4	Takazumi Katayama	JAP	Suzuki
5	Barry Sheene	GB	Yamaha
6	Johnny Cecotto	VEN	Yamaha
7	Franco Uncini	ITA	Suzuki
8	Philippe Coulon	SWI	Suzuki
9	Michel Frutschi	SWI	Yamaha
10	Carlo Perugini	ITA	Suzuki

Round 3 — GP France - Paul Ricard 25/05
#	Rider	Country	Bike
1	Kenny Roberts	USA	Yamaha
2	Randy Mamola	USA	Suzuki
3	Marco Lucchinelli	ITA	Suzuki
4	Graziano Rossi	ITA	Suzuki
5	Graeme Crosby	NZ	Suzuki
6	Takazumi Katayama	JAP	Suzuki
7	Michel Rougerie	FRA	Suzuki
8	Kork Ballington	SA	Kawasaki
9	Johnny Cecotto	VEN	Yamaha
10	Patrick Pons	FRA	Yamaha

Round 4 — Dutch TT - Assen 28/06
#	Rider	Country	Bike
1	Jack Middelburg	NL	Yamaha
2	Graziano Rossi	ITA	Suzuki
3	Franco Uncini	ITA	Suzuki
4	Boet van Dulmen	NL	Yamaha
5	Randy Mamola	USA	Suzuki
6	Johnny Cecotto	VEN	Yamaha
7	Patrick Fernandez	FRA	Yamaha
8	Graeme Crosby	NZ	Suzuki
9	Henk de Vries	NL	Suzuki
10	Patrick Pons	FRA	Yamaha

Round 5 — GP Belgium - Spa 06/07
#	Rider	Country	Bike
1	Randy Mamola	USA	Suzuki
2	Marco Lucchinelli	ITA	Suzuki
3	Kenny Roberts	USA	Yamaha
4	Graeme Crosby	NZ	Suzuki
5	Wil Hartog	NL	Suzuki
6	Franco Uncini	ITA	Suzuki
7	Carlo Perugini	ITA	Suzuki
8	Patrick Pons	FRA	Yamaha
9	Boet van Dulmen	NL	Yamaha
10	Bernard Fau	FRA	Suzuki

Round 6 — GP Finland - Imatra 27/07
#	Rider	Country	Bike
1	Wil Hartog	NL	Suzuki
2	Kenny Roberts	USA	Yamaha
3	Franco Uncini	ITA	Suzuki
4	Randy Mamola	USA	Suzuki
5	Kork Ballington	SA	Kawasaki
6	Patrick Pons	FRA	Yamaha
7	Carlo Perugini	ITA	Suzuki
8	Philippe Coulon	SWI	Suzuki
9	Sadao Asami	JAP	Yamaha
10	Raymond Roche	FRA	Yamaha

Round 7 — GP Great Britain - Silverstone 10/08
#	Rider	Country	Bike
1	Randy Mamola	USA	Suzuki
2	Kenny Roberts	USA	Yamaha
3	Marco Lucchinelli	ITA	Suzuki
4	Graziano Rossi	ITA	Suzuki
5	Johnny Cecotto	VEN	Yamaha
6	Franco Uncini	ITA	Suzuki
7	Kork Ballington	SA	Kawasaki
8	Philippe Coulon	SWI	Suzuki
9	Jack Middelburg	NL	Yamaha
10	Dave Potter	GB	Yamaha

Round 8 — GP W. Germany - Nürburgring 24/08
#	Rider	Country	Bike
1	Marco Lucchinelli	ITA	Suzuki
2	Graeme Crosby	NZ	Suzuki
3	Wil Hartog	NL	Suzuki
4	Kenny Roberts	USA	Yamaha
5	Randy Mamola	USA	Suzuki
6	Johnny Cecotto	VEN	Yamaha
7	Franco Uncini	ITA	Suzuki
8	Jack Middelburg	NL	Yamaha
9	Carlo Perugini	ITA	Suzuki
10	Gustav Reiner	GER	Suzuki

1980 Riders' 500 World Championship
#	Rider	Country	Bike	Pts
1	Kenny Roberts	USA	Yamaha	87
2	Randy Mamola	USA	Suzuki	72
3	Marco Lucchinelli	ITA	Suzuki	59
4	Franco Uncini	ITA	Suzuki	50
5	Graziano Rossi	ITA	Suzuki	38
6	Wil Hartog	NL	Suzuki	31
6	Johnny Cecotto	VEN	Yamaha	31
8	Graeme Crosby	NZ	Suzuki	29
9	Jack Middelburg	NL	Yamaha	20
10	Takazumi Katayama	JAP	Suzuki	18

1980 Manufacturers' 500 World Championship
#	Make	Pts
1	Suzuki	108
2	Yamaha	102
3	Kawasaki	13

ANNUAL DATA

SUZUKI RIDERS in the World Championship GP 500 - 1974/1983

YEAR	RIDER	NATION	SUZUKI CODE	TEAM	N° FRAME	N° ENGINE	ENGINE	VICTOR.	CLASS.	P.TS
1974	Barry Sheene	GBR	RG 500 XR14	Suzuki Motor Co			56X50,5		6	30
1974	Paul Smart	GBR	RG 500 XR14	Suzuki Motor Co			56X50,5			
1974	Jack Findlay	AUS	RG 500 XR14	SAIAD Suzuki Italia			56X50,5		5	34
1974	Guido Mandracci	ITA	RG 500 XR14	SAIAD Suzuki Italia			56X50,5			

YEAR	RIDER	NATION	SUZUKI CODE	TEAM	N° FRAME	N° ENGINE	ENGINE	VICTOR.	CLASS.	P.TS
1975	Teuvo Länsivuori	FIN	RG 500 XR14	Suzuki Motor Co		1011	56X50,5		4	40
1975	Barry Sheene	GBR	RG 500 XR14	Suzuki Motor Co	1026?		56X50,5	2	6	30
1975	John Newbold	GBR	RG 500 XR14	Team Heron Suzuki			56X50,5		8	24
1975	Stan Woods	GBR	RG 500 XR14	Team Heron Suzuki			56X50,5		16	12
1975	Roberto Gallina	ITA	RG 500 XR14				56X50,5			
1975	Armando Toracca	ITA	RG 500 XR14				56X50,5			
1975	Marcel Ankonè	NED	SUZUKI						28	4
1975	Nico Cereghini	ITA	SUZUKI							
1975	Egid Schwemmer	GER	SUZUKI							
1975	Remo Bianconcini	ITA	SUZUKI							
1975	Roger Sutcliffe	GBR	SUZUKI							
1975	Mick Poxon	GBR	SUZUKI							
1975	Bernie Toleman	GBR	SUZUKI							
1975	Bill Robertson	GBR	SUZUKI							
1975	Derek Loan	GBR	SUZUKI							
1975	Rob Bron	NED	SUZUKI							

YEAR	RIDER	NATION	SUZUKI CODE	TEAM	N° FRAME	N° ENGINE	ENGINE	VICTOR.	CLASS.	P.TS
1976	Barry Sheene	GBR	RG 500 XR14	Texaco Heron Suzuki	1101	1101	54X54	5	1	72 (87)
1976	John Newbold	GBR	RG 500 XR14	Texaco Heron Suzuki		1011	56x50,5	1	5	31 (34)
1976	John Williams	GBR	RG 500 XR14	Texaco Heron Suzuki			56x50,5	1	9	24
1976	Teuvo Länsivuori	FIN	RG 500 MK I	Life Racing Team			56x50,5		2	48 (54)
1976	Pat Hennen	USA	RG 500 MK I	Colemans			56x50,5	1	3	46
1976	Marco Lucchinelli	ITA	RG 500 MK I	Gallina Corse			56x50,5		4	40
1976	Philippe Coulon	SUI	RG 500 MK I	Frankonia Suzuki?			56x50,5		6	28
1976	Giacomo Agostini	ITA	RG 500 MK I	Team Agostini Marlboro			56x50,5		7	26
1976	Jack Findlay	AUS	RG 500 MK I	Meuaui Racing Team?			56x50,5		8	25
1976	Phil Read	GBR	RG 500 MK I	Team Life International			56x50,5		10	22
1976	Marcel Ankonè	NED	RG 500 MK I				56x50,5		11	21
1976	Stuart Avant	NZL	RG 500 MK I	Colemans			56x50,5		12	20
1976	Tom Herron	IRL	RG 500 XR14	Texaco Heron Suzuki			56x50,5		13	17
1976	Chas Mortimer	GBR	RG 500 MK I	Team Sarome			56x50,5		14	16 (18)
1976	Michel Rougerie	FRA	RG 500 MK I	Ecurie ELF			56x50,5		14	16
1976	Dieter Braun	GER	RG 500 MK I	Boeri Dainese?			56x50,5		17	15
1976	Wil Hartog	NED	RG 500 MK I	Riemersma Racing			56x50,5		21	10
1976	Virginio Ferrari	ITA	RG 500 MK I	Gallina Corse			56x50,5		21	10
1976	Alex George	GBR	RG 500 MK I				56x50,5		25	9
1976	Boet Van Dulmen	NED	RG 500 MK I				56x50,5		25	9
1976	Alan North	RSA	RG 500 MK I				56x50,5		31	4
1976	Christian Estrosi	FRA	RG 500 MK I				56x50,5		34	3
1976	Helmut Kassner	GER	RG 500 MK I				56x50,5		34	3
1976	Nico Cereghini	ITA	RG 500 MK I	Sacchi			56x50,5			
1976	Armando Toracca	ITA	RG 500 MK I	Gallina Corse			56x50,5			
1976	Roberto Gallina	ITA	RG 500 MK I	Gallina Corse			56x50,5			
1976	Johnny Bengtsson	SWE	SUZUKI							
1976	Goran Alden	SWE	SUZUKI							
1976	Jules Nies	BEL	SUZUKI							
1976	Jean-Paul Boinet	FRA	SUZUKI							
1976	Renè Guili	FRA	SUZUKI							
1976	Walter Hofmann	GER	SUZUKI							
1976	Franz Heller	GER	SUZUKI							
1976	Horst Lotz	GER	SUZUKI							
1976	Michel Renson	BEL	SUZUKI							
1976	Ron Robinson	GBR	SUZUKI							
1976	Francois Hollebecq	BEL	SUZUKI							
1976	Giorgio Avveduti	ITA	SUZUKI							
1976	Mario Fiorentino	ITA	SUZUKI							
1976	Mario Necchi	ITA	SUZUKI							
1976	Vittorio Gornati	ITA	SUZUKI							
1976	Germano Paganini	ITA	SUZUKI							
1976	Carlo Piazza	ITA	SUZUKI							

RG 500 STATISTICS

GP WITH SUZUKI	RACING NUMBERS	NOTES
FRA, AUT, NAT, NED, BEL, SWE, TCH	5 NAT-SWE,6,7,11 AUT,30,32 FRA	
FRA, AUT, NAT, TT, NED, SWE, TCH	16 NED,43	
FRA, AUT, NAT, TT, NED, BEL, SWE, FIN, TCH	4,5 FRA,6 NAT,7 SWE,23 NED	
NED, BEL	24 NED,92 BEL	

GP WITH SUZUKI	RACING NUMBERS	NOTES
FRA, AUT, GER, NED, BEL, SWE, FIN, TCH	1 FRA,3 NED	
AUT, NAT, NED, BEL, SWE, FIN, TCH	6 NED,7,9 NAT,12 BEL	
AUT, GER, NAT, NED, BEL, SWE	14 NED	
AUT, GER, NAT	4?	
NAT	130 NAT	
SWE, TCH		SWE with XR05 Twin Cylinders
FRA, GER, TCH	25,37 NED	
FRA, NAT	17 FRA	
GER		
NAT		
TT		
TT		
TT		
TT		
NED	35,40 NED	

GP WITH SUZUKI	RACING NUMBERS	NOTES
FRA, AUT, NAT, NED, BEL, SWE	7	
NAT, NED, BEL, SWE, FIN, TCH, GER	8,3,6,7	
FRA, AUT, TT, NED, BEL	2 TT,5,30 NED	
FRA, AUT, NAT, NED, BEL, SWE, FIN, TCH, GER	4,2,3	
AUT, NAT, NED, BEL, SWE, FIN, TCH, GER	54,22,25,28,40,45,66	
FRA, AUT, SWE, FIN, TCH, GER	33,17,30,32,34,40	
FRA, AUT, NAT, NED, BEL, SWE, FIN, TCH, GER	40,18,22,23,38,43,51,71	
NAT, NED, BEL, FIN, TCH	1	FRA, AUT, GER MV AGUSTA. No points with SUZUKI
FRA, AUT, NAT, TT, NED, BEL, SWE, FIN, TCH, GER	10,5,6	
FRA, AUT, NAT, NED, BEL	2,9	
FRA, NAT, NED, BEL, SWE, FIN, TCH, GER	12,27,28,33,43,	
FRA, AUT, NAT, NED, SWE, FIN	11,25,32,35,42,47,56	
FIN	14	Retired, with Works Suzuki from John Williams
SWE, FIN, TCH, GER	11,8,10	
FRA, AUT, NAT, NED, BEL	21,2	
FRA, AUT, NAT, BEL, SWE, FIN, TCH, GER	13,10,12,14,30	
AUT, NED, SWE	34,31,48	
NAT, FIN, TCH, GER	28,26,31,40	
NED, SWE, FIN, GER	8	
BEL, FIN, TCH, GER	14 TCH,27 BEL,29 GER	FRA, AUT, NAT, NED Yamaha
GER		
FRA, NED, SWE, FIN, TCH	24,21,48,52	
FRA, AUT, NED, BEL, TCH, GER	41,19,39,44,63	
FRA, NAT, BEL	18 BEL, 49 FRA-NAT	
AUT	9	
FRA, TCH	34	one for Rossi in italian championship Team OECE?
FRA, SWE, FIN	30	
SWE		
FRA, BEL	36 FRA	
FRA, NED	26	
FRA	48	
GER		
GER		
GER		
GER		
FRA, BEL, TCH	37	
NAT		
NAT		
NAT		
NAT		
NAT		
NAT		

YEAR	RIDER	NATION	SUZUKI CODE	TEAM	N° FRAME	N° ENGINE	ENGINE	VICTOR.	CLASS.	P.TS
1977	Barry Sheene	GBR	RG 500 XR14	Texaco Heron Suzuki	1201,1202	1201,1202	54X54	6	1	107
1977	Pat Hennen	USA	RG 500 XR14	Texaco Heron Suzuki		1203	54X54	1	3	67
1977	Steve Parrish	GBR	RG 500 XR14	Texaco Heron Suzuki			54X54		5	39
1977	Gianfranco Bonera	ITA	RG 500 MK II	Nava Olio Fiat			56X50,5		7	37
1977	Virginio Ferrari	ITA	RG 500 MK II	Nava Olio Fiat			56X50,5		12	21
1977	Philippe Coulon	SUI	RG 500 MK II				56X50,5		8	36
1977	Teuvo Länsivuori	FIN	RG 500 MK II	Life Racing Team	11087	11087	56X50,5		9	35
1977	Marco Lucchinelli	ITA	RG 500 MK II	Life Racing Team			56X50,5		11	25
1977	Wil Hartog	NED	RG 500 MK II	Riemersma Racing			56X50,5	1	10	30
1977	Michel Rougerie	FRA	RG 500 MK II	ELF			56X50,5		13	21
1977	Armando Toracca	ITA	RG 500 MK II	Ceramiche della Robbia			56X50,5		13	21
1977	Max Wiener	AUT	SUZUKI	MSC Rottenegg					15	20
1977	Jack Findlay	AUS	RG 500 MK I	Hermetite Racing Int.			56X50,5	1	16	17
1977	Alex George	GBR	SUZUKI	Hermetite Racing Int.					17	15
1977	Helmut Kassner	GER	SUZUKI	Boeri Dainese Giudici					18	9
1977	Steve Wright	GBR	SUZUKI						19	6
1977	Franz Heller	GER	SUZUKI						19	6
1977	Christian Estrosi	FRA	SUZUKI						19	6
1977	Michael Schmid	AUT	SUZUKI						22	5
1977	John Newbold	GBR	SUZUKI						23	4
1977	Derek Chatterton	GBR	SUZUKI						23	4
1977	Anton Mang	GER	SUZUKI						23	4
1977	John Williams	GBR	SUZUKI						23	4
1977	Boet Van Dulmen	NED	SUZUKI						27	3
1977	Jean Philippe Orban	BEL	SUZUKI						28	2
1977	Franz Rau	GER	SUZUKI						28	2
1977	Kevin Wrettom	GBR	SUZUKI						30	1
1977	Jack Middelburg	NED	SUZUKI							
1977	Marcel Ankonè	NED	SUZUKI							
1977	Gianni Rolando	ITA	SUZUKI							
1977	Werner Nenning	AUT	SUZUKI							
1977	Bosse Granath	SWE	SUZUKI							
1977	Stuart Avant	NZL	SUZUKI							
1977	Børge Nielsen	DEN	SUZUKI							
1977	Harald Merkl	GER	SUZUKI							
1977	Hervè Regout	BEL	SUZUKI							
1977	Carlo Perugini	ITA	SUZUKI							
1977	Hans Braumandl	AUT	SUZUKI							
1977	Les Van Breda	RSA	SUZUKI							
1977	Graziano Rossi	ITA	SUZUKI							
1977	Mario Necchi	ITA	SUZUKI							
1977	Bernard Fau	FRA	SUZUKI							
1977	John Woodley	NZL	SUZUKI							
1977	Markku Matikainen	FIN	SUZUKI							
1977	Carlos de San Antonio	ESP	SUZUKI							
1977	Andrè Pogolotti	FRA	SUZUKI							
1977	Hervè Moineau	FRA	SUZUKI							
1977	Claude Ben El Hadj	FRA	SUZUKI							
1977	Willem Zoet	NED	SUZUKI							
1977	Dave Potter	GBR	SUZUKI							
1977	Alan North	RSA	SUZUKI							
1977	Alf Graarud	NOR	SUZUKI							
1977	Odd Larne Lände	SWE	SUZUKI							
1977	Ron Haslam	GBR	SUZUKI							
1977	George Fogarty	GBR	SUZUKI							
1977	John Weeden	GBR	SUZUKI							
1977	Steve Manship	GBR	SUZUKI							
1977	Jean-Paul Boinet	FRA	SUZUKI							
1977	Rob Bron	NED	SUZUKI							
1977	Ingo Riemer	GER	SUZUKI							
1977	Daniel Rouge	FRA	SUZUKI							
1977	Gregorio Mariani	ITA	SUZUKI							
1977	Cesare Leali (Naeli)	ITA	SUZUKI							
1977	Florian Bürki	SUI	SUZUKI							
1977	Francesco Pisanelli	ITA	SUZUKI							
1977	Dudley Robinson	GBR	SUZUKI							
1977	Bengt Slydal	SWE	SUZUKI							
1977	Goran Alden	NOR	SUZUKI							
1977	Teuvo Laasko	FIN	SUZUKI							
1977	Bernard Regoni	FRA	SUZUKI							
1977	Nico Cereghini	ITA	RG 500 MK II				56X50,5			

GP WITH SUZUKI	RACING NUMBERS	NOTES
VEN, AUT, GER, NAT , FRA, NED, BEL, SWE, FIN, TCH, GBR	7	
VEN, AUT, GER, NAT , FRA, NED, BEL, SWE, FIN, TCH, GBR	3	
VEN, AUT, GER, NAT , FRA, NED, BEL, SWE, FIN, TCH, GBR	1 GBR,8 VEN,11 BEL,12 FRA,15 SWE,16 GER,19 NAT,21 FIN,24 TCH	
VEN, AUT, GER, NAT , FRA, NED, BEL, SWE, FIN, TCH, GBR	22 BEL,13,21 FIN	
VEN, AUT, GER, NAT , FRA, NED, BEL, SWE, FIN, TCH	1,2,12,14,22 BEL	
VEN, AUT, GER, NAT , FRA, NED, BEL, SWE	5 NED,6,16 VEN,27 BEL	
VEN,AUT, GER, NAT , FRA, NED, BEL, SWE, FIN, TCH, GBR	2,41 BEL	
AUT, GER, NAT , FRA, NED, BEL, SWE, FIN, TCH, GBR	4,19,23 BEL	
VEN, AUT, GER, NAT , FRA, NED, BEL, SWE, FIN, TCH	19 BEL,22 GBR,30 NED,45	
AUT, GER, NAT , FRA, NED, BEL, SWE, FIN, TCH, GBR	12,16,21 NED,31 BEL	
AUT, GER, NAT , FRA, NED, BEL, SWE, FIN, TCH	15 GBR,17 NED,19 FRA, 23 TCH,24 BEL SWE,26 FIN, 46 NAT	
AUT, GER, NAT, FRA, NED, BEL, SWE, TCH, GBR	17 BEL,46	
AUT, GER, NAT , NED, BEL, SWE, FIN, TCH, GBR	8	NICO BAKKER monoshock frame
AUT, GER, NAT , FRA, NED, SWE, FIN, TCH, GBR	24	
AUT, GER, NAT , FRA, NED, BEL, SWE, TCH, GBR	37	
GBR		
AUT, NAT, GER, BEL, TCH	21 GER,29 TCH,37 BEL,47 FRA,48 AUT	
VEN, AUT, GER, NAT , FRA, NED, SWE, FIN, GBR	13 NED,16	
AUT, TCH	28 TCH,33 AUT	
AUT, GER, NAT , FRA, NED, BEL, SWE, GBR	5	
GBR		
NAT, GER, FRA, SWE	26 NAT,30 FRA,33 SWE,49 GER	
AUT, GER, NAT , FRA, NED, BEL, SWE, FIN, TCH, GBR	8 TCH,9,10 FRA,14 BEL	
AUT, GER, NAT, FRA, TCH, GBR	15 TCH,18 FRA,23 GBR,27 NAT,58 GER	
AUT, GER, NAT , FRA, NED, BEL, SWE, FIN, TCH	49 BEL	
GER, NED, TCH, GBR	19 NED,40 GBR,43 TCH	
GBR		
NED		
VEN, AUT, GER, NED	10 AUT,11 NED,47 GER	
VEN, AUT, NAT , FRA, NED, BEL, FIN, TCH	20 NED,25 BEL,34 TCH,68 FRA	
AUT, TCH		
AUT, GER, NED, BEL, SWE, FIN, TCH	6 BEL	
AUT, GER, NAT , FRA, NED, FIN, GBR	11 AUT,12 NED,-GBR,36 FRA,42 GER	
GER, NAT , FRA, NED, BEL, SWE, FIN, TCH, GBR	11 GER,20 FIN-TCH,26 NED,27 FRA,31 SWE,38 GBR,53 BEL	
GER, BEL, TCH		
GER, BEL, GBR	50 BEL	
GER, NAT		
AUT, GER, TCH		
GER, NED, BEL, GBR		
NAT, FRA, FIN		
NAT		
GER, NAT, FRA, FIN		
FRA, BEL, GBR	15 BEL	
AUT, NAT, FRA, BEL, SWE, FIN	34 FIN,35 FRA,38 SWE,42 BEL	
FRA		
FRA		
FRA		
FRA		
NED, BEL		
NED, BEL		
BEL	33 BEL	
SWE		
SWE, FIN, TCH, GBR	35 SWE,38 TCH,43 GBR	
GBR		
GBR		
GBR		
GBR		
GBR		
NED		
FRA		
FRA		
NAT		
NAT, FRA		
GER, AUT		
NAT		
GER		
SWE, FIN		
SWE		
FIN		
FIN		
GER, NAT, FRA	65 FRA	

YEAR	RIDER	NATION	SUZUKI CODE	TEAM	N° FRAME	N° ENGINE	ENGINE	VICTOR.	CLASS.	P.TS
1978	Barry Sheene	GBR	RGA 500 XR22	Texaco Heron Suzuki	1008	1008	54x54	2	2	100
1978	Pat Hennen	USA	RGA 500 XR22	Texaco Heron Suzuki			54x54	1	6	51
1978	Steve Baker	USA	XR14 – XR22	Nava Olio Fiat			54x54		7	42
1978	Virginio Ferrari	ITA	XR14 – XR22	Nava Olio Fiat			54x54	1	11	22
1978	Wil Hartog	NED	XR14 – XR22	Nimag Riemersma-Team Heron			54x54	2	4	65
1978	Teuvo Länsivuori	FIN	RG 500 MK III				56X50,5		8	39
1978	Marco Lucchinelli	ITA	RG 500 MK III	CAGIVA			56X50,5		9	30
1978	Michel Rougerie	FRA	RG 500 MK III-XR22	Team ELF-Team Heron Suzuki					10	23
1978	Steve Parrish	GBR	RG 500 MK III	Team Castrol			56X50,5		12	20
1978	Boet Van Dulmen	NED	RG 500 MK III				56X50,5		13	15
1978	Steve Manship	GBR	RG 500 MK III				56X50,5		14	12
1978	Christian Estrosi	FRA	RG 500 MK III				56X50,5		15	11
1978	Graziano Rossi	ITA	RG 500 MK III	Team OECE			56X50,5		16	7
1978	John Newbold	GBR	RG 500 MK III	Ray Hamblin			56X50,5		16	7
1978	Gianni Rolando	ITA	RG 500 MK III				56X50,5		19	6
1978	Gerhard Vogt	GER	SUZUKI						20	5
1978	Philippe Coulon	SUI	RG 500 MK III				56X50,5		20	5
1978	Leandro Becheroni	ITA	SUZUKI						22	4
1978	Alex George	GBR	SUZUKI	Haags Motor Centrum					22	4
1978	Jürgen Steiner	GER	SUZUKI						22	4
1978	Jean Philippe Orban	BEL	SUZUKI						25	3
1978	Carlo Perugini	ITA	SUZUKI						26	2
1978	Tom Herron	IRL	SUZUKI						26	2
1978	Gianfranco Bonera	ITA	SUZUKI						26	2
1978	Bruno Kneubuhler	SUI	SUZUKI						26	2
1978	Dennis Ireland	NZL	SUZUKI						30	1
1978	Jack Middelburg	NED	SUZUKI	F&S Properties						
1978	John Woodley	NZL	SUZUKI	Sid Griffiths						
1978	Clive Padgett	GBR	SUZUKI							
1978	Nico Cereghini	ITA	RG 500 MK III	Sacchi			56X50,5			
1978	John Williams	GBR	SUZUKI	Appleby Glade						
1978	Max Wiener	AUT	SUZUKI	Jim Beam Team						
1978	Les Van Breda	RSA	SUZUKI	Holters Bouwmat.						
1978	Markku Matikainen	FIN	SUZUKI							
1978	Franz Rau	GER	SUZUKI							
1978	Bosse Granath	SWE	SUZUKI	Tranemo Färg						
1978	Dick Alblas	NED	SUZUKI							
1978	Helmut Kassner	GER	SUZUKI							
1978	Børge Nielsen	DEN	SUZUKI							
1978	Jack Findlay	AUS	RG 500 MK III		11221	11221	56X50,5			
1978	Franz Heller	GER	SUZUKI							
1978	Roberto Coli	ITA	SUZUKI							
1978	Greg Johnson	AUS	SUZUKI							
1978	Peter Sjöström	SWE	SUZUKI							
1978	Odd Larne Lände	SWE	SUZUKI							
1978	Michael Schmidt	AUT	SUZUKI							
1978	Eduard Coormans	BEL	SUZUKI							
1978	Franz Shermer	GER	SUZUKI							
1978	Carlos de San Antonio	ESP	SUZUKI							
1978	Cees Scheepens	NED	SUZUKI							
1978	Renè Gutknecht	SUI	SUZUKI							
1978	Jon Ekerold	RSA	SUZUKI	SUZUKI Deutschland						
1978	Hans Braumandl	AUT	SUZUKI							
1978	Werner Nenning	AUT	SUZUKI							
1978	Dave Potter	GBR	SUZUKI	Team BP-Broad Motors						
1978	Eddie Roberts	GBR	SUZUKI							
1978	Marc Fontan	FRA	SUZUKI							
1978	Michel Frutschi	SUI	SUZUKI							
1978	Lorenzo Ghiselli	ITA	SUZUKI							
1978	Walter Hoffmann	GER	SUZUKI							
1978	Horst Lahfeld	GER	SUZUKI							
1978	Gregorio Mariani	ITA	SUZUKI							
1978	Carlo Paganini	ITA	SUZUKI							
1978	Horst Scherer	GER	SUZUKI							
1978	Kewin Stowe	GBR	SUZUKI							
1978	Jan Verwey	GER	SUZUKI							
1978	Walter Villa	ITA	RG 500 MK III				56X50,5			
1978	Graham Wood	GBR	SUZUKI							
1978	Andres Pèrez Rubio	ESP	SUZUKI							
1978	Bernd Dawicki	GER	SUZUKI							
1978	Bengt Slydal	SWE	SUZUKI							
1978	Sergio Pellandini	SUI	SUZUKI							
1978	Herbert Prügl	AUT	SUZUKI							
1978	Roger Marshall	GBR	SUZUKI?							
1978	Hans-Otto Butenuth	GER	SUZUKI							
1978	Tako Hase	JPN	SUZUKI							
1978	Hans-Günter Schöne	GER	SUZUKI							
1978	Lars Johansson	SWE	SUZUKI							
1978	Walter Kaletsch	GER	SUZUKI							

GP WITH SUZUKI	RACING NUMBERS	NOTES
VEN, ESP, AUT, FRA, NAT, NED, BEL, SWE, FIN, GBR, GER	7	
VEN, ESP, AUT, FRA, NAT	3	
VEN, ESP, AUT, NAT, NED, BEL, SWE, FIN, GBR, GER	1 GER,2 NED-FIN,3 BEL	from NAT with XR22
VEN, ESP, AUT, FRA, NAT, NED, BEL, SWE, FIN, GBR, GER	12,15 FIN	GER with Team Heron XR22
ESP, AUT, FRA, NAT, NED, BEL, SWE, FIN, GBR, GER	10,11 FIN,15 BEL	from NED with Team HERON XR22
ESP, AUT, FRA, NAT, NED, BEL, SWE, FIN, GBR, GER	5 AUT,9 NED,48 FRA	
ESP, AUT, FRA, NAT, NED, BEL, SWE, FIN, GBR, GER	11	
ESP, AUT, FRA, NAT, NED, BEL, SWE, FIN, GBR, GER	13 NED-GBR,14 AUT-FIN-FRA,30 BEL	BEL with Team HERON XR22
VEN, ESP, AUT, FRA, NAT, NED, BEL, SWE, FIN, GBR, GER	3 NED,5 ESP-FRA,6 AUT-SWE-FIN-GBR	
ESP, AUT, FRA, NAT, NED, BEL, SWE, FIN, GBR, GER	9 SWE,14 ESP,18 AUT,23 GBR,29 NAT-GER,34 NED	
GBR	43 GBR	
ESP, FRA, NAT	24, 25 NAT	
FRA, NAT, NED, BEL, FIN, GBR, GER	19 NAT,27 NED,29 BEL,31 FRA,40 GER	
ESP, AUT, NAT, NED, BEL, GBR	17 NED,47 AUT	
ESP, NAT, NED, GBR, GER	20 NAT, 22 GBR,39 AUT-NED,42 GER	
FRA, NED, BEL, FIN, GBR, GER	26 NED	
ESP, AUT, FRA, NAT, NED, BEL, SWE, FIN, GBR, GER	1 AUT,3 GBR,5 FIN,6 NED,8 GER, 16 FRA,42 SWE	
VEN, FRA	9 VEN,41 GBR	
ESP, AUT, FRA, NAT, NED, BEL, SWE, FIN, GBR, GER	19 NED,22 AUT	
AUT, SWE, FIN, GER	39 FIN,40 AUT	
ESP, AUT, FRA	43 AUT	
FRA, NAT	26 NAT, 48 FRA	
ESP, AUT, BEL	9	
AUT, FRA, NED, GBR, GER	5 NED,49 AUT	
ESP, AUT, FRA, NAT, NED, BEL, SWE, FIN, GBR, GER	17 AUT, 23 NED,24 FIN, 28, 41	
BEL, SWE, FIN, GBR	21 GBR,36 SWE,46 BEL	
AUT, NED, SWE, GBR, GER	33 NED,42 AUT	
FRA, NED, BEL, SWE, FIN, GBR	24 NED,28 AUT	
FIN	30 FIN	
NAT		
NED, BEL ,GBR	16 GBR,20 NED,38 BEL	
ESP, AUT, NED, BEL, SWE, FIN, GBR, GER	15 NED,20 AUT,24 GER	
ESP, AUT, FRA, NED, BEL, SWE, FIN, GBR, GER	22 NED, 39 GER, 50 AUT	
AUT, SWE, FIN	23 SWE,44 AUT	
AUT, FRA, NAT, NED, BEL, SWE, FIN, GBR, GER	21 FIN,25 NED,34 GBR,37 FRA,39 AUT,45 GER	
AUT, NED, BEL, SWE, FIN	33 AUT	
NED, BEL, SWE, FIN, GBR, GER	35 NED	
AUT	23 AUT	
AUT, FRA, NAT, NED, BEL, FIN, GER	25 FRA,30 NED,35 GER,38 AUT	
AUT, FRA, NAT, NED, BEL, GBR, GER	16 NED, 21 AUT	
AUT, BEL	25 AUT	
NAT	38 NAT	
BEL		
AUT, SWE, GBR, GER	24 GER,38 GBR,45 AUT	
SWE	22	
AUT, GER	34 AUT	
BEL		
GER		
ESP, AUT, NAT, BEL, SWE, GER	17 SWE,41 GER, 48 AUT	
NED, BEL	37 NED	
FRA, GER		
ESP, AUT, BEL	15 AUT	
AUT, NED, GER	36 AUT	
AUT, GBR	35 AUT	
NED, GBR		
ESP, FRA		
GBR		
GER		
NAT		
FIN	38 FIN	
GER		
NAT		
NAT		
GER		
GBR		
GER		
AUT	27 AUT	
GBR		
ESP		
GER		
SWE		
NAT		
AUT	37 AUT	
GBR		
GER		
GER		
GER		
GER		
GER		

YEAR	RIDER	NATION	SUZUKI CODE	TEAM	N° FRAME	N° ENGINE	ENGINE	VICTOR.	CLASS.	P.TS
1979	Barry Sheene	GBR	RGB 500 XR27B-BFR	Texaco Heron Suzuki	1005	1005	54x54	3	3	87
1979	Tom Herron	IRL	RGB 500 XR27B	Texaco Heron Suzuki			54x54		10	28
1979	Steve Parrish	GBR	RGB 500 XR27B	Texaco Heron Suzuki			54x54		12	19
1979	Virginio Ferrari	ITA	RGB 500 XR27B	Nava Olio Fiat			54x54	1	2	89
1979	Wil Hartog	NED	RGB 500 XR27B	Nimag Riemersma			54x54	1	4	66
1979	Franco Uncini	ITA	RG 500 MK IV	Jen Organs	11302	11302 – 11340	54x54		5	51
1979	Boet Van Dulmen	NED	RG 500 MK IV				54x54	1	6	50
1979	Jack Middelburg	NED	RG 500 MK IV				54x54		7	36
1979	Randy Mamola	USA	RG 500 MK IV	Serge Zago Team			54x54		8	29
1979	Philippe Coulon	SUI	RG 500 MK IV				54x54		8	29
1979	Mike Baldwin	USA	RG 500 MK IV				54x54		13	17
1979	Dennis Ireland	NZL	RG 500 MK IV				54x54	1	14	16
1979	Michel Rougerie	FRA	RG 500 MK IV				54x54		14	16
1979	Bernard Fau	FRA	RG 500 MK IV				54x54		16	13
1979	Marco Lucchinelli	ITA	RG 500 MK IV				54x54		18	11
1979	Gary Lingham	GBR	SUZUKI						19	10
1979	Gustav Reiner	GER	SUZUKI						21	8
1979	Hiroyuki Kawasaki	JPN	SUZUKI	Suzuki Motor Co			54x54		22	6
1979	Henk De Vries	NED	SUZUKI						22	6
1979	Gerhardt Vogt	GER	SUZUKI						22	6
1979	Roberto Pietri	VEN	SUZUKI						25	5
1979	Josef Hage	GER	SUZUKI						25	5
1979	Jacky Matagne	BEL	SUZUKI						27	4
1979	Max Wiener	AUT	SUZUKI						27	4
1979	Carlo Perugini	ITA	RG 500 MK IV				54x54		29	3
1979	Sergio Pellandini	SUI	SUZUKI						31	2
1979	Guy Cooremans	BEL	SUZUKI						31	2
1979	John Woodley	NZL	SUZUKI						31	2
1979	Peter Sjöström	SWE	SUZUKI						35	1
1979	Seppo Rossi	FIN	SUZUKI						35	1
1979	Mick Grant	GBR	SUZUKI						35	1
1979	John Newbold	GBR	SUZUKI						35	1
1979	Giovanni Pelletier	ITA	RG 500 MK IV	Cappelletti			54x54		35	1
1979	Gianni Rolando	ITA	RG 500 MK IV	Team Naldoni	11304	11304	54x54			
1979	Lennart Bäckström	SWE	SUZUKI							
1979	Franck Gross	FRA	SUZUKI							
1979	Alan North	RSA	SUZUKI							
1979	Elmar Renner	GER	SUZUKI							
1979	Markku Matikainen	FIN	SUZUKI							
1979	Willem Zoet	NED	SUZUKI							
1979	Alex George	GBR	SUZUKI							
1979	Werner Nenning	AUT	SUZUKI							
1979	Steve Ward	GBR	SUZUKI							
1979	Hans-Otto Butenuth	GER	SUZUKI							
1979	Max Nöthiger	AUT	SUZUKI							
1979	Raffaele Pasqual	ITA	SUZUKI							
1979	Peter Sköld	SWE	SUZUKI							
1979	Dick Alblas	NED	SUZUKI							
1979	Herbert Schieferecke	GER	SUZUKI							
1979	George Fogarty	GBR	SUZUKI							
1979	Alain Röthlisberger	SUI	SUZUKI							
1979	Jürgen Steiner	GER	SUZUKI							
1979	Didier De Radigues	BEL	SUZUKI							
1979	Corrado Tuzii	ITA	SUZUKI							
1979	King Wong-Kwong	GER	SUZUKI							
1979	Jochen Schmidt	GER	SUZUKI							
1979	Michel Rastel	FRA	SUZUKI							
1979	Michael Schmid	AUT	SUZUKI							
1979	Carlos de San Antonio	ESP	SUZUKI							
1979	Richard Schulze	AUT	SUZUKI							
1979	Stefano Bonetti	ITA	SUZUKI							
1979	Børge Nielsen	DEN	SUZUKI							
1979	Leandro Becheroni	ITA	SUZUKI							
1979	Lorenzo Ghiselli	ITA	SUZUKI							
1979	Seppo Ojala	FIN	SUZUKI							
1979	Carlo Prati	ITA	SUZUKI							
1979	Toni Garcia	ESP	SUZUKI							
1979	Eddie Grant	GBR	SUZUKI							
1979	Sandro Moro	ITA	SUZUKI							
1979	Timo Pohjola	FIN	SUZUKI							
1979	Gregg Barsdorf	AUT	SUZUKI							
1979	Chris Fisker	DEN	SUZUKI							
1979	Odd Larne Lände	NOR	SUZUKI							
1979	Carlo Paganini	ITA	SUZUKI							
1979	Erik Björn Paulsen	DEN	SUZUKI							
1979	Max Steiner	GER	SUZUKI							
1979	Graham Wood	GBR	SUZUKI							
1979	Stan Woods	GBR	SUZUKI							
1979	Philippe Chaltin	BEL	SUZUKI							
1979	Steve Manship	GBR	SUZUKI							
1979	Gregorio Mariani	ITA	SUZUKI							
1979	Kenny Blake	AUS	SUZUKI							
1979	Roger Marshall	GBR	SUZUKI							

GP WITH SUZUKI	RACING NUMBERS	NOTES
VEN, AUT, GER, NAT, ESP, YUG, NED, BEL, SWE, FIN, GBR, FRA	7	
VEN, AUT, GER, NAT, ESP	18 VEN,20	
VEN, AUT, GER, NAT, ESP, YUG, NED, BEL, SWE, FIN, GBR, FRA	6 AUT-ESP-FIN,12 YUG-NED-SWE,22 GER	
VEN, AUT, GER, NAT, ESP, YUG, NED, BEL, SWE, FIN, GBR, FRA	8 BEL,9 FIN,11,12	
VEN, AUT, GER, NAT, ESP, YUG, NED, BEL, SWE, FIN, GBR, FRA	2 FIN,3,5,10	
VEN, AUT, GER, NAT, ESP, YUG, NED, BEL, SWE, FIN, GBR, FRA	8 NAT,12 GBR,18 FIN,23 NED,40 YUG,43 SWE,49 BEL,53 FRA	
AUT, GER, NAT, ESP, YUG, NED, BEL, SWE, FIN, GBR, FRA	10 SWE-FIN,12 AUT,14 BEL-SPA,16 NAT,17 NED,18 YUG	
AUT, GER, NAT, ESP, YUG, NED, BEL, SWE, FIN, GBR	21 FIN,28 GBR,30 NED,33 BEL,39 YUG,52 GER,62 NAT	
NED, BEL, SWE, FIN, GBR, FRA	17,41 FRA,46 NED,48 SWE,54 BEL	
AUT, GER, NAT, ESP, YUG, NED, BEL, SWE, FIN, GBR, FRA	13 SWE,14 NED-FIN,15 YUG,19 GER,20 AUT,21 ESP	
AUT, GER, NAT, ESP	27 NAT,46 SPA	
VEN, AUT, GER, NAT, YUG, NED, BEL, SWE, FIN, GBR, FRA	28 ESP-YUG,30 BEL,32 NED,46 SWE,47 AUT,60 GER	
VEN, GER, NAT, ESP, YUG, NED, BEL, SWE, FIN, GBR, FRA	6 NAT,10 YUG-BEL	
AUT, GER, NAT, ESP, NED, BEL	26 NED	
AUT, GER, NAT, ESP, YUG, NED, BEL, SWE, FIN, GBR, FRA	9 AUT-NAT-YUG,44 NED	
BEL, GBR		
AUT, GER, ESP, NED, BEL, SWE, FIN, FRA	32 BEL, 35 NED	
AUT, GER, NAT, ESP	29 BEL	
GER, ESP, NED, BEL, GBR, FRA	17 GER,25 ESP,42 NED	
VEN, AUT, GER, ESP, NED, BEL, FIN, GBR, FRA	31 NED	
VEN, GBR, FRA		
BEL, GBR, FRA		
BEL		
AUT, GER, NAT, YUG, NED, BEL, SWE, FIN, GBR, FRA	15 NED	
AUT, GER, NAT, YUG, BEL, GBR, FRA	42 AUT,52 YUG,53 GER	
VEN, NAT, ESP, YUG, BEL, FRA	19 SPA,34 YUG	
BEL		
GBR, FRA		
AUT, GER, NAT, ESP, YUG, NED, BEL, SWE, FIN, GBR, FRA	20 SWE,27 ESP,32 AUT,37 NED,46 YUG,59 GER	
AUT, GER, NAT, ESP, YUG, NED, BEL, SWE, FIN, GBR, FRA	16 NED	
VEN, AUT, GER		
BEL, GBR		
VEN, GER, NAT, ESP, YUG, BEL, GBR, FRA	55 YUG	
AUT, GER, NAT, YUG, NED, BEL, GBR, FRA	19 FRA, 30 YUG, 33 NAT, 38 NED, 45 GER	
ESP, SWE, FIN, GBR, FRA	24 SWE,31 ESP	
YUG, BEL, FRA		
AUT, SWE	19 AUT, 42 SWE	
AUT, GER, BEL		
AUT, FIN	37 AUT	
YUG, NED, BEL, SWE, FIN, FRA	40 NED	
AUT, GER, NAT, NED, BEL, GBR	9 NED	
NAT, YUG, NED	34 NED	
GBR		
GER		
GER, ESP		
NAT, YUG		
SWE, FIN		
NED	39 NED	
GER		
GBR		
FRA		
AUT, NAT, NED	29 NED	
YUG		
NAT, GBR		
GER, FRA		
AUT, YUG		
FRA		
GER		
VEN, AUT, YUG, BEL, FRA	38 YUG	
AUT		
GER, NAT		
AUT, GER, YUG, NED, BEL, FIN, FRA	25 FIN,26 AUT,36 NED, 54 GER	
FRA		
NAT, ESP		
GER, FIN		
GER, NAT, YUG	57 GER	
ESP, YUG, BEL, GBR		
NAT		
GER, NAT		
BEL, SWE ,FIN		
AUT		
SWE		
SWE		
NAT		
SWE		
GER		
GBR		
GBR		
BEL		
BEL		
NAT		
BEL, SWE		
GBR		

YEAR	RIDER	NATION	SUZUKI CODE	TEAM	N° FRAME	N° ENGINE	ENGINE	VICTOR.	CLASS.	P.TS
1979	Dave Potter	GBR	SUZUKI							
1979	Ikujiro Takai	JPN	SUZUKI							
1979	Kevin Stowe	GBR	SUZUKI							
1979	Mario Prattichizzo	ITA	SUZUKI							
1979	Giovanni Pretto	ITA	SUZUKI							
1979	Tony Head	GBR	SUZUKI							
1979	Ron Haslam	GBR	SUZUKI							
1979	Rod Scivyer	GBR	SUZUKI							

YEAR	RIDER	NATION	SUZUKI CODE	TEAM	N° FRAME	N° ENGINE	ENGINE	VICTOR.	CLASS.	P.TS
1980	Randy Mamola	USA	RGB 500 XR34	Texaco Heron Suzuki	1101,1103	1101,1103	54x54	2	2	72
1980	Graeme Crosby	NZL	RGB 500 XR34	Texaco Heron Suzuki			54x54		8	29
1980	Marco Lucchinelli	ITA	RGB 500 XR34	Nava Olio Fiat			54x54	1	3	59
1980	Graziano Rossi	ITA	RGB 500 XR34	Nava Olio Fiat			54x54		5	38
1980	Franco Uncini	ITA	RG 500 MK V	Jen Organs			54x54		4	50
1980	Wil Hartog	NED	RGB 500 XR34	Riemersma Racing			54x54	1	6	31
1980	Takazumi Katayama	JPN	RG 500 MK V	Sarome			54x54		10	18
1980	Carlo Perugini	ITA	RG 500 MK V	Team Gattino ?			54x54		11	17
1980	Philippe Coulon	SUI	RG 500 MK V	Marlboro Frankonia Nava			54x54		13	11
1980	Michel Rougerie	FRA	RG 500 MK V	Ecurie Stè Pernod			54x54		17	4
1980	Christian Estrosi	FRA	RG 500 MK V				54x54		19	3
1980	Henk De Vries	NED	RG 500 MK V				54x54		20	2
1980	Gustav Reiner	GER	RG 500 MK V				54x54		23	1
1980	Bernard Fau	FRA	RG 500 MK V	GME Motul GPA			54x54		23	1
1980	Sergio Pellandini	SUI	RG 500 MK V				54x54		23	1
1980	Franck Gross	FRA	SUZUKI							
1980	Willem Zoet	NED	RG 500 MK V	Stimorol?			54x54			
1980	Lennart Bäckström	SWE	SUZUKI							
1980	John Newbold	GBR	SUZUKI							
1980	Seppo Rossi	FIN	RG 500 MK V	MAN 2000?			54x54			
1980	Markku Matikainen	FIN	SUZUKI							
1980	Guido Paci	ITA	SUZUKI							
1980	Stuart Avant	AUS	SUZUKI							
1980	Werner Nenning	AUT	SUZUKI							
1980	Mick Grant	GBR	SUZUKI							
1980	Steve Parrish	GBR	SUZUKI							
1980	Roger Marshall	GBR	SUZUKI							
1980	Max Wiener	AUT	SUZUKI	Jim Beam Team						
1980	Joseph Hage	GER	SUZUKI							
1980	Peter Sjöström	SWE	SUZUKI							
1980	Peter Amman	GER	SUZUKI							
1980	Phil Henderson	GBR	SUZUKI							
1980	Jürgen Steiner	GER	SUZUKI							
1980	Gerhard Vogt	GER	SUZUKI							
1980	Michael Schmid	AUT	SUZUKI							
1980	Rolf Schneider	GER	SUZUKI							
1980	Gianni Rolando	ITA	SUZUKI							
1980	Carlo Prati	ITA	SUZUKI							
1980	Jon Ekerold	RSA	SUZUKI							
1980	Elmar Renner	GER	SUZUKI							
1980	Clemens Driesch	GER	SUZUKI							
1980	Adelio Faccioli	ITA	SUZUKI							
1980	Klaus Klein	GER	SUZUKI							
1980	Alain Nies	BEL	SUZUKI							
1980	Fritz Reitmaier	GER	SUZUKI							
1980	Peter Sköld	SWE	SUZUKI							
1980	Dick Alblas	NED	SUZUKI							
1980	Philippe Chaltin	BEL	SUZUKI							
1980	Carlos de San Antonio	ESP	SUZUKI							
1980	Antonio Garcia	ESP	SUZUKI							
1980	Gary Lingham	GBR	SUZUKI							
1980	Timo Pohjola	FIN	SUZUKI							
1980	Didier De Radigues	BEL	SUZUKI							
1980	Gianfranco Bonera	ITA	SUZUKI							
1980	Børge Nielsen	DEN	SUZUKI							
1980	Albert Siegers	NED	SUZUKI							
1980	Dennis Ireland	NZL	SUZUKI							
1980	Masaru Iwasaki	JPN	SUZUKI							
1980	Walter Koschine	GER	SUZUKI							
1980	Henk Twikler	NED	SUZUKI							
1980	Fabio Biliotti	ITA	SUZUKI							
1980	Corrado Tuzii	ITA	SUZUKI							
1980	Jaques Agopian	FRA	SUZUKI							

NED, GBR	21 NED	
YUG, SWE, GBR		
ESP		
NAT		
NAT		
BEL, SVE		
GBR		
GBR		

GP WITH SUZUKI	RACING NUMBERS	NOTES
NAT, ESP, FRA, NED, BEL, FIN, GBR, GER	8 GER,10 NED,15	
NAT, ESP, FRA, NED, BEL, GBR, GER	4,37 GER, 40	
NAT, ESP, FRA, NED, BEL, FIN, GBR, GER	2 GBR,10,11 BEL,15 FIN,21 GER,22 SPA,28 FRA	
NAT, ESP, FRA, NED, BEL, FIN, GBR, GER	9 NED,16 BEL,18 FIN,22,28	
NAT, ESP, FRA, NED, BEL, FIN, GBR, GER	5,57	
NAT, ESP, NED, BEL, FIN, GBR, GER	3,4 GER	
NAT, ESP, FRA	11 SPA,40	
NAT, ESP, FRA, NED, BEL, FIN, GBR, GER	18 NED,22 NAT,24 GER, 27 GBR,40 BEL,45,59 FRA	
NAT, ESP, FRA, NED, BEL, FIN, GBR, GER	9 FRA-GER,10 BEL,11 FIN,12 NAT,19 NED,28 GBR	
NAT, ESP, FRA, NED, BEL, FIN, GBR	14 FIN	
NAT, ESP, FRA, NED, BEL, FIN	27 NAT	
NED, BEL, GBR	37 GBR,40 NED	
BEL, GBR, GER	32 GER	
NAT, ESP, FRA, BEL, FIN, GBR	28,41 FIN	
NAT, ESP, FRA, GER	26,42 GER,51 NAT	
FRA, BEL, FIN, GER	27 GER,43 FIN	
FRA, NED, BEL, FIN, GBR, GER	36 NED,61 FRA,62 BEL	
FIN	35 FIN	
GBR		
NAT, ESP, FRA, BEL, FIN, GBR, GER	20 FIN,44	
NAT, ESP, FRA, NED, BEL, FIN		
NAT, FRA	60 FRA	
BEL, GBR, GER	38 GBR,53 GER,63 BEL	
FRA, GBR		
NED, FIN		
NED, BEL, GBR, GER	11 GER,14 NED,16 GBR,38 BEL	
GBR		
FRA, FIN, GER	17 FIN	
BEL, GER	33 GER	
ESP, FRA, BEL, FIN, GBR	36 FRA,48 BEL,56 GBR	
GER		
GBR		
GER		
GBR		
FRA, GER		
GER		
NAT, ESP, FRA, GBR	23 NAT,24 GBR,49 FRA	
NAT, GER		
NED, GBR, GER		
ESP, FRA, GER	3 GER	
GER	57 GER	
FIN		
GER		
FRA, BEL		
GER		
FIN		
NED		
BEL		
ESP		
ESP		
ESP		
FIN	36 FIN	
ESP		
FRA		
FRA	22	
BEL		
BEL	32	
BEL		
BEL		
BEL		
NAT		
NAT		
FRA		

YEAR	RIDER	NATION	SUZUKI CODE	TEAM	N° FRAME	N° ENGINE	ENGINE	VICTOR.	CLASS.	P.TS
1981	Marco Lucchinelli	ITA	Rgr 500 XR35	Nava Olio Fiat	1008,1009	1008,1009	54x54	5	1	105
1981	Randy Mamola	USA	Rgr 500 XR35	Texaco Heron Suzuki	1003	1003,1004	54x54	2	2	94
1981	Graeme Crosby	NZL	Rgr 500 XR35	Texaco Heron Suzuki			54x54		5	68
1981	Jack Middelburg	NED	RG 500 MK VI	Sarome			54x54	1	7	60
1981	Hiroyuki Kawasaki	JPN	Rgr 500 XR35	Suzuki Motor Co			54x54		10	19
1981	Bernard Fau	FRA	RG 500 MK VI	Team Zago			54x54		11	14
1981	Franco Uncini	ITA	RG 500 MK VI-XR34				54x54		13	12
1981	Willem Zoet	NED	RG 500 MK VI				54x54		14	10
1981	Seppo Rossi	FIN	RG 500 MK VI				54x54		15	9
1981	Giovanni Pellettier	ITA	RG 500 MK VI				54x54		16	8
1981	Stuart Avant	AUS	RG 500 MK VI				54x54		19	4
1981	Sergio Pellandini	SUI	RG 500 MK VI				54x54		19	4
1981	Wil Hartog	NED	RGB 500 XR34	RIEMERSMA RACING			54x54		23	2
1981	Franck Gross	FRA	SUZUKI						23	2
1981	Sadao Asami	JAP	SUZUKI						26	1
1981	Kimmo Kopra	FIN	SUZUKI						26	1
1981	Keith Huewen	GBR	SUZUKI						26	1
1981	Chris Guy	GBR	SUZUKI						26	1
1981	Graziano Rossi	ITA	RG 500 MK VI				54x54			
1981	Philippe Coulon	SUI	SUZUKI							
1981	Leandro Becheroni	ITA	SUZUKI							
1981	Peter Sjöström	SWE	SUZUKI							
1981	Dick Alblas	NED	SUZUKI							
1981	Lars Johansson	SWE	SUZUKI							
1981	Walter Migliorati	ITA	RG 500 MK VI				54x54			
1981	Alain Röthlisberger	SUI	SUZUKI							
1981	Timo Pohjola	FIN	SUZUKI							
1981	Børge Nielsen	DEN	SUZUKI							
1981	Roberto Pietri	VEN	SUZUKI							
1981	Dale Singleton	USA	SUZUKI							
1981	Raymond Roche	FRA	SUZUKI							
1981	Andreas Hofmann	SUI	SUZUKI							
1981	Christian Estrosi	FRA	SUZUKI							
1981	Fabio Biliotti	ITA	SUZUKI							
1981	Jean Lafond	FRA	SUZUKI							
1981	Henk de Vries	NED	SUZUKI							
1981	Marco Greco	BRA	SUZUKI							
1981	Raffaele Pasqual	ITA	SUZUKI							
1981	Jacques Agopian	FRA	SUZUKI							
1981	Michael Schmid	AUT	SUZUKI							
1981	Jochen Schmid	GER	SUZUKI							
1981	Marco Papa	ITA	SUZUKI							
1981	Peter Sköld	SWE	SUZUKI							
1981	Lennart Bäckström	SWE	SUZUKI							
1981	Barry Woodland	GBR	SUZUKI							
1981	Philippe Chaltin	BEL	SUZUKI							
1981	Dennis Ireland	AUS	SUZUKI							
1981	Gerhard Vogt	GER	SUZUKI							
1981	Gary Lingham	GBR	SUZUKI							
1981	Mike Baldwin	USA	SUZUKI							
1981	Adelio Faccioli	ITA	SUZUKI							
1981	Sergio Bertocchi	ITA	SUZUKI							
1981	Steve Henshaw	GBR	SUZUKI							
1981	Klaus Klein	GER	SUZUKI							
1981	Seppo Korhonen	FIN	SUZUKI							
1981	John Newbold	GBR	SUZUKI							
1981	Bengt Slydal	SWE	SUZUKI							
1981	Corrado Tuzii	ITA	SUZUKI							
1981	Günther Dreier	GER	SUZUKI							
1981	Antonio Grecco	ITA	SUZUKI							
1981	Willem Zoet	NED	SUZUKI							
1981	Alain Nies	BEL	SUZUKI							
1981	Gianni Rolando	ITA	SUZUKI							
1981	Alex George	GBR	SUZUKI							

GP WITH SUZUKI	RACING NUMBERS	NOTES
AUT, GER, NAT, FRA, YUG, NED, BEL, RSM, GBR, FIN, SWE	3,5 AUT	from GBR 56x50,7mm
AUT, GER, NAT, FRA, YUG, NED, BEL, RSM, GBR, FIN, SWE	3 AUT	from NED ALUMINUM frame, from GBR 56x50,7 mm
AUT, GER, NAT, FRA, YUG, NED, BEL, RSM, GBR, FIN, SWE	2 NAT,4	
AUT, GER, NAT, FRA, YUG, NED, BEL, RSM, GBR, FIN, SWE	8 FIN,9 NED	
AUT, GER, NAT, FRA	43	
FRA, YUG, NED, BEL, RSM, GBR, FIN, SWE	57 BEL, 66 NAT	AUT, GER Yamaha
AUT, GER, NAT, FRA, YUG, NED, BEL, RSM, GBR, FIN, SWE	2 AUT,4 NAT, 12, 19	from YUG Hartog's 1980 XR34
YUG, NED, BEL, RSM	43 BEL	
AUT, GER, NAT, FRA, YUG, NED, BEL, RSM, FIN, SWE	37 BEL,39 AUT	
AUT, GER, NAT, YUG, NED, BEL, RSM, FIN, SWE	49 AUT	
AUT, GER, NAT, FRA, NED, BEL, GBR	32 AUT-NAT-NED,36 GBR,38 FRA,48 BEL,51 GER	
AUT, GER, NAT, YUG, RSM, GBR, FIN, SWE	19 GER,20 AUT-NAT,21 SWE,24 GBR,26 YUG	FRA, BEL Yamaha, NED Kawasaki
AUT, GER	8 AUT	
NAT, FRA, YUG, BEL, FIN	58 BEL	
BEL?		remaining with Yamaha, 1 point in NED
GER, FRA, YUG, NED, BEL, RSM, FIN, SWE	61 GER	
GER, NAT, FRA, BEL, RSM, GBR	21 GBR,27 BEL,37 GER,46 FRA,53 NAT,63 RSM	
GBR		
GBR, SWE, FIN		previous with Morbidelli, then Uncini's Suzuki
AUT, GER, NAT, FRA, YUG, NED, BEL, RSM, GBR, FIN, SWE	12 BEL,14,17 GER-YUG,22 GBR	
NAT		
GER, NAT, FRA, BEL, RSM, GBR, FIN, SWE	27 SWE,32 GER,33 NAT,35 FIN,36 FRA,38 GBR,40 BEL	
NED	38 NED	
SWE		
AUT, GER, NAT, FRA, YUG, RSM	37 AUT	
AUT, GER, NAT, FRA, YUG, RSM, SWE		
FIN		
YUG, BEL, RSM, FIN , SWE	32 YUG,33 BEL-SWE	
NAT, FRA, GBR		
NED, BEL, GBR		
NAT, FRA		AUT, GER Yamaha
GER, FRA		GBR Yamaha
AUT		GER, NAT, FRA, YUG, NED, BEL, RSM, GBR Yamaha
NAT, RSM		
FRA		
AUT, GER, NED	15 NED,19 AUT,41 GER	
GER, YUG, BEL		
FRA		
FRA, BEL		
AUT, GER, NAT		
YUG, RSM		
NAT		
SWE		
AUT, FRA	33 AUT,41 FRA	
GBR		
BEL		
BEL, GBR		
GER		
BEL, GBR	27 GBR,59 BEL	
FRA		
GER, NAT		
YUG		
GBR		
GER		
FIN		
GBR		
SWE		
GBR		
GER		
FRA		
YUG, NED, BEL, NAT		
BEL		
FIN		NAT, FRA, YUG, RSM, SWE Lombardini
GBR		

YEAR	RIDER	NATION	SUZUKI CODE	TEAM	N° FRAME	N° ENGINE	ENGINE	VICTOR.	CLASS.	P.TS
1982	Franco Uncini	ITA	Rgr 500 XR40	Team Gallina	1107	1107	56X50,7	5	1	103
1982	Loris Reggiani	ITA	Rgr 500 XR35/40	Team Gallina	1109	1109	54X54		13	21
1982	Randy Mamola	USA	Rgr 500 XR35/40	Suzuki Racing LTD	1103	1102	56X50,7	1	6	65
1982	Virginio Ferrari	ITA	Rgr 500 XR40	Suzuki Racing LTD	1105	1111	54X54		11	25
1982	Boet Van Dulmen	NED	RGB-RGr 500 XR35?	Michael Hordo Racing			54X54		12	23
1982	Sergio Pellandini	SUI	SUZUKI						15	15
1982	Jack Middelburg	NED	Rgr 500 XR35/40	Riemersma			56X50,7		16	13
1982	Franck Gross	FRA	SUZUKI						17	12
1982	Leandro Becheroni	ITA	RGB 500 MK I				54X54		18	11
1982	Stuart Avant	AUS	SUZUKI						21	6
1982	Philippe Coulon	SUI	SUZUKI						21	6
1982	Seppo Rossi	FIN	SUZUKI						23	5
1982	Philippe Robinet	FRA	SUZUKI						24	4
1982	Chris Guy	GBR	SUZUKI						24	4
1982	Victor Palomo	ESP	SUZUKI						26	3
1982	Andreas Hofmann	SUI	SUZUKI						26	3
1982	Peter Sjöström	SWE	SUZUKI						28	1
1982	Raymond Roche	FRA	SUZUKI						28	1
1982	Jon Ekerold	RSA	SUZUKI						28	1
1982	Lorenzo Ghiselli	ITA	RGB 500 MK I				54X54			
1982	Wolfgang Von Muralt	SUI	SUZUKI							
1982	Hiroyuki Kawasaki	JPN	SUZUKI							
1982	Bernard Fau	FRA	SUZUKI							
1982	Dave Dean	GBR	SUZUKI							
1982	Reinhold Roth	GER	SUZUKI							
1982	Gary Lingham	GBR	SUZUKI							
1982	Fabio Biliotti	ITA	SUZUKI							
1982	Roberto Pietri	VEN	SUZUKI							
1982	Børge Nielsen	DEN	SUZUKI							
1982	Ernst Gschwender	GER	SUZUKI							
1982	Walter Migliorati	ITA	SUZUKI							
1982	Bengt Slydal	SWE	SUZUKI							
1982	Marco Papa	ITA	SUZUKI							
1982	Peter Huber	SUI	SUZUKI							
1982	Iwao Ishikawa	JPN	SUZUKI							
1982	Corrado Tuzii	ITA	SUZUKI							
1982	Marco Greco	BRA	SUZUKI							
1982	Peter Sköld	SWE	SUZUKI							
1982	Alfons Amerschläger	GER	SUZUKI							
1982	Benny Mortensen	DEN	SUZUKI							
1982	Carlos Morante	ESP	SUZUKI							
1982	Josef Ragginger	AUT	SUZUKI							
1982	Steve Williams	GBR	SUZUKI							
1982	Steve Henshaw	GBR	SUZUKI							
1982	Pierluigi Rimoldi	ITA	SUZUKI							
1982	Hans Steinhögl	AUT	SUZUKI							
1982	Henk De Vries	NED	SUZUKI							
1982	Kjeld Sörensen	DEN	SUZUKI							
1982	Josef Hage	AUT	SUZUKI							
1982	Esko Kuparinen	FIN	SUZUKI							
1982	Peter Looijesteijn	NED	SUZUKI							
1982	Norman Brown	IRL	SUZUKI							
1982	Cai Hedstrum	SWE	SUZUKI							
1982	Pauli Freudenlund	SWE	SUZUKI							
1982	Klaus Klein	AUT	SUZUKI							
1982	Risto Korhonen	FIN	SUZUKI							
1982	Gerhard Treusch	GER	SUZUKI							
1982	Mark Salle	GBR	SUZUKI							
1982	Rinus van Kasteren	NED	SUZUKI							
1982	Gustav Reiner	GER	SUZUKI							
1982	Keith Huewen	GBR	SUZUKI							
1982	Gina Bovaird	USA	SUZUKI							
1982	Maurice Coq	FRA	SUZUKI							
1982	Oliviero Cruciani	ITA	SUZUKI							
1982	Guido del Piano	ITA	SUZUKI							
1982	Chris Fisker	DEN	SUZUKI							
1982	Paul Iddon	GBR	SUZUKI							
1982	Dennis Ireland	AUS	SUZUKI							
1982	Ulrich Lang	GER	SUZUKI							
1982	Christian Le Liard	FRA	SUZUKI							
1982	Louis-Luc Maisto	FRA	SUZUKI							
1982	Maurizio Massimiani	ITA	SUZUKI							
1982	Rob McElnea	GBR	SUZUKI							
1982	Attilio Riondato	ITA	RGB 500 MK I				54X54			
1982	Barry Woodland	GBR	SUZUKI							
1982	Dick Alblas	NED	SUZUKI							
1982	Jan-Olof Odeholm	SWE	SUZUKI							
1982	Clive Padgett	GBR	SUZUKI							
1982	Johan Van Eijk	NED	SUZUKI							

GP WITH SUZUKI	RACING NUMBERS	NOTES
ARG, AUT, ESP, NAT, NED, BEL, YUG, GBR, SWE, RSM, GER	10,13,14,15,18,41	ARG with XR40 (54x54mm)
ARG, AUT, ESP, NED, BEL, YUG, GBR, SWE, RSM, GER	24,27	from NED XR40, from SWE XR4050 (56x50,7mm)
ARG, AUT, ESP, NAT, NED, BEL, YUG, GBR, SWE, RSM, GER	2	ARG with XR3550 (56x50,7mm)
ARG, AUT, NED, YUG, GBR, SWE, RSM, GER	24,31,47	SWE with XR4050 (56x50,7mm)
ARG, AUT, YUG, GBR, SWE, RSM, GER	12	NED, BEL Yamaha
ARG, AUT, FRA, ESP, NAT, NED, BEL, YUG, GBR, SWE, RSM, GER	32 FRA	
ARG, AUT, ESP, NED, BEL, YUG, RSM, GER	4	XR35 ex Crosby'81, from NED XR40,RSM XR4070
FRA, ESP, NAT, BEL, YUG, GBR, GER	23 GER, 29 FRA	
AUT, FRA, NAT, NED, BEL, YUG, GBR, RSM, GER	12 BEL,20 YUG-RSM,23 GBR,32 NED,40 FRA, 48 GER, 51 AUT	
AUT, FRA, NED, BEL, GBR, GER	11 BEL,19 FRA-NED, 22 GBR,47 GER	
ARG, AUT, FRA, ESP, NAT, NED, BEL, YUG, GBR, SWE, RSM, GER		
ARG, AUT, ESP, NAT, NED, BEL, YUG, GBR, SWE, RSM, GER	37 BEL	
FRA, NED, GBR, SWE, GER	9, 50 FRA	
AUT, FRA, NED, BEL, YUG, GBR, SWE, RSM		
FRA, ESP, NAT, NED, BEL, YUG, RSM, GER		
AUT, FRA, NAT, NED, GBR, SWE, RSM, GER	41 FRA	
AUT, FRA, ESP, NAT, NED, BEL,YUG, SWE, RSM, GER	36 AUT	
FRA, NAT, NED, BEL	26 NED	
ARG, AUT, FRA, NED, BEL		YUG, GBR, RSM, GER Cagiva
AUT, FRA, ESP, NAT, NED, RSM		
FRA, BEL, YUG, SWE, GER	44 FRA	
NED, BEL, YUG		
ARG, AUT, FRA, ESP	14 FRA	
GBR		
AUT, NAT, NED, YUG, RSM	21 RSM, 39 NED	
BEL, GBR		
NAT, BEL, YUG, GBR, RSM		
GBR		
FRA, NED, SWE		
GER		
AUT, NED, RSM, GER		
ESP, YUG, SWE, RSM		
AUT, FRA,ESP, GBR, RSM		
BEL, YUG, RSM, GER		
GBR		
NAT		
ARG, FRA, ESP	48 FRA	
SWE		
GER	24 GER?	
SWE		
ESP		
AUT		
GBR		
GBR		
RSM		
AUT		
NED, GER	12 GER	
SWE		
AUT		
SWE		
AUT, NED, GER		
GBR		
SWE		
SWE		
GER	35 GER	
SWE		
GER		
GBR		
NED		
AUT, BEL, YUG, GER	17 GER, 39 YUG	
AUT, NED, GBR		
FRA		
FRA		
RSM		
NAT		
SWE		
GBR		
GBR		
GER		
FRA	37 FRA	
FRA		
RSM		
GBR		
RSM		
GBR		
NED		
SWE		
GBR		
NED		

YEAR	RIDER	NATION	SUZUKI CODE	TEAM	N° FRAME	N° ENGINE	ENGINE	VICTOR.	CLASS.	P.TS
1983	Randy Mamola	USA	Rgr 500 XR45	HB Suzuki Racing LTD	2005-2007	2002-2005-2006	56X50,7		3	89
1983	Anton Mang	GER	RGB MKII-Rgr XR40	HB Suzuki Racing LTD			56X50,7		18	2
1983	Franco Uncini	ITA	Rgr 500 XR45	HB Gallina Corse	2004-2008	2003-2004-2008	56X50,7		9	31
1983	Boet van Dulmen	NED	RGB MKII-Rgr XR45	HB Gallina Corse	2008?	2008?	56X50,7		11	17
1983	Sergio Pellandini	SUI	RGB MKII-Rgr XR45	Carimati Pezzani – HB Gallina	2004?	2004?	56X50,7		13	11
1983	Barry Sheene	GBR	RGB MKII-Rgr XR40	HB Racing Team Heron			56X50,7		14	9
1983	Keith Huewen	GBR	RGB 500 MK II	HB Racing Team Heron			54X54		15	7
1983	Paul Lewis	AUS	SUZUKI						19	1
1983	Mark Salle	GBR	SUZUKI						19	1
1983	Wolfgang Von Muralt	SUI	SUZUKI							
1983	Leandro Becheroni	ITA	SUZUKI							
1983	Loris Reggiani	ITA	SUZUKI	HB Suzuki Racing LTD						
1983	Stuart Avant	AUS	SUZUKI							
1983	Walter Migliorati	ITA	SUZUKI	Moto Club Carate						
1983	Philippe Coulon	SUI	SUZUKI							
1983	Norman Brown	IRL	SUZUKI	Hector Neill racing						
1983	Chris Guy	GBR	SUZUKI							
1983	Peter Sjöström	SWE	SUZUKI							
1983	Gustav Reiner	GER	SUZUKI							
1983	Eero Hyvärinen	FIN	SUZUKI							
1983	Henk de Vries	NED	SUZUKI	Henk de Vries Motoren						
1983	Franck Gross	FRA	SUZUKI							
1983	Rob Punt	NED	SUZUKI	M Woestenburg						
1983	Massimo Broccoli	ITA	SUZUKI							
1983	Louis-Luc Maisto	FRA	SUZUKI							
1983	Kevin Wrettom	GBR	SUZUKI							
1983	Ernst Gschwender	GER	SUZUKI	MO Motul Racing Team						
1983	Marco Greco	BRA	SUZUKI							
1983	Marco Papa	ITA	SUZUKI							
1983	Steve Henshaw	GBR	SUZUKI	Harold Coppock						
1983	Paolo Ferretti	ITA	RGB 500 MK II				54X54			
1983	Peter Huber	SUI	SUZUKI							
1983	Gary Lingham	GBR	SUZUKI	Myers Motorcycles						
1983	Lorenzo Ghiselli	ITA	RGB 500 MK II?							
1983	Alan Irwin	GBR	SUZUKI	D McManus						
1983	Steve Parrish	GBR	SUZUKI							
1983	Rinus van Kasteren	NED	SUZUKI							
1983	Børge Nielsen	DEN	SUZUKI							
1983	Andreas Hofmann	SUI	SUZUKI							
1983	Bengt Slydal	SWE	SUZUKI							
1983	Francisco Rico	ESP	SUZUKI							
1983	Alfons Amerschläger	GER	SUZUKI	Skoal Bandit Heron Suzuki						
1983	Franz Kaserer	AUT	SUZUKI							
1983	Dennis Ireland	NZL	SUZUKI							
1983	Con Law	GBR	SUZUKI							
1983	Peter Sköld	SWE	SUZUKI							
1983	Johan van Eijk	NED	SUZUKI							
1983	Wolfgang Schwarz	GER	SUZUKI	ES Motorradzubeh Racing						
1983	Lars Johansson	SWE	SUZUKI							
1983	Josè Parra	ESP	SUZUKI							
1983	Josef Ragginger	AUT	SUZUKI							
1983	Esko Kuparinen	FIN	SUZUKI							
1983	Dave Dean	GBR	SUZUKI							
1983	Kjeld Sörensen	DEN	SUZUKI							
1983	Jan-Olof Odeholm	SWE	SUZUKI							
1983	Jean Lafond	FRA	SUZUKI							
1983	Simon Buckmaster	GBR	SUZUKI							
1983	Bernard Denis	BEL	SUZUKI							
1983	Marco Grino	ESP	SUZUKI							
1983	Harry Heutmekers	NED	SUZUKI							
1983	Walter Hoffmann	GER	SUZUKI	Deutsche Tecalemit						
1983	Klaus Klein	AUT	SUZUKI	Dieter Braun Team						
1983	Risto Korhonen	FIN	SUZUKI							
1983	Peter Linden	SWE	SUZUKI							
1983	Rob McElnea	GBR	SUZUKI							
1983	John Pace	AUS	SUZUKI							
1983	Attilio Riondato	ITA	SUZUKI							
1983	Markus Ober	GER	SUZUKI							

In these tables you can see the data from the official factory and privateer riders who raced on a Suzuki RG 500 (SUZUKI where the specific version cannot be determined - Ed.). You can also see the riders who only took part in test sessions but did not manage to qualify or weren't able to take part in the race.

GP WITH SUZUKI	RACING NUMBERS	NOTES
RSA, FRA, NAT, GER, ESP, AUT, YUG, NED, BEL, GBR, SWE, RSM	6	
AUT, GBR, SWE, RSM	16	
RSA, FRA, NAT, GER, ESP, AUT, YUG, NED	1	
RSA, FRA, NAT, GER, ESP, AUT, YUG, NED, BEL, GBR, SWE, RSM	12	from GBR XR45 UNCINI (2008?)
RSA, FRA, NAT, GER, ESP, AUT, YUG, NED, BEL, GBR	15	from GBR XR45 UNCINI (2004?)
RSA, FRA, NAT, GER, AUT, YUG, NED, BEL, GBR, SWE, RSM	7	from AUT XR40
FRA, NAT, GER, ESP, AUT, YUG, NED, BEL, GBR, SWE, RSM	29 BEL-GBR,34 AUT,35 YUG,36 NED,37 RSM,47 FRA,54 GER	
GBR		
NED, BEL ,GBR		
RSA, FRA, NAT, GER, ESP, AUT, YUG, NED, BEL, GBR, SWE, RSM		
RSA, FRA, NAT, GER, ESP, AUT, YUG, GBR, SWE, RSM	33 BEL,38 FRA,40 AUT,43 RSM,44 YUG,49 NED,55 GER	
RSA, GBR, SWE, RSM	14 GBR	
FRA, GER, NED, BEL	34 BEL,40 NED,46 FRA,47 GER	
FRA, NAT, GER, AUT, YUG, NED, RSM		
RSA, FRA, NAT, GER, ESP, AUT, YUG, NED, BEL, GBR, SWE, RSM	33 GBR,37 BEL,40 RSM,41 FRA-AUT,46 YUG-NED,49 GER	
NED, BEL ,GBR		
RSA, FRA, NAT, GER, ESP, AUT, YUG, NED, BEL, GBR, SWE, RSM		
FRA, NAT, GER, AUT, NED, BEL, GBR, SWE, RSM	41 NAT-GBR,42 RSM,49 BEL,50 FRA,51 AUT,53 NED,57 GER	
RSA, FRA, NAT, GER, ESP, AUT, YUG	17 GER - YUG	
FRA, YUG, NED, BEL		
GER, NED	51 GER,55 NED	
YUG		BEL, GBR, RSM Honda
NED, BEL, GBR	58 NED	
RSM		
FRA		
GBR		
FRA, NAT, GER, AUT, YUG, NED, BEL, RSM	38 NAT, 48 NED	
RSA, FRA, NAT, GER, ESP, YUG, GBR		
NAT		
GBR		
NAT, AUT, RSM		FRA Yamaha, GER Honda
NAT, GER, YUG, BEL, GBR		
RSA, GBR	45 GBR	
NAT		
GBR		
NED	42 NED	remaining with Yamaha
NED		
GER, AUT, YUG, NED, BEL, SWE, RSM	40 YUG,47 BEL,49 RSM,53 GER,54 NED,55 AUT	
FRA, NAT, GER, ESP, AUT, GBR, RSM		
AUT, YUG, BEL, GBR, SWE		
ESP		
RSA, GER, ESP, AUT	34 GER	NAT Yamaha
NAT, GER, AUT, YUG, NED, BEL, RSM	51 NAT	
GER, NED, BEL, GBR		
BEL, GBR		
SWE		
NED, BEL		
RSA, GER	35 GER	
SWE		
ESP		
AUT, YUG		
SWE		
NAT, GER, GBR		
SWE		
SWE		
FRA, GER, BEL		Fior-Suzuki
GBR		
BEL		
ESP		
GER		
GER		
GER		
SWE		
SWE		
GBR	25 GBR	
GBR		
RSM		
ESP, FRA, BEL		

ABBREVIATIONS							
ARG:	Argentine	DEN:	Denmark	IRL:	North Ireland	NZL:	New Zeland	TCH:	Cecoslovacchia
AUS:	Australia	ESP:	Spain	ITA:	Italy	POR:	Portugal	TT:	Tourist Trophy
AUT:	Austria	FIN:	Finland	JPN:	Japan	RSA:	South Africa	USA:	United States
BEL:	Belgium	FRA:	France	NAT:	Nations	RSM:	San Marino	VEN:	Venezuela
BRA:	Brazil	GBR:	Great Britain	NED:	Netherlands	SUI:	Switzerland	YUG:	Yugoslavia
		GER:	West Germany	NOR:	Norway	SWE:	Sweden		

THANKS TO

I kept this part for the conclusion, but it is no less important than the rest. Without the help and the inspiration of many people, I would never have started and finished this book.
I would like to thank my parents again for having supported and put up with my passion for motorcycling;
Ferrari, Lucchinelli, Rossi, Uncini and Ciamberlini for the interviews and for everything they did for the world of motorcycles;
Simona for her moral support, and for also her technical expertise, "Word" and "Excel" expertise, and for proofreading;
Francesco Merzari, the person who introduced to me the Suzuki RG 500 world and made it possible in so many ways for me to publish this book. And, as well as Francesco, I would also like to thank all the other members of the **IMOLA CLASSIC RACING TEAM, Massimo Broccoli, Adriano Poggi and Giuliano Galassi;**
Dario Ballardini, with his deep knowledge of motorcycling, for the forward, for helping me in the drafting and corrections of the book and for his myriad other suggestions;
Luca Martignani, for graphic support and for how he, alongside **Lorenza Grandi,** photographed the motorcycles.
Massimiliano Renzi for graphic support ;
Claudio Ghini - another 'Imolese' with the motorcycle bug - for the photographic material;
Alfio Tosi for technical advice;
Chiara Stelitano , Traduco Srl and "myself" for the English translation.

BIBLIOGRAPHY

BOOKS:
TEAM SUZUKI – Ray Battersby
RACERS Volume 12 RG 500 & RGB 500
BARRY - Steve Parrish and Nick Harris
FIM MotoGP Results 1949-2013 Guide - W. Haefliger

MAGAZINES:
Motosprint
La Moto
Legend Bike
Moto Storiche D'Epoca

WEB SITES:
www.motogp.com
www.autosport.com
www.jumpingjack.nl
www.speciali.raisport.rai.it
www.wikipedia.org
www.highsider.com
www.gazzetta.it/speciali/motociclismo
www.pit-lane.biz

archivio © F.Merzari

MASSIMO CUFFIANI - Was born and lives in Imola. He has started to work as a designer and graphic designer since 1994, mainly and luckily of motorbikes!

1 - "Rocket" Haslam. Leon, the son, raced for us with Italjet.
2 - What a show "Lucky"! Great!
3 - Mr. Pellino won for us...
4 - Yes, this is "Super" Uncini in his studio.
5 - Ferrari, he's always in good shape...and what elegance.
6 - "Beasts" from SBK, Pedercini and Borciani.
7 - 7 - 7 - 7 - 7 Always only one 7... "Barry" forever.
8 - Massimo + Massimo...but there's only one Broccoli!
9 - The fastest goggles in the World Championship: Steve Baker.
10 - Special party with Bautista and Dovizioso.
11 - "Tomo" Koyama with his lucky "Grid Girl"...
12 - A young Pirro and Pellino with "my" Italian tricolour Malaguti.
13 - Umberto Masetti, the legend.

Until 2000 he worked for CAGIVA GROUP (DUCATI, MV AGUSTA, HUSQVARNA), then until 2003 for ITALJET and ITALJET RACING, from 2003 until today for ENGINES ENGINEERING (MALAGUTI RACING, LONCIN RACING, LAMBRETTA RACING, MAHINDRA RACING).

14 - With Graziano Rossi remembering the good times... the 2 strokes!
15 - I'm not sure, maybe "Dovi" didn't like my autograph...
16 - Valencia 2011, Webb and Mahindra got the pole position...
17 - What can I say?...just "Fast Freddie"!!!
18 - Young and wild: Webb e Schrotter.
19 - Ladies and gentlemen, Mr. Virginio Ferrari!
20 - Instead, Masbou liked blonde Grid Girls...
21 - Gabor forgive me for the cold in the Wind Tunnel...
22 - We miss Claudio Castiglioni and his dreams...
23 - Japanese champions: Harada and the lamented Abe.
24 - "Barox" I want my helmet back!!!

Photo credits: pag. 52-53 archivo © Claudio Ghini; pag.258-259 archivo © Massimo Cuffiani.
Where not expressly stated otherwise, the author has been unable to trace them back to their respective owners.
The author is available to those holding the copyright to any unidentified image or written sources, the origin of which has been unintentionally omitted.

ISBN 978-88-27861-67-7
© 2018 Massimo Cuffiani
www.suzukirg500.it - info@suzukirg500.it

All rights of electronic storage, translation, reproduction and total or partial adaptation by any means (including pictures, microfilms and electrostatic copies) are reserved for all countries.

© Massimo Cuffiani